D0477497

NEWMAN COLLEGE
BARTLEY GREEN
BIRMINGHAM, 32.

| CLASS | 665·7 |
|---|---|
| ACCESSION | 46895 |
| AUTHOR | BRI |

N 0090366 3

# The changing pattern of world energy consumption*

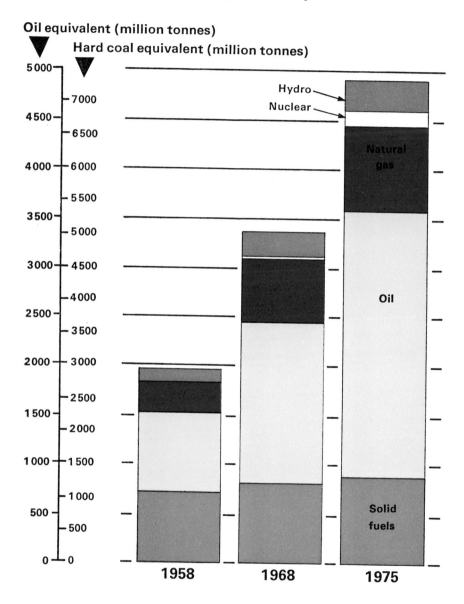

Oil equivalent (million tonnes)

Hard coal equivalent (million tonnes)

Hydro

Nuclear

Natural gas

Oil

Solid fuels

1958    1968    1975

*Excluding the USSR, China and Eastern Europe

# FOREWORD

The rapidly increasing demand in mankind's primary energy requirements continues to be met mainly by the increased production of petroleum oils and gases (see frontispiece). It is probable that this situation will persist until the last decade of this millennium. Even then, by the year 2000, although nuclear energy should be making the greater contribution towards meeting the annual increase in demand, hydrocarbon oils and gases should still be satisfying more than half of the total requirement.

Gas consumption throughout the world is likely to keep pace with the expanding primary energy requirement. The manufactured element, at present mainly high-flame-speed gas, is likely to fall to a low level from 1972 onwards owing to the exploitation of natural-gas discoveries. However, on current predictions of natural gas resources, the manufactured element should stage a recovery in the form of natural-gas substitutes, starting about 1980.

Our book *Gasmaking* was first published in 1959 and revised in 1965. In the few years that elapsed between these editions, the revolutionary trend away from gas-making processes based on solid feedstocks towards those based on hydrocarbon oils and gases, as predicted in the first edition, was confirmed by events. So much so that, in most countries, the use of solid feedstocks for gas-making projects would now be considered only in exceptional circumstances. Before the full impact of this revolution was felt, however, the scale of natural-gas discoveries made on land and off-shore in North-West Europe was such as to threaten the virtual extinction of town-gas manufacture in areas close to the gas fields, and to raise issues regarding the integration of manufactured gas and natural-gas supplies further afield.

The object of *Gas Making and Natural Gas* is to present in a single volume a brief treatment of the basic aspects of gas manufacture, natural-gas supply and the integration of natural gas and manufactured gas supplies.

*Britannic House*
*London EC2Y 9BU*                                       *April 1972*

v

# CONTENTS

|  |  | Page |
|---|---|---|
| *Part One* | **Gas Making from Solid, Liquid and Gaseous Feedstocks** | |
| *Introduction* | | 1 |
| *Chapter 1* | Town Gas, Synthesis Gas, Commercial Hydrogen and their Characteristics | 3 |
| *Chapter 2* | Materials Available for Gas Making | 15 |
| *Chapter 3* | Carbonization and the Application of Liquid Hydrocarbons to Carbonizing Plants | 19 |
| *Chapter 4* | Gasification of Solid Fuels | 26 |
| *Chapter 5* | Carburetted-Water-Gas Process | 52 |
| *Chapter 6* | Oil Gasification and Hydrocarbon-Gas Reforming: Thermal-Cracking Processes | 63 |
| *Chapter 7* | Oil Gasification and Hydrocarbon-Gas Reforming: Catalytic Processes –General Principles | 72 |
| *Chapter 8* | Oil Gasification and Hydrocarbon-Gas Reforming: Cyclic Catalytic Processes | 81 |
| *Chapter 9* | Oil Gasification and Hydrocarbon-Gas Reforming: Continuous Catalytic Steam Reforming | 99 |
| *Chapter 10* | Oil Gasification and Hydrocarbon-Gas Reforming: Partial-Combustion Processes | 135 |
| *Chapter 11* | Oil Gasification and Hydrocarbon-Gas Reforming: the Non-Catalytic Hydrogasification of Hydrocarbon Oils | 151 |

# PART ONE  GAS MAKING FROM SOLID, LIQUID AND GASEOUS FEEDSTOCKS

## Introduction

The function of the gas manufacturing industry normally is to transform solid or liquid materials into gaseous fuels that are relatively free from impurities, consistent in quality, and convenient and efficient in use. This transformation involves two main operations; the reduction in size of large molecules, loosely termed cracking, and the reduction in carbon/hydrogen ratio. Cracking is achieved by heating. The carbon/hydrogen ratio is reduced by the addition of hydrogen, which may be in the form of steam or a gas rich in hydrogen, normally derived from steam. Alternatively the reduction may be obtained by the removal of carbon or high-carbon-content tar.

Less commonly synthesis gas, hydrogen or high-flame-speed town gas is made by using natural gas as a feedstock, in which case all that is involved is catalytic reaction with steam followed by appropriate degrees of carbon-monoxide conversion and carbon-dioxide removal.

All these processes are carried out at high temperatures and sometimes, to speed up the reactions, under pressure and/or with catalysts.

Petroleum is more easily handled and is lower in carbon/hydrogen ratio than coal and other solid fuels. As might be expected, therefore, it can be cracked and hydrogenated or reacted with steam more cheaply and efficiently than can coal. Normally the lighter the petroleum derivative employed, the lower its carbon/hydrogen ratio and the more suitable it is for processing in this way. Furthermore, with distillate fuels use can be made of catalysts, which are virtually excluded from processes based on residual oil and solid fuel owing to the presence of impurities in such feedstocks.

The carbonization of coal for the production of coke for use in metallurgy, especially in blast furnaces, is likely to continue for several decades. Competition from auxiliary liquid and gaseous fuels, from alternative direct-reduction processes for the production of iron and, to a smaller extent, from petroleum coke will, however, prevent coking from keeping pace with metal production.

Economic considerations, other than those concerned with gas manufacture costs, are significant in areas where indigenous coal competes with imported hydrocarbon oils and gases. The savings involved in supplanting solid gas-making materials are so great, however, that these considerations appear to carry progressively less weight.

1

It is apparent that the most economical use to make of any solid fuel, where it *must* be consumed as a matter of policy, is to burn it with air to develop heat. Used in this way it competes more closely with petroleum hydrocarbons, whereas to use it for making town gas or synthesis gas would place it at a great disadvantage relative to oil.

# Chapter 1    Town Gas, Synthesis Gas, Commercial Hydrogen and their Characteristics

## Description of Town Gas

Town gas is fuel gas distributed in pipes to domestic, commercial and industrial consumers. It is normally sold at a declared calorific value subject to legal requirements, which also usually demand almost complete elimination of hydrogen sulphide from the gas. Whether manufactured or derived from natural sources, town gases are mainly mixtures in various proportions of the gases set out in Table 1.

The non-combustible constituents result mainly from the controlled or uncontrolled dilution of the gas with waste gas and air, although the production of some carbon dioxide is usually inherent in gas-making processes. As these heavy diluents add to the cost of gas distribution, their presence should be reduced to the economic minimum.

The ideal qualities demanded of town gas are that it should be consumable in 'neat flame' (non-aerated) burners without carbon formation, in aerated burners without lighting back, and in both types of burner without the flame 'lifting off', ie leaving the burner. The gas should also be non-toxic and free from sulphur other than that required to give it a characteristic odour.

Gases manufactured from solid fuels commonly have excessive carbon monoxide and organic sulphur contents, but high-flame-speed gases made from desulphurized feedstocks in the more complex modern processes, after carbon-monoxide conversion, conform to the ideal in all respects. Satisfactory neat-flame burners for the range of domestic appliances have yet to be developed for natural gas; otherwise it also can meet all these requirements.

Undesirable impurities in town gas are the organic sulphur compounds (mainly carbon disulphide, thiophene and carbon oxysulphide), nitrogenous gum and unstable polymerizing hydrocarbons. Organic sulphur compounds present a problem, most of all in the case of gases made from solid fuels and heavy fuel oil, and various processes for their removal are in operation. The organic sulphur content of town gases made from light distillates and hydrocarbon gases in cyclic processes is normally sufficiently low to render desulphurization unnecessary. However, in some continuous reforming processes a

3

Table 1   Characteristics of the principal constituents of town gas and natural gas
(Courtesy of the UK Gas Council's London Research Station)

| | Chemical formula | Ideal-gas calorific values | | | Ideal-gas specific gravity | *Compressibility factor 'Z' | Summation factor | Calculated maximum Weaver flame speed 'S' (hydrogen =100) |
| | | $Btu_{15}/ft^3$ at 60°F and 30 inches Hg (1013·74 mb) | | MJ/m³ at 15°C and 1013·25 mb | Dry | | $\sqrt{(1-Z)}$ | |
| | | Saturated | Dry | Dry | | | | |
|---|---|---|---|---|---|---|---|---|
| Carbon dioxide | $CO_2$ | nil | nil | nil | 1·519 | 0·994 | 0·064 0 | nil |
| Oxygen | $O_2$ | nil | nil | nil | 1·104 | 0·999 | 0·028 3 | nil |
| Nitrogen | $N_2$ | nil | nil | nil | 0·967 | 0·999 3 | 0·016 4 | nil |
| Hydrogen | $H_2$ | 318·7 | 324·4 | 12·10 | 0·069 6 | 1·001 | — | 100 |
| Carbon monoxide | CO | 315·3 | 320·8 | 11·97 | 0·967 | 0·999 5 | 0·022 4 | 18 |
| Methane | $CH_4$ | 992·9 | 1 010·5 | 37·69 | 0·554 | 0·998 | 0·043 6 | 14 |
| Ethane | $C_2H_6$ | 1 739·6 | 1 770·2 | 66·03 | 1·038 | 0·992 | 0·091 7 | 17 |
| Propane | $C_3H_8$ | 2 475·3 | 2 519·2 | 93·97 | 1·522 | 0·982 | 0·134 2 | 16 |
| n-Butane | $C_4H_{10}$ | 3 206·7 | 3 263·6 | 121·74 | 2·006 | 0·966 | 0·184 1 | 16 |
| iso-Butane | $C_4H_{10}$ | 3 197·2 | 3 253·9 | 121·38 | 2·006 | 0·970 | 0·172 3 | 16 |
| Ethylene | $C_2H_4$ | 1 573·1 | 1 601·0 | 59·72 | 0·968 | 0·994 | 0·077 5 | 30 |
| Propylene | $C_3H_6$ | 2 294·3 | 2 334·7 | 87·09 | 1·452 | 0·984 | 0·126 9 | 30 |
| Benzene | $C_6H_6$ | 3 679·6 | 3 744·8 | 139·69 | 2·696 | 0·929 | 0·266 5 | 25 |

*These factors are applicable to gases under both UK Gas Industry and IGU standard conditions.

further factor emerges, namely the need to protect the process cata-lyst, and for this reason almost complete desulphurization of the feed-stock may be required. This yields a sulphur-free gas, which normally has to be stenched with an odoriferous sulphur compound.

The data shown in Table 1 are designed to assist the determination of calculated calorific values. The compressibility factors of the gases shown indicate the ratio of the real to the ideal-gas volume under the conditions used to express standard gas volumes. At the lower partial pressures of the individual constituents of manufactured town gas these factors would approach more closely to $1 \cdot 0$. A sufficiently accur-ate calculation of the calorific value or density of such mixed gases can therefore usually be obtained by using the ideal-gas values each multiplied by its volumetric fraction and divided by the total.

The real calorific values of individual indicated gases are obtained by dividing the ideal values by the compressibility factors. The real calorific values of mixtures are obtained by multiplying the mol fractions of the constituents by their ideal values and adding them. The result so obtained is then divided by the compressibility factor of the mixture, $Z_m$.

$$Z_m = 1 - [X_1 \sqrt{(1-Z_1)} + X_2 \sqrt{(1-Z_2)} + \ldots]^2 \\ + 5 \times 10^{-4} [2X_H - X_H^2]$$

where $X_1$, $X_2$ ... are the constituent mol fractions
$$(\text{Total } X_1 + X_2 \ldots \ldots X_H = 1 \cdot 0)$$

$X_H$ ........is the hydrogen mol fraction

$Z_1$, $Z_2$ ... are the constituents' compressibility factors

Differences between the calorific values and specific gravities shown in respect of gas analyses throughout this book, and the real-gas values determined by the above method, are small, *ie* with few exceptions within $\pm 0.2\%$. In some cases these differences result from the fact that the values shown were measured, rather than calculated. When calorific values are expressed unqualified in the text they are on the following bases:

$Btu/ft^3 = Btu_{15}/ft^3$ at 60°F and 30 inHg (1 013·74 mbar) saturated
$\qquad\quad$ = UK Gas Industry Standard (saturated)

$MJ/m^3 = MJ/m^3$ at 15°C and 1 013·25 mbar dry
$\qquad\quad$ = International Gas Union Standard

Town gas supplies fall into three categories, two major and one minor as follows:

## 1 High-Flame-Speed Town Gas
Calorific value range 450 to 550 Btu/ft$^3$ (17·0 to 20·9 MJ/m$^3$)
Weaver flame-speed factor 32 to 45; see page 11.

All coal-gas-based town gas and some oil-based gas supplies are in this category.

Gas made by the carbonization of coal has a calorific value in the range 500 to 600 Btu/ft$^3$ (18·98 to 22·78MJ/ m$^3$) and is approximately 50% hydrogen, which is responsible for its high flame-speed. It is commonly diluted with carburetted water-gas and/or producer gas. Provided the degree of dilution is limited, no adjustment of consumers' appliances is involved. As will be shown later, high-flame-speed gases having physical properties similar to coal gas can be made from hydrocarbon oils and gases.

Typical Wobbe Number limits for a 500 Btu/ft$^3$ (18·98 MJ/m$^3$) town gas are 700 to 770 UK units (26·57 to 29·23 SI units) – see page 8.

## 2 Low-Flame-Speed Town Gas
Calorific value range 850 to 1 100 Btu/ft$^3$ (32·2 to 41·7 MJ/m$^3$)
Weaver flame-speed factor 13 to 25

This category is based on natural gas and is quantitatively the most important, owing to its widespread use in North America. Its use is, however, now developing rapidly in Europe and the USSR. It consists almost entirely of natural gases of flame-speed factors within the narrow limits 13 to 16. Oil-based gas or liquefied-petroleum-gas/air mixture of high calorific values and having flame-speed factors in the range 15 to 24 are used for 'standby' or 'peak shaving'.

A rare type of town gas consisting of undiluted propane and/or butane is piped to a few small communities. Although its flame speed is within the limits shown above, its calorific value is roughly three-fold, ie 3 000 Btu/ft$^3$ (114 MJ/m$^3$).

## 3 Intermediate Gas Types
Calorific value range 550 to 850 Btu/ft$^3$ (20·8 to 32·2 MJ/m$^3$)
Weaver flame-speed factor 25 to 32

Town gases in the calorific value range between these limits are uncommon. They were, and still are, used to a small extent in America in areas where, for example, coke-oven gas is readily available and natural-gas supplies are limited. Generally, conditions favour abrupt change from high-flame-speed gas to low-flame-speed gas.

The foregoing arbitrary classification is regarded as more logical than the international classification currently in use (1), which is as follows:

|                          | Family |
|--------------------------|--------|
| Town gas                 | 1 (a)  |
| Coke-oven gas            | 1 (b)  |
| Hydrocarbon/air          | 1 (c)  |
| Natural gas              | 2      |
| Liquefied petroleum gas  | 3      |

Typical characteristics of town gases in the two main categories described are given in Table 2. There is no typical intermediate gas; gases in this category are produced by a variety of means and expedients.

*Table 2    Town-gas characteristics*

|  | High-flame-speed gases | | | | | Low-flame-speed gases (Natural gas) | |
|---|---|---|---|---|---|---|---|
|  | Coal gas | Coal-gas/ CWG mixture | Cyclic-reformer gas | Continuous-reformer gas | | A North Sea gas | Dutch Slochteren |
|  |  |  |  | CRG-enriched | GRH-enriched |  |  |
| **Composition** | | | | | | | |
| $CO_2$     % vol | 2·0 | 4·2 | 5·0 | 14·2 | 13·3 | 0·6 | 0·9 |
| $O_2$ | 0·5 | 0·6 | 0·4 | nil | nil | — | — |
| $C_nH_m$ | 3·5 | 3·8 | 7·4 | nil | 0·4 | — | — |
| $CO$ | 7·5 | 14·8 | 20·3 | 3·3 | 5·5 | — | — |
| $H_2$ | 51·8 | 48·7 | 49·8 | 48·6 | 55·9 | — | — |
| $CH_4$ | 27·0 | *20·0 | *11·5 | 33·7 | 17·9 | 90·0 | 81·7 |
| $C_2H_6$ | 1·2 | — | — | — | 7·0 | 5·1 | 2·7 |
| $C_3H_8$ and higher | — | — | — | — | — | 1·6 | 0·7 |
| $N_2$ | 6·5 | 6·6 | 5·6 | 0·2 | — | 2·7 | 14·0 |
| Total | 100·0 | 100·0 | 100·0 | 100·0 | 100·0 | 100·0 | 100·0 |
| Specific gravity (air=1·0) | 0·422 | 0·482 | 0·550 | 0·467 | 0·470 | 0·618 | 0·643 |
| Calorific value   Btu/ft³stp(sat) | 550 | 500 | 500 | 500 | 500 | 1033 | 881 |
| Btu/ft³stp(dry) | 559·8 | 508·9 | 508·9 | 508·9 | 508·9 | 1051 | 897 |
| $MJ/m^3$(st) | 20·88 | 18·98 | 18·98 | 18·98 | 18·98 | 39·20 | 33·44 |
| Wobbe number (UK) | 846 | 720 | 674 | 730 | 730 | 1315 | 1100 |
| (SI) | 32·12 | 27·33 | 25·59 | 27·71 | 27·71 | 49·92 | 41·76 |
| Weaver flame-speed factor 'S' (hydrogen=100) | 43·6 | 40·1 | 40·4 | 35·1 | 39·9 | 14·1 | 13·0 |

* Includes higher paraffins

7

## Description of Synthesis Gas and Commercial Hydrogen

Large quantities of hydrogen-rich gas are used throughout the world for the synthesis of ammonia, hydrocarbons and, on a smaller scale, such products as methanol. Ammonia synthesis requires a relatively pure mixture of one part of nitrogen to three parts of hydrogen. The other syntheses commonly require a mixture of one part of carbon monoxide to two parts of hydrogen, although lower hydrogen ratios are sometimes used. Some degree of dilution with inert gases and methane can, in most cases, be tolerated.

Hydrogen is used on an increasing scale for the hydro-desulphurization and hydro-cracking of hydrocarbon oils, for the hydrogenation of fats and, on a small scale at present, for the hydrogenation of coal.

Typical characteristics of the gases used commercially for syntheses and hydrogenation are given in Table 3.

## The Interchangeability of Gases

### 1   High-Flame-Speed Gases

Although gas-burning appliances have considerable flexibility in use, mixtures of various types of fuel gases made regardless of considerations other than the maintenance of the declared calorific value cannot be consumed satisfactorily.

An important criterion in respect of combustion and service is the ratio of the calorific value of the gas to the square root of its specific gravity, *ie* cal val $\div \sqrt{\text{sp gr}}$. This is termed the Wobbe Number, and is an index of the thermal input to an appliance at a given gas pressure. Since the air requirement of most combustible gases is approximately the same on a thermal basis, the Wobbe Number is also a rough index of the air requirement. It is also needed for the calculation of the gas modulus (2), $M = \sqrt{p}/W$ (where $p$ is the gas pressure and $W$ is the Wobbe Number), which must remain constant if a given degree of pre-aeration is to be achieved in an aerated burner.

In practice it has been found that, with town gas, the maintenance of the Wobbe Number within the limits $\pm 5\%$ ensures satisfactory operation of appliances, provided that the gas is debenzolized. Variations of $+8$ to $-10\%$ in the Wobbe Number occurring in emergencies have resulted in few complaints.

On the other hand, if gas composition were allowed to vary beyond certain limits, unsatisfactory combustion would result even if the

Wobbe Number remained constant. The reason for this is that there are three requirements that must be met. Firstly, there must be an adequate thermal input of gas of a given air demand into an appliance, so that combustion is complete and little carbon monoxide is produced. Secondly, it is necessary to ensure that the flame speed is not so slow that the flames of either aerated or non-aerated burners lift off the burner. Thirdly, the flame speed must not be so fast that aerated burners light back.

In order to satisfy these requirements it is necessary to relate the flame speed of the gas to the Wobbe Number. This is done for a type of town gas (G4 Group Gas UK Standard) in Figure 1, in which the thermal inputs (Wobbe Number) are shown as horizontal lines, the triangular area representing the limits within which the characteristics must lie if satisfactory combustion conditions are to be achieved in British Standard appliances.

In practice, the flame-speed factor of high-flame-speed gas is dominated by, and is almost proportional to, the hydrogen content. The flame-speed variation in Figure 1, within the limits of the area of

*Table 3  Typical compositions of gases used commercially for syntheses and hydrogenation*

| | Hydrogen for hydrocracking | | Hydrogen for edible oil hydrogenation | Ammonia synthesis gas | Methanol synthesis gas | Hydrogen for electronics etc (small scale) |
| | From partial combustion | From steam reforming | | | | |
|---|---|---|---|---|---|---|
| **Composition** | | | | | | |
| $H_2$    mol % | 98·4 | 96·5 | 99·5 | 74·2 | 68·5 | >99·999 |
| CO | — | — | — | — | 14·6 | |
| $CO_2$ | — | — | — | — | 13·0 | Purified |
| $CH_4$ | 1·2 | 3·5 | 0·5 | 0·7 | 3·9 | by |
| $N_2$ | 0·2 | nil | nil | 24·8 | — | palladium |
| Ar | 0·2 | nil | nil | 0·3 | — | diffusion |
| Total | 100·0 | 100·0 | 100·0 | 100·0 | 100·0 | — |
| **Trace impurities** | | | | | | |
| $CO_2$   ppm mol | }<20 | }<20 | — | }<5 | | — |
| CO    „   „ | | | <10 | | | |
| Sulphur   ppm w/w | <2 | <2 | 1 | <2 | <2 | — |

satisfactory combustion, is roughly equivalent to a variation of hydrogen content from 40 to 65% by volume.

From Figure 1 it will be seen that inert gases and carbon monoxide reduce the flame speed and Wobbe Number, whereas hydrogen does the reverse. It will also be seen that hydrocarbons reduce flame speed but raise the Wobbe Number.

The boundary line of satisfactory combustion in Figure 1 connects the points below which an acceptably low carbon-monoxide/carbon-dioxide ratio (0·02:1) will be achieved in the products of combustion. It does not guarantee that small quantities of soot will not be produced by the flames of non-aerated burners.

Aromatic hydrocarbons are the most prone to endowing gas mixtures with this propensity for producing soot at the points where non-aerated burner flames impinge on the surfaces of gas appliances, but other hydrocarbons can have a contributory effect. A test has been

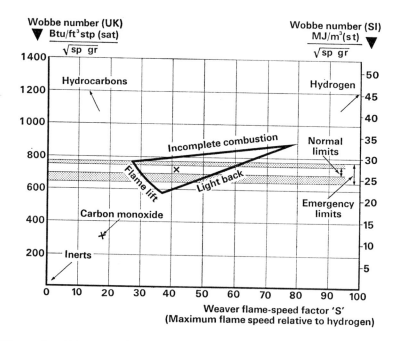

*Figure 1   Diagram showing limits of satisfactory combustion in UK appliances adjusted to consume gas in the Wobbe Number range 700 to 760 (26·6 to 28·8 SI)*
*(Based on UK Gas Council Research Communication GC85)*

10

developed which is of value in the control of this quality (3). The apparatus comprises a 56 mm internal-diameter silica tube connected to a gas supply, centred in a 38 mm internal-diameter heat-resisting glass tube. The combustion air supply is fed to the base of the annulus below a sintered glass disc used to steady the air flow. A diffusion flame is produced by burning gas at a standard thermal rate at the top of the inner tube. Starting from a position using excess combustion air, the air flow is reduced until the flame tip begins first to waver, then to lose definition and open, and finally to lengthen. The air rate is taken at the point when the flame tip begins to open up, and is used to produce an index of the sooting propensity.

Methods of using gas analysis to calculate the type of flame speed or combustion factor used as the horizontal co-ordinate in Figure 1 were developed by Weaver (4) and Delbourg (5 & 6). This is a calculated flame-speed factor, based mainly on empirical data and expressed on an arbitrary scale in which the factor for hydrogen is deemed to be 100. It is sometimes referred to as the 'Weaver flame-speed'. Gilbert and Prigg (7) give the details of Weaver's method and also formulae, relating to British gas-testing apparatus and methods, for the determination of the limits of complete combustion, light-back and flame-lift. These allow the complete prediction diagram to be plotted.

This method of prediction of combustion characteristics, although adequate for giving an indication of the type of combustion defects that might be expected as a result of change in the composition of a town gas, is not sufficiently accurate to eliminate the need for practical testing with the gas appliances concerned.

## 2   Low-Flame-Speed Gases

A prediction diagram for natural gas and natural-gas substitutes using the same flame-speed factor $S$ as that referred to under high-flame-speed gases is given by Harris and Lovelace (8) Figure 2. The positions of several types of natural gas are indicated on this diagram.

The test limit gases upon which this diagram is based are as follows:
*NGA Methane*
*NGB Test Gas for complete combustion (enriched methane)*
*NGC Test Gas for light-back (methane diluted with hydrogen-rich gas)*
*NGD Test Gas for flame-lift (methane diluted with nitrogen)*

These limit gases, the characteristics of which are given in Table 4, must be defined having regard to the technical and economic limitations on the degree of flexibility that can be built into gas-consuming appliances.

11

The points in the graph $X^1-X^{10}$ indicate the characteristics of the four substitute natural gases described on lines 1, 4, 7 and 10 of Table 5. All were subjected to carbon-dioxide removal and enriched with propane to produce the approximate Wobbe Number of the reference gas NGA. In practice it is unlikely to be desirable to go to this extreme with regard to substitute-gas quality. The extent to which the characteristics of these substitute gases vary with a lower degree of carbon-dioxide removal and increased enrichment are also demonstrated in Table 5.

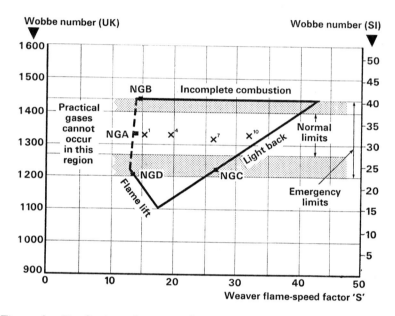

*Figure 2    Prediction diagram for natural gas (Courtesy of the Institution of Gas Engineers)*

## 3  Intermediate Gas Types

As already stated, these gases form a minor category. However, their appearances in parts of Europe, particularly in the UK, was regarded as a possibility, owing to the greater cost of the lean, high-hydrogen-content, component of high-flame-speed town gas, compared with the hydrocarbon-enrichment component. In addition there may be local political and economic obstacles to an abrupt change-over to town gas based exclusively on low-flame-speed hydrocarbon gases.

The extent under UK conditions to which the calorific value and Wobbe Number of town gas could be raised without the need arising to change from the neat (*ie* non-pre-aerated) types of burner in use was examined (9). The result was disappointing in that it demonstrated the small extent to which high-flame-speed gas can be enriched and the hydrogen content reduced without provoking the need to change over to pre-aerated burners.

The development of neat-flame domestic burners that can operate on low-flame-speed gas is, however, currently subject to intensive research.

Table 4    *Properties of the natural-gas test gases used in defining Figure 2 (8) (Courtesy of the Institution of Gas Engineers)*

| Test Gas | | NGA (Reference) | NGB (Complete combustion) | NGC (Light-back) | NGD (Flame-lift) |
|---|---|---|---|---|---|
| Composition | | | | | |
| CH$_4$ | % vol | 100 | 87 | 65 | 92·5 |
| H$_2$ | | | | 35 | |
| N$_2$ | | | | | 7·5 |
| C$_3$H$_8$ | | | 13 | | |
| Calorific value | | | | | |
| | Btu/ft$^3$stp(sat) | 995 | 1187 | 758 | 920 |
| | MJ/m$^3$(st) | 37·77 | 45·06 | 28·78 | 34·92 |
| Specific gravity | | 0·555 | 0·681 | 0·385 | 0·585 |
| Wobbe number (UK) | | 1335 | 1440 | 1222 | 1203 |
| | (SI) | 50·68 | 54·66 | 46·39 | 45·66 |
| Flame-speed factor | | 14·0 | 14·5 | 26·7 | 13·4 |
| Lift pressure | cm water gauge | 17·3 | 18·8 | >22·9 | 14·0 |
| Reversion pressure | cm water gauge | 6·1 | 6·3 | 8·6 | 5·1 |
| Sooting number | | 10·8 | 14·5 | 8·6 | 9·0 |
| Maximum burning velocity | cm/s | 35·5 | 36·0 | 46·5 | 32·5 |

Table 5   Properties of natural-gas substitutes (Propane-enriched) (Courtesy of the Institution of Gas Engineers)

| Process | Composition of propane-enriched gas % vol | | | | | | | Calorific value | | Specific gravity | Wobbe number | | Flame-speed factor | Lift pressure cm water gauge | Reversion pressure cm water gauge | Sooting number | Maximum burning velocity cm/s |
| | $CO_2$ | CO | $CH_4$ | $C_2H_6$ | $H_2$ | Enriching $C_3H_8$ | Added air | Btu/ft³ stp (sat) | MJ/m³ (st) | | UK | SI | | | | | |
|---|---|---|---|---|---|---|---|---|---|---|---|---|---|---|---|---|---|
| CRG with methanation | nil | nil | 95·7 | – | 3·5 | 0·8 | – | 983 | 37·32 | 0·546 | 1330 | 50·49 | 15·0 | >22·9 | 7·2 | 11·0 | 35·0 |
| | 4·8 | nil | 88·1 | – | 3·2 | 3·9 | – | 983 | 37·32 | 0·623 | 1245 | 47·26 | 14·7 | 16·0 | 5·3 | 11·3 | 34·5 |
| | 17·6 | – | 67·8 | – | 2·5 | 12·1 | – | 983 | 37·32 | 0·829 | 1081 | 41·04 | 13·9 | 10·2 | 3·8 | 10·7 | 32·0 |
| CRG without methanation | nil | 0·9 | 72·3 | – | 18·8 | 8·1 | – | 983 | 37·32 | 0·546 | 1330 | 50·49 | 19·7 | >22·9 | 7·6 | 14·3 | 40·5 |
| | 4·5 | 0·7 | 66·9 | – | 17·4 | 10·5 | – | 983 | 37·32 | 0·618 | 1250 | 47·45 | 19·0 | >22·9 | 5·6 | 11·9 | 39·0 |
| | 16·6 | 0·6 | 52·3 | – | 13·7 | 16·8 | – | 983 | 37·32 | 0·814 | 1091 | 41·42 | 17·1 | 12·7 | 4·8 | 12·2 | 35·5 |
| Gas recycle hydrogenator | nil | 3·0 | 34·1 | 12·9 | 38·4 | 11·6 | – | 983 | 37·32 | 0·556 | 1318 | 50·03 | 26·3 | >22·9 | 11·2 | 12·9 | 49·0 |
| | 4·4 | 2·8 | 31·6 | 12·0 | 35·6 | 13·6 | – | 983 | 37·32 | 0·625 | 1243 | 47·19 | 24·5 | >22·9 | 9·4 | 12·7 | 45·0 |
| | 16·4 | 2·2 | 24·8 | 9·4 | 28·0 | 19·2 | – | 983 | 37·32 | 0·818 | 1087 | 41·27 | 21·5 | >22·9 | 5·7 | 11·5 | 42·0 |
| Enriched ICI lean gas | nil | 2·6 | 11·7 | 0·8 | 58·3 | 26·6 | – | 983 | 37·32 | 0·544 | 1332 | 50·57 | 32·3 | >22·9 | 18·3 | 16·0 | 54·5 |
| | 3·6 | 2·5 | 11·0 | 0·7 | 54·8 | 27·4 | – | 983 | 37·32 | 0·603 | 1266 | 48·06 | 30·6 | >22·9 | 11·2 | 15·3 | 52·0 |
| | 14·1 | 2·0 | 9·0 | 0·6 | 44·7 | 29·6 | – | 983 | 37·32 | 0·772 | 1119 | 42·48 | 26·3 | >22·9 | 8·1 | 13·0 | 45·0 |
| Propane/air | – | – | – | – | – | 39·7 | 60·3 | 983 | 37·32 | 1·207 | 894 | 33·94 | 16·0 | 19·8 | 3·6 | 9·7 | 40·5 |
| | – | – | – | – | – | 60·8 | 39·2 | 1505 | 57·13 | 1·316 | 1312 | 49·81 | 16·0 | 16·3 | 6·4 | 21·0 | 40·5 |

14

# Chapter 2    Materials Available for Gas Making

Practically the whole range of solid, liquid and gaseous fuels found in nature can be converted into town gas, industrial fuel gas, synthesis gas or, indirectly, into hydrogen. In addition, substances derived from the heat treatment of natural fuels, such as coke, semi-coke, char (carbonized non-agglomerating coal or lignite) and various tars, may also be used. Materials of more recent origin that have been used to a small extent include peat, wood and such agricultural wastes as seed husks and shells, corn cobs, wood bark and sugar-cane refuse. It has even been claimed that a town gas supply was maintained in an emergency

*Table 6    Typical properties of solid fuels*

| | Dry ash-free basis | | | | | | Carbon/ hydrogen ratio | Natural basis calorific value | |
| | Ultimate analysis % wt | | | | Approximate analysis % wt | | | Btu/lb | MJ/kg |
| | C | H | O | N+S | Volatile matter | Fixed carbon | | | |
| Wood | 50·0 | 6·0 | 43·0 | 1·0 | 80·0 | 20·0 | 8·3 | 6 260 | 14·6 |
| Peat | 57·5 | 5·5 | 35·0 | 2·0 | 68·4 | 31·6 | 10·4 | 6 840 | 15·9 |
| Coals | | | | | | | | | |
| Lignite* | 70·0 | 5·0 | 23·0 | 2·0 | 52·6 | 47·4 | 14·0 | 9 310 | 21·6 |
| Bituminous Cat. I | 77·0 | 5·5 | 15·0 | 2·5 | 42·1 | 57·9 | 14·0 | 11 090 | 25·8 |
| „    „    II | 82·0 | 6·0 | 9·5 | 2·5 | 36·8 | 63·2 | 13·7 | 13 480 | 31·3 |
| „    „    III | 86·0 | 5·5 | 6·0 | 2·5 | 31·6 | 68·4 | 15·6 | 14 400 | 33·5 |
| „    „    IV | 88·0 | 5·0 | 4·5 | 2·5 | 26·3 | 73·7 | 17·6 | 14 400 | 33·5 |
| Semi-bituminous | 90·5 | 4·5 | 3·0 | 2·0 | 18·8 | 81·2 | 20·1 | 14 960 | 34·8 |
| Semi-anthracite | 93·0 | 3·5 | 2·0 | 1·5 | 10·4 | 89·6 | 26·6 | 14 710 | 34·2 |
| Anthracite | 94·0 | 3·0 | 1·5 | 1·5 | 4·1 | 95·9 | 31·3 | 14 870 | 34·6 |
| Manufactured fuels | | | | | | | | | |
| Charcoal | 93·0 | 2·5 | 3·0 | 1·5 | 10·1 | 89·9 | 37·2 | 14 490 | 33·7 |
| Coke | 95·0 | 1·0 | 2·0 | 2·0 | 1·1 | 98·9 | 95·0 | 13 210 | 30·7 |
| Semi-coke | 93·0 | 3·0 | 2·0 | 2·0 | 8·6 | 91·4 | 31·0 | 13 450 | 31·3 |

\* Soft, uncompacted lignites are sometimes referred to as brown coal.

Based on 'Technical Data on Fuel' by H. M. Spiers

15

by carbonizing coffee in one instance and old rubber tyres in another. Currently a project for the carbonization of used rubber tyres is under consideration in the USA.

The principal materials used are set out in the following paragraphs.

## Solid Gas-Making Materials

In Table 6 are listed the solid materials used in gas making, together with their typical properties which may, however, vary considerably from one specimen to another. The most notable differences in comparison with liquid fuels are the relatively high carbon/hydrogen ratios and oxygen contents. The coals are arranged in order of increasing rank or geological age, and it is interesting to note, by comparing anthracite and semi-coke, that a few hours of heat treatment appear to be equivalent, in their effect on the ultimate analysis, to the passage of several geological eras.

*Table 7   Typical characteristics of liquid hydrocarbon feedstocks*

| | Specific gravity (H$_2$O=1·0) | Calorific value | | | Carbon/ hydrogen ratio | Sulphur % w/w |
| | | Therms | | MJ per kg | | |
| | | per gallon | per ton | | | |
|---|---|---|---|---|---|---|
| Petroleum oils | | | | | | |
| Light distillate (115)* | 0·67 | 1·38 | 460 | 47·8 | 5·2 | 0·02 |
| (160)* | 0·72 | 1·45 | 450 | 46·7 | 5·6 | 0·04 |
| (170)* | 0·73 | 1·47 | 450 | 46·7 | 5·7 | 0·06 |
| Gas oil | 0·84 | 1·65 | 440 | 45·7 | 6·4 | 0·5 |
| Crude oil | 0·86 | 1·66 | 430 | 44·6 | 6·8 | 2·0 |
| Fuel oil, 950 seconds | | | | | | |
| Redwood I (UK Class F) | 0·96 | 1·77 | 410 | 42·6 | 7·4 | 3·4 |
| Fuel oil, 3 500 seconds | | | | | | |
| Redwood I (UK Class G) | 0·97 | 1·77 | 405 | 42·1 | 7·7 | 3·4 |
| Other materials | | | | | | |
| Shale oil | 0·95 | 1·65 | 390 | 40·5 | 9·0 | 2·3 |
| Brown-coal tar | 1·00 | 1·70 | 380 | 39·5 | 8·0 | 0·8 |

* Temperature (°C) at which 95% distills

16

The most important group of solid fuels comprises the bituminous coals, including all coals that agglomerate and a number that do not.

With a few exceptions the so-called inert constituents, *ie* moisture and ash, are the most variable characteristics of solid fuels within each group. Therefore, to avoid confusion, the analyses are expressed on a dry, ash-free basis and, for the same reason, the natural-basis calorific values are related to the normal minimum inerts contents.

## Liquid Gas-Making Materials

The term *liquid gas-making materials* virtually means petroleum oils, although shale oil and tar are occasionally used. Crude petroleum oils vary considerably in quality throughout the world, and Table 7 shows typical characteristics of products derived from mixed crudes.

## Gaseous Gas-Making Materials

### 1  Natural Gases
The hydrocarbon contents of natural gases, except in rare instances, fall within the limits set out below:

$CH_4$            60·0 to 99·0% volume

$\left.\begin{array}{l} C_2H_6 \\ C_3H_8 \\ C_4H_{10} \end{array}\right\}$ in total    0 to 30·0% volume

Information on natural gases, including some physical characteristics, is given in greater detail in Chapter 14.

### 2  Refinery Gases and Liquefied Petroleum Gases
Tail gas and other gases resulting from refinery operations, and consisting mainly of hydrogen and the lower paraffins and olefins up to '$C_4$', are sometimes used, reformed and/or unreformed, in town-gas mixtures and for the production of synthesis gas. Liquefied propane and butane are also used for these purposes.

Tail gases, even from a given source, can be highly variable in composition and physical characteristics. Commercial liquefied petroleum gases are relatively constant in quality, especially with regard to physical characteristics. Details of examples of these materials are given in Table 8.

*Table 8  Typical chemical and physical characteristics of refinery gases, propane and butane*

| | | Refinery gases | | | Commercial propane | | |
|---|---|---|---|---|---|---|---|
| | | Low calorific value | Intermediate calorific value | High calorific value | For enriching | For gas-making | Commercial butane |
| **Composition** | | | | | | | |
| $CH_4$ | mol % | 12·0 | 21·4 | 17·2 | nil | nil | 0·1 |
| $C_2H_6$ | | 13·0 | 18·6 | 17·8 | 1·5 | nil | 7·2 |
| $C_2H_4$ | | nil | 2·5 | 4·0 | nil | nil | nil |
| $C_3H_8$ | | 13·0 | 16·0 | 20·7 | 45·0 | 92·5 | 0·5 |
| $C_3H_6$ | | 2·0 | 5·4 | 14·9 | 52·0 | 5·0 | 4·2 |
| $C_4H_{10}$ | | 2·0 | 12·4 | 21·9 | } 1·5 | } 2·5 | 87·0 |
| $C_4H_8$ | | 1·0 | nil | nil | | | 1·0 |
| $CO_2$ | | nil | 0·1 | 0·3 | nil | nil | nil |
| $H_2$ | | 56·0 | 21·8 | 0·2 | nil | nil | nil |
| $N_2$ | | 1·0 | 1·8 | 3·0 | nil | nil | nil |
| Total | | 100·0 | 100·0 | 100·0 | 100·0 | 100·0 | 100·0 |
| **As gas** | | | | | | | |
| Hydrogen sulphide | gr/100ft³ | trace | 30 | 50 | nil | nil | nil |
| | g/m³ | trace | 0·70 | 1·14 | nil | nil | nil |
| Organic sulphur | gr/100ft³ | 5 | 5 | 7 | 3 | 2 | 5 |
| | g/m³ | 0·12 | 0·12 | 0·16 | 0·07 | 0·05 | 0·12 |
| Calorific value (gross) | Btu/ft³ | 1 000 | 1 620 | 2 181 | 2 386 | 2 476 | 3 052 |
| | MJ/m³ | 37·9 | 61·5 | 82·8 | 90·6 | 94·0 | 115·8 |
| Specific gravity (air = 1·0) | | 0·54 | 0·96 | 1·35 | 1·47 | 1·53 | 1·96 |
| **As liquid** | | | | | | | |
| Specific gravity (water = 1·0) | | — | — | — | 0·52 | 0·51 | 0·58 |
| Calorific value (gross) | Btu/lb | — | — | — | 21 440 | 21 250 | 21 350 |
| | MJ/kg | — | — | — | 49·8 | 49·4 | 49·6 |

18

*Chapter 3*    **Carbonization and the Application of Liquid Hydrocarbons to Carbonizing Plants**


The high-temperature carbonization of coking coal is a process of destructive distillation, effected at a temperature of approximately 1 000°C, in which the greater part of the volatile matter of the coal is driven off, leaving a coke residue.

The coal to be carbonized is charged into refractory retorts or ovens, which are usually heated by the combustion of producer gas in surrounding flues and maintained at a maximum temperature of 1 400°C. The weight of the coal charge may range from 0·5 to 30 tonnes, but usually its thickness on the minor axis is approximately 30 cm, and a typical carbonizing time is twelve hours.

The chemical processes that take place during carbonization are complex, and result in successive endothermic and exothermic phases which, on balance, are only slightly exothermic. Heat, equivalent to 35 to 65% of the thermal value of the gas made, has therefore to be used to provide the sensible heat for the coke residue, sensible and latent heat for the gas and for the losses involved in the process of heat transfer. It is because of these and other factors that the overall thermal efficiency of coal-gas manufacture by carbonization is considerably lower than that of oil-gas processes. However, the value of the conversion of coal into coke should be considered in this context, even although it cannot be expressed in terms of heat.

Coal gas, after cooling and de-tarring, usually contains 0·5 to 1·5% by volume of hydrogen sulphide and a similar amount of hydrocyanic acid and ammonia, compared with 0 to 0·5% by volume of hydrogen sulphide and negligible amounts of nitrogenous impurities contained in the various gases made from petroleum feedstocks. Therefore, the purification of coal gas is more costly.

On carbonization, 100 heat units of coal normally yield 25 heat units of gas, and 59 heat units of coke and tar. The difference of 16 is the heat used for carbonization and ancillary processes. The steaming of the retorts increases gas yield in the form of water gas, by up to 3 heat units per 100, at the expense of the coke yield. Typical coal-gas analyses are given in Table 2.

Brief details of the principal carbonizing techniques used throughout the world are set out in the following pages. The use of these processes for the purpose of town gas or synthesis gas manufacture is rapidly diminishing, but coke ovens for the production of blast-furnace coke are likely to operate on the current scale for a decade or so.


## Carbonizing Processes

### 1   Horizontal Retorts and Vertical Chambers

A typical horizontal retort is built of silica refractory segments and is 20 feet (6 metres) in length. Its ⌂-shaped cross-sectional dimensions are 24 inches (60 cm) for the base and 16 inches (40 cm) for the vertical height. They are normally constructed in settings of eight to ten retorts which are mechanically charged and discharged.

The disadvantages of this system are the arduous nature of the tasks carried out in bad conditions by the large labour force required, the large ground space taken up, and the atmospheric pollution arising. As a result, this process may now be regarded as obsolete.

Continuous vertical retorts are roughly 25 feet (7·5 metres) in length. The cross-section at the top may be 50 or 100 inches (1·27 or 2·54 metres) on the major axis and 10 inches (250 mm) on the minor. They are built mainly of silica refractories, tapering to the top in varying degrees in order to assist the downward flow of the carbonizing charge, and are usually arranged in rows of two to four, according to size, in the line of their major horizontal axes.

The capacities of the retorts range from 1·5 to 4·5 tonnes compared with 0·7 tonnes for the typical horizontal retort. Coal is fed continuously by gravity into the top of the retort, from which the gas issues, and coke is mechanically extracted continuously, or at short intervals, from the bottom.

The carbonized coke charge is partly cooled by heat exchange to the air used for producer gas combustion, following which a minimum amount of steaming of the charge from the bottom is then required to quench the coke further, before it reaches the extraction mechanism. Part of the sensible heat of the coke charge is passed up by this means through the retort to assist carbonization or water-gas manufacture. If desired, the steaming rate can be increased to produce still further dilution with water-gas. This results in an increased unit-basis yield of a poorer, heavier gas, and a lower coke yield.

The heating of the retorts is carried out by the combustion of producer gas in vertical or horizontal flues between the rows of retorts. In the latter case the waste gas rises to the top of the setting through a series of similar horizontal flues arranged one above the other between

20

the retorts. The waste gases pass to atmosphere through a waste-heat boiler, without the stage of heat transfer to secondary air, which is achieved by recuperators in the case of horizontal and intermittent vertical retorts, or regenerators in the case of coke ovens.

Continuous-vertical-retort installations are more compact than horizontal-retort systems. The coke produced is more porous and better suited to domestic use than other high-temperature cokes. The atmospheric pollution arising from the process is negligible compared with that from horizontal retorts. The advantages of this system, on balance, are such that this is likely to be the last carbonizing process to disappear from works manufacturing town gas.

Intermittent-vertical-retort systems differ in principle from continuous vertical systems in that the coal charge is static during carbonization and the hot coke is then completely discharged and replaced by a fresh coal charge, as it is in horizontal retorts and coke ovens. They also differ in that the waste gases are subject to heat exchange in a recuperator with the air required for producer-gas combustion. Slight steaming of the charge is normally practised and the gas resembles horizontal-retort gas slightly diluted with water-gas.

Gas, coke and tar qualities and yields, and gas-making efficiency are similar to those of horizontal-retort installations. In respect of such factors as capital and maintenance costs, the low process-labour requirement and the absence of atmospheric pollution, they are similar to the continuous vertical installations.


## 2　Coke Ovens

The primary function of coke ovens (Figure 3) is the manufacture, from crushed strongly-coking coals, of coke for the steel industry. In some countries the gas made by these coking installations is integrated with the output of the gas industry. Coke ovens are usually designed to be fired with coal gas (rich gas), or producer gas (lean gas) as desired. For many years the process of firing with producer gas was practised in order to free the coal gas for use in town supplies, and, latterly, instances have been reported of the use of light hydrocarbon distillates for under-firing where these can be obtained at an attractive price (10 & 11). The conversion of town gas systems to natural gas usually results in the oven gas having to be used on the cokery or integrated steelworks, possibly for coke-oven firing.

When producer gas is used for the heating of the ovens it is made in external mechanical coke-burning producers of a type described in Chapter 4.

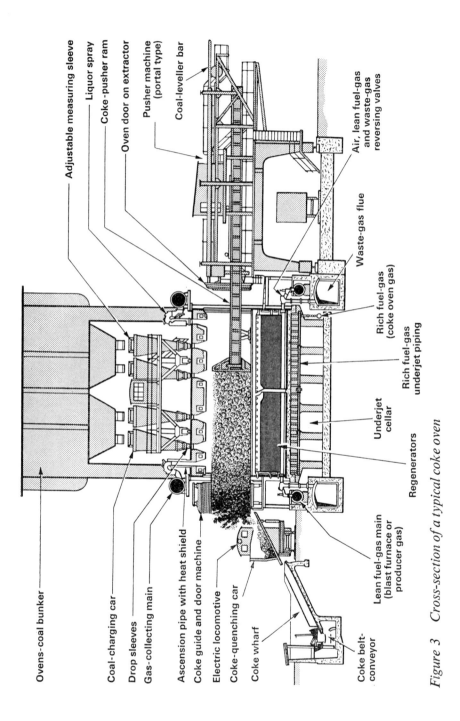

Ovens - coal bunker

Coal-charging car

Drop sleeves

Gas-collecting main

Ascension pipe with heat shield

Coke guide and door machine

Electric locomotive

Coke-quenching car

Coke wharf

Coke belt-conveyor

Lean fuel-gas main (blast furnace or producer gas)

Regenerators

Rich fuel-gas underjet piping

Underjet cellar

Rich fuel-gas (coke oven gas)

Waste-gas flue

Air, lean fuel-gas and waste-gas reversing valves

Coal-leveller bar

Pusher machine (portal type)

Oven door on extractor

Coke-pusher ram

Liquor spray

Adjustable measuring sleeve

*Figure 3   Cross-section of a typical coke oven*

22

The coke-oven plant has a characteristic system of flues below the oven chambers for the efficient interchange of heat from the issuing waste gases to the incoming air and producer gas. These are termed regenerators, in which heat exchange is effected by passing the cold secondary air and producer gas up flues which have previously been heated by the downward passage of waste gas through them. The directions of flow of air and producer gas for combustion, and of waste gas, are reversed every thirty minutes.

The advantages of coke ovens over other systems for gas manufacture are the lower capital and maintenance cost per unit of gas made and the low process-labour requirement. The thermal efficiency of gas manufacture is normally at a high level, such as can be obtained only with difficulty from other carbonizing plants.

The disadvantages are that they are economical only in large installations, they lack flexibility of output, and there is difficulty in producing a coke as suitable for domestic purposes as that obtained from horizontal and vertical retorts.

## 3   Low-Temperature Carbonization

When coking coals are heated (12) a degree of decomposition takes place up to approximately 300°C, with the coal still retaining its normal physical form. Following this, more destructive changes take place over the range 300 to 600°C during which the coal is at first deformed and then becomes plastic. During this phase, all the tarry and condensible volatile matter is driven off, which leads to the formation of a semi-coke. This semi-coke may then be gradually converted into coke by heating over the range 600 to 1 000°C. During this third phase, most of the remaining hydrogen and oxygen is expelled from the coal, taking with it part of the carbon in combination. By forgoing or drastically curtailing the final phase, semi-cokes may be produced which are smokeless in combustion and which are more easily ignited and more flexibly consumed in domestic grates than high-temperature cokes.

Low-temperature carbonization is usually carried out in narrow metal retorts. Special coals or mixtures of coal and low-temperature coke breeze are used.

# The Use of Heavy Oil and Light Distillates in Carbonizing

## 1 Carbonization of Coal/Oil Mixtures

The phenomenal wetting power of petroleum oils, including fuel oils, on coking coal has been known for many years, and the addition of up to 0·5% by weight of such oils to dusty coal for the purpose of reducing dust in coal handling has proved beneficial in some instances.

More recently, mixtures of coking coal and fuel oil containing up to 5·0% oil have been successfully carbonized in horizontal retorts, resulting in a 10·0% increase in gas output from the plant and a 15·0% reduction in the coal required for a given gas output. An estimated gas yield of 1·0 therm per gallon (23 MJ/l) indicates, as may be expected, a higher overall efficiency of gas production from the oil than that obtained from coal alone. The coal/oil mixture was made by adding the heated fuel oil to the coal in a rotating mixer similar in principle to a concrete mixer.

Similar results on a reduced scale have been reported from the addition of up to a maximum of 3% of heavy oil to coal charged into vertical retorts.

Success in improving the gas, benzene and tar yields, and coke quality by the addition of hydrocarbon materials to coke-oven charges has been reported (13 & 14).

## 2 The Use of Light Distillate Feedstocks (LDF) in Vertical Retorts

At a number of gas-works in England (15), light-distillate-feedstock/steam mixtures have been reformed by passage through partly carbonized coal charges in intermittent and continuous vertical retorts. Increases in the thermal output of the carbonizing plant of up to 30% have been achieved by this means, in instances where the normal carbonizing practice involved relatively high steaming rates and long carbonizing periods. Worthwhile although much smaller increases in thermal output are obtainable from systems operating with minimum steaming and maximum coal throughputs. These increased gas outputs are achieved with little change in Wobbe Number and other characteristics of the mixed gas made.

A gas yield is obtained of approximately 0·95 to 1·00 therm per gallon (23 MJ/l) of light distillate feedstock used, on the assumption that the yield of coal-gas and water-gas is unchanged. There is also a slight increase in the net dry coke yield.

In the case of continuous vertical retorts, the rate of carbonization of the coal is appreciably accelerated when light distillate feedstock is used. This, together with the deposition of feedstock carbon on the surface of the coke, would produce a deterioration in coke quality unless it was offset by appropriate adjustment of coal travel rate and/or combustion chamber temperatures. If this is done the coke quality is restored almost to normal.

### 3 Reforming of Liquefied Petroleum Gases in Vertical Retorts

Results similar to those obtained from the reforming of light distillates in the coke charge of intermittent retorts have been achieved using liquefied petroleum gases (16).

### 4 Catalytic Reforming of Butane in Vertical Retorts

An interesting expedient has been reported from a gas works in Australia where a surplus of carbonizing plant in the form of continuous vertical retorts was available together with an economical supply of butane.

A number of these retorts were charged with a crude catalyst made by impregnating 3 inch × 2 inch (75 mm × 50 mm) prisms of insulating brick with nickel nitrate. The retorts were heated to 1 000°C at the first and second combustion chamber levels using butane, and then fed internally with a mixture of 1 volume of butane, 2 volumes of air and 7 volumes of steam.

The butane was reformed into a lean gas with a calorific value of 270 Btu/ft$^3$ (10·2 MJ/m$^3$) which was subsequently cold-enriched to 520 Btu/ft$^3$ (19·7 MJ/m$^3$). Regeneration of the catalyst by the use of steam was carried out for four or five hours at approximately weekly intervals.

Retorts used in this way may be described as continuous refractory-tube catalytic reformers. The volumetric output obtained was 50% above the coal-gas rating, but the overall cold-enriched-gas yield at 75 to 78 heat units per 100 heat units of total feedstock was roughly 10% less than is obtainable using plant specifically designed for the purpose.

25

# Chapter 4    Gasification of Solid Fuels

Although it is not possible to deal comprehensively in this book with all the gasification processes in use, the best known have been set out in the following pages under the headings listed. These are based on differences in characteristics so selected as to produce a grouping convenient for the purpose of description.

Typical characteristics of gases produced by the principal conventional solid-fuel gasification processes are given in Table 9. Similar characteristics for gas produced by the principal commercial unconventional process, namely Lurgi, are given in Table 10.

*Table 9    Typical characteristics of gas produced by the conventional solid-fuel gasification processes*

| Description of gas | | Producer gas | | Blue water-gas | Conventional total-gasification gas | |
|---|---|---|---|---|---|---|
| Plant make or type | | Marischka | Two stage (IFE) | Power-gas | Gaz Integrale | |
| Fuel | | Coke | Coal | Coke | Coal | Coal + Oil |
| Composition | | | | | | |
| $CO_2$ | % vol | 5·7 | 3·4 | 5·0 | 8·0 | 7·0 |
| $O_2$ | | — | 0·2 | — | 0·2 | 0·2 |
| $C_nH_m$* | | — | — | — | 0·6 | 6·8 |
| CO | | 27·3 | 30·0 | 41·0 | 28·5 | 27·2 |
| $CH_4$† | | 0·4 | 2·6 | 0·5 | 6·5 | 11·8 |
| $H_2$ | | 10·6 | 16·1 | 50·0 | 52·2 | 40·0 |
| $N_2$ | | 56·0 | 47·7 | 3·5 | 4·0 | 7·0 |
| Total | | 100·0 | 100·0 | 100·0 | 100·0 | 100·0 |
| Calorific value (gross) | Btu/ft³stp(sat) | 125 | 173 | 295 | 335 | 485 |
| | MJ/m³(st) | 4·74 | 6·57 | 11·18 | 12·72 | 18·41 |
| Specific gravity (air=1·0) | | 0·90 | 0·83 | 0·54 | 0·52 | 0·63 |
| Wobbe number (UK) | | 132 | 190 | 401 | 465 | 611 |
| (SI) | | 5·00 | 7·20 | 15·20 | 17·62 | 23·19 |

\* Unsaturated hydrocarbons

† Includes higher paraffins, if any

# Processes Involving Air or Oxygen

There are many commercial processes designed to gasify completely the combustible matter in solid fuels using steam/air and/or oxygen. The fuels range from agricultural wastes, wood, peat, brown coal, lignite and coke to non-coking or weakly coking coals. Strongly coking coals, because of their agglomerating power, are unsuitable for most of these processes.

The basic reactions involved are expressed as follows:

(i)   *The producer-gas reaction*
$$C + O_2 \rightarrow CO_2 \quad / \quad CO_2 + C \rightleftharpoons 2CO$$

This is strongly exothermic and, therefore, can readily be maintained in continuous operation.

*Table 10   Characteristics of gas produced from a weakly coking British coal at approximately 20 bars pressure by the Lurgi process*

| | | Crude gas (H$_2$S-free basis) | Purified CO-converted gas | Diluted purified gas plus butane (16 bars gauge) |
|---|---|---|---|---|
| Composition | | | | |
| CO$_2$ | % vol | 25·6 | 2·1 | 1·5 |
| O$_2$ | | — | — | 0·2 |
| C$_4$H$_{10}$ | | — | — | 5·8 |
| C$_n$H$_m$ | | 0·6 | 0·4 | 0·6 |
| CO | | 24·4 | 9·8 | 6·9 |
| CH$_4$ | | 10·3 | 13·6 | 9·6 |
| H$_2$ | | 37·3 | 71·8 | 50·4 |
| N$_2$ | | 1·8 | 2·3 | 25·0 |
| Total | | 100·0 | 100·0 | 100·0 |
| Calorific value (gross) | Btu/ft$^3$stp(sat) | 312 | 404 | 477 |
| | MJ/m$^3$(st) | 11·82 | 15·33 | 18·08 |
| Specific gravity   (air=1·0) | | 0·738 | 0·280 | 0·549 |
| Wobbe number (UK) | | — | — | 642 |
| (SI) | | — | — | 24·33 |
| Flame-speed factor | | — | — | 34·4 |

From T. S. Ricketts 'The Operation of the Westfield Lurgi Plant and High-Pressure Grid System', IGE Communication 633

27

(ii)  *The water-gas reaction*

$C + H_2O \rightarrow CO + H_2$

This is strongly endothermic and, if predominant, is usually alternated in a cycle of operations with the exothermic producer gas reaction.

A quantity of carbon dioxide will be produced in both reactions. This quantity depends on the effect of temperature and pressure upon the equilibrium in the reversible producer-gas reaction ($CO_2 + C \rightleftharpoons 2CO$), and, in the case of water-gas, in the water-gas shift or controlling reaction ($CO + H_2O \rightleftharpoons CO_2 + H_2$). Carbon dioxide production will be still further increased according to the extent to which the reactions fall short of these equilibria, and this, in turn, is determined by the reactivity of the fuel and the speed of diffusion of the reacting gases towards it.

Plants employing predominantly the continuous producer-gas reaction are termed 'Producer-Gas Plants'; those employing only the water-gas reaction in the gas-making phase are termed 'Blue-Water-Gas Plants', and those in which the above-mentioned reactions are preceded or accompanied in the same plant by the carbonization of the fuel used are customarily termed 'Complete' or 'Total Gasification Plants'. This latter term may also be applied without discrimination to all these processes.

Prior to 1950 the plants were mainly operated at approximately atmospheric pressure, air being used to supply the oxygen required, but trends subsequently developed towards the use of oxygen, or air/oxygen mixtures, in most cases at pressures higher than atmospheric. The main object of this was to increase the gasification rate per unit of plant cross-section and the pressure of the product gas.

The increased output obtained by the use of oxygen arises not only from the increased partial pressures of the reacting gases, resulting from the complete or partial exclusion of the diluent nitrogen, but also from the fact that producer gas made from oxygen has approximately the same calorific value as water gas. Thus the two reactions can proceed simultaneously in continuous operation without degrading the calorific value of the gas made, so increasing the output of a given generator relative to that obtainable if it were operated cyclically. The effect of the use of oxygen, or oxygen-enriched air, for the blast on the plant output is still further enhanced if the steam content of that blast is maintained at a level low enough, or the blast temperature high enough, to permit liquefaction (*ie* slagging) of the ash.

All these gasification processes have much greater outputs per unit of plant cross-section than carbonizing plants. In addition all the fuel, which has to be heated, is gasified – another advantage over carbonization. Mainly as a result of these factors, complete gasification processes operate at a higher thermal efficiency than carbonizing processes. The losses involved in the manufacture of producer gas may be as low as 10% or 15% of the thermal value of the gas made when it is utilized as a hot fuel gas *in situ*. In the manufacture of cold gases, however, the heat used to supply all losses usually approaches 25%, and in the case of blue-water-gas manufacture it rises to 50% or more of the thermal value of the gas made.

As the gases made, even when undiluted with nitrogen, consist mainly of carbon monoxide and hydrogen, they are higher in density and lower in calorific value than coal gas, and much lower in Wobbe Number than either coal gas or natural gas. Consequently, most of them are too costly to store or transmit and too toxic to be distributed alone in town-gas systems. They are, therefore, mainly used as industrial fuel gases or synthesis gases, and only to a small extent as diluents for high-flame-speed town gas. A possible exception to the foregoing generalization is the product of the Lurgi generator when coal-fed and operated under high pressure with steam and oxygen. Here the enrichment arising from the hydrogenation of the coal makes the gas more acceptable as a component of town gas.

The up-grading of these low-grade industrial fuel and synthesis gases by means of the catalytic conversion of carbon monoxide and hydrogen to methane, in order to render them more acceptable as town gases, though technically possible, is at the present time uneconomical owing to the capital cost and heat losses involved, the latter arising basically from the strongly exothermic nature of the methanation reaction. Apart from the costs and heat losses involved in methane synthesis, enrichment in the form of hydrocarbons in the range methane to light distillate is normally available at a lower cost per heat unit than that of the raw synthesis gas made from solid fuel.

## 1    Producer-Gas Process

The fuel to be gasified, which is mainly coke or coke breeze (although certain coals are used), is contained in a vessel which may be an annular boiler, or a refractory-lined steel shell, or it may be built entirely of refractory materials.

The air blast, which is continuous, is normally saturated with steam at a temperature of approximately 50°C. The object of using steam in the blast is to control, by means of the endothermic water-gas reaction, the temperature of the combustion zone, which in turn controls the degree of fusion of the ash, and the temperatures of the grate and the exit producer-gas. There is also, in effect, a conversion of sensible heat of producer-gas into potential heat of water-gas, which is important in cases where the producer-gas is subject to sensible heat loss before combustion. The admixture of water-gas also raises the calorific value of the gas made, slightly above that possible using the producer-gas reaction alone. The use of coal, as for example in the Demag and Power-Gas coal-fed producers, also results in enrichment of the producer-gas.

A typical example of a low-pressure air-blown coke-fed producer is given in Figure 4.

The high efficiency with which producer-gas is made, together with the low capital cost of the air-blown plants, resulted in its being until recently the most widely used industrial fuel gas. It is normally used where it is made, sometimes without prior cooling and treatment. Its low calorific value and high density, arising from the fact that its main constituent is nitrogen, make it unsuitable for distribution as town gas, for which it was only used as a diluent for calorific-value adjustment.

The increasing availability for use as bulk fuel of natural gas, LPG, and town gas made from hydrocarbon oils, and the high cost and scarcity of coke, are rendering obsolete the conventional producer gas described above.

## 2 Blue-Water-Gas Process

In the blue-water-gas process a producer, usually fed with coke, and similar to those described in the preceding section, is blown with steam (the 'make' or 'run' phase) during which the gas passes through a water seal and condenser into a relief holder. Then, in the blast phase, it is blown with air to atmosphere to restore the temperature of the fuel bed lowered by the water-gas reaction.

When operated to produce blue water-gas as the final product, the producer-gas made during the blast phase is burnt on the outlet of the generator, the waste gas then passing through a waste-heat boiler to atmosphere. Despite this heat recovery, a large proportion of the total heat of the blast gas is lost to atmosphere by radiation and as sensible heat of water-gas and waste gas. As a result the gasification efficiency is the lowest of all fixed-fuel-bed gasification processes.

Blue water-gas has no role in the modern town-gas works based on hydrocarbon oils, and for ammonia synthesis it is rapidly being replaced, in rare cases by the solid fuel processes described in Section 4,

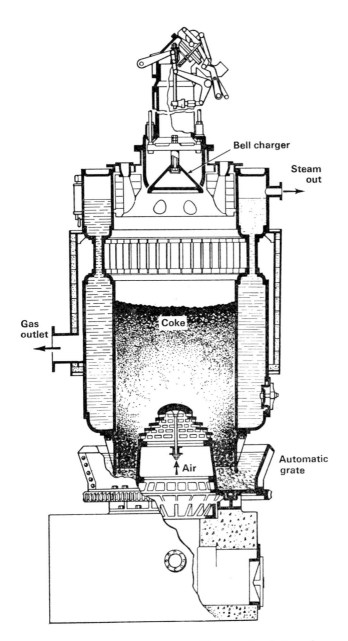

Bell charger

Steam
out

Gas
outlet

Coke

Air

Automatic
grate

*Figure 4    Marischka low-pressure air-blown coke-fed producer*

but more frequently by the high-pressure hydrocarbon reforming processes described in Chapter 6.

## 3 Conventional Complete-Gasification Processes

In this group of processes, coal, usually graded nuts or cobbles, is carbonized in a continuous vertical retort superimposed upon a cyclically operated water-gas generator into which the resulting coke or char gravitates and is gasified. The fuels used fall into a narrow range of fusing but non-agglomerating or weakly agglomerating coals. The gas made is a mixture of coal-gas and water-gas of lower calorific value, higher density and higher carbon monoxide content than is normal for coal-gas-based town gas. In spite of this, town-gas supplies in several instances were based on this gas. It is also used more appropriately, as far as gas quality is concerned, but less appropriately with respect to capital cost, in admixture with coal-gas to meet seasonal demands.

The earliest complete gasification plant of this type was the 'Double Gas' plant of Strache of Vienna. Other plants of this type, of similar design, are the 'Tulley' and 'Power-Gas' complete gasification plants.

Two-stage processes in which the rich gas from the first stage was taken off separately, and recycled in order to decompose the hydrocarbons present, were developed for synthesis-gas manufacture. Examples of these are:

Pintsch Hillebrand Process
Koppers Recycling Process
Viag Synthesis-Gas Process
Bubiag Didier Process.

All the complete gasification processes described in this Section have been superseded by the modern unconventional processes based on the use of either solid fuels or, as is more likely, hydrocarbon feedstocks.

## 4 Unconventional Complete Gasification Processes: Oxygen or Air Based

The processes detailed in Sections 1 to 3, all of which are commercial, have been arbitrarily described as 'conventional', on the basis that they operate at low pressure with fixed fuel-beds and solid-ash removal, and that air and steam are used as the gasifying media. The processes, some of which are sub-commercial, described in this section as 'unconventional', either operate at high pressure, employ fuel in a fluidized or suspended state, produce a fluid ash (slag), use steam/oxygen, or oxygen-enriched air as a gasifying medium, or

32

employ a combination of these departures from conventional methods. Most of these unconventional techniques have the effect of speeding up the reactions involved and, therefore, it is not surprising to find that the processes dealt with under this heading have higher specific fuel throughputs than conventional processes. This, together with the fact that most unconventional processes use oxygen, which must be made on a large scale if its cost is to be economical, renders most of them suitable only for the larger projects.

The types of industrial fuel-gas and synthesis-gas made are too low in Wobbe Number for use alone as high-flame-speed town gas, but this may be overcome by increasing the hydrogen content by means of a shift-catalyst treatment, preceded by catalytic methanation or followed by enrichment with propane, butane or hydrocarbon gases made from liquid hydrocarbons. The relatively high cost of the lean gas, even when based on low-priced solid fuel, together with the heat losses involved in methanation, is likely to result, in most cases, in hydrocarbon sources providing the most economical enrichment.

*(a)   The Lurgi Process*
The gas-making vessel of the Lurgi plant resembles that of a conventional producer-gas or water-gas plant in that it consists of a boiler-jacketed generator with a fixed fuel-bed, provided with a stirring mechanism, on a rotating grate from which the ash is removed in a solid state (Figure 5). Its unconventional features are that it is designed for pressures in the range 20 to 30 bars, and that the gasifying medium is a mixture of superheated steam and oxygen, which allows continuous autothermic operation while producing gas of medium calorific value.

The high gasification pressure employed facilitates the interaction of hydrogen with the coal substance, producing a high yield of methane relative to that obtainable from low-pressure gasification. Dent (17) states that, contrary to the view held earlier, the Sabatier reaction, in so far as it operates, would tend to decompose methane formed by the hydrogenation reaction rather than synthesize methane. The reactions referred to are as follows:

$$C + 2H_2 \rightleftharpoons CH_4 \text{ (coal hydrogenation)}$$
$$CO + 3H_2 \rightleftharpoons CH_4 + H_2O \text{ (Sabatier synthesis)}$$

A high steam/oxygen ratio is maintained to ensure that ash sintering or fusion is avoided. The steam/oxygen ratio also affords a means of control of the hydrogen/carbon-monoxide ratio in the gas made. In a particular case, using a high-ash-content, non-coking coal, a minimum

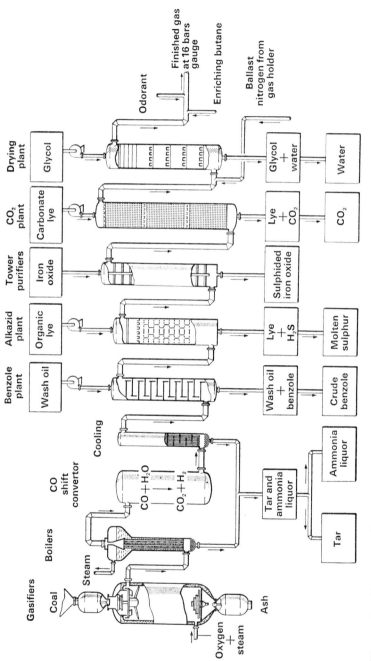

*Figure 5   Diagram of a Lurgi generator with gas treatment train*

34

hydrogen/carbon-monoxide ratio of 1·7:1 was obtained by increasing the oxygen content of the blast, short of fusing the ash. This ratio was increased to 2·4:1 by reducing the oxygen content until the ash presented difficulties owing to its fine state.

A number of alternative processes are available for the treatment and purification of the gas carried out under pressure. The pressure of the purified gas is then a starting point for the higher pressures demanded for the various syntheses or, in the case of town gas, it could provide for the pressure losses of gas transmission. If, however, the gas is required at low pressure, some recovery of power could be achieved by passing it through an expansion turbine. In a typical gas treatment system, the gas leaving the generator is sprayed with hot liquor to assist the deposition of grit and heavy tar, after which it passes into a waste-heat boiler where the bulk of its sensible heat and the bulk of the latent heat of the steam is recovered as low-pressure steam. It is then subjected to carbon monoxide shift conversion, final cooling, benzole recovery, first-stage hydrogen sulphide removal by 'Alkazid', final-stage hydrogen sulphide removal using pressure towers, and carbon dioxide removal by 'Vetrocoke'. The carbon monoxide conversion of the incompletely cooled, unpurified gas is effected by means of a cobalt/molybdenum-oxide catalyst operated in the sulphided state.

The characteristics of the crude, purified and enriched purified gas produced by a plant with a purification system slightly different from that described are given in Table 10. The gas described was used for town-gas production, but gas with suitable carbon-monoxide/hydrogen ratios for various syntheses can readily be produced by control of the steam/oxygen ratio, the carbon monoxide conversion and gas treatment processes.

With the aid of fuel-bed stirring, a range of solid fuels can be gasified, including materials having high ash and sulphur contents. Medium and strongly agglomerating coals and all materials below 2 mm in size are the exceptions.

Gasification rates vary from 100 to 400 lb/ft$^2$ (490 to 1 960 kg/m$^2$) of fuel/grate-area per hour according to the type of fuel used and the pressure employed, compared with a maximum of 60 lb/ft$^2$ (290 kg/m$^2$) per hour for an air-blown, and 150 lb/ft$^2$ (730 kg/m$^2$) per hour for an oxygen-blown, solid-ash producer operated at atmospheric pressure.

The thermal value of the gas made from a low-coking coal, is equivalent to 81 % of the coal fed to the generator, and tar and other products are obtained equivalent to a further 8 %, giving a total recovery on this basis of 89 %. These results were obtained when tar, equivalent to 4·0% wt of the coal carbonized, was recycled by injection into the fuel bed. However, a considerable quantity of heat or energy is required for oxygen and steam production, and a method of expressing the thermal efficiency of the process, which takes this and all other net energy demands into account, thus affording a sounder basis for comparison with conventional processes, is the Pexton efficiency of gas production (18). On this basis of comparison the Lurgi process has an estimated gas production efficiency of 67% for the production of a 400 Btu/ft$^3$ (15·18 MJ/m$^3$) gas compared with an index of 62% for the production of a 600 Btu/ft$^3$ (22·78 MJ/m$^3$) gas by carbonization.

The upgrading of the calorific value of the Lurgi gas to render it interchangeable with high-flame-speed town gas can be effected by the addition of natural gas, propane or, if the pressure of the enriched gas permits, butane. The resulting overall efficiency of town-gas production will vary according to the calorific value of the enricher and the degree of enrichment.

In recent years Lurgi plants have been installed in South Africa, Australia and the UK. In common with other solid-fuel gasification processes, the economic viability of this process is seriously threatened in many areas by the continuous reforming of light distillate feedstock.

Together with the Shell, Texaco and continuous tubular hydrocarbon-reforming processes, the Lurgi process has the advantage of producing gas at pressure. This confers a considerable cost advantage relative to low-pressure processes for the production of synthesis gas or town gas for high-pressure distribution.

*(b)   Winkler-Type Processes*
In these synthesis-gas processes a bed of 0·8 mm fuel particles is maintained in a state of agitation by means of the steam/oxygen or steam/air/oxygen blast, under conditions in which ash that is not blown over with the make-gas is sintered and falls to the bottom of the fuel bed, where it is extracted. The operating pressure is approximately 1 bar.

The original Winkler process was continuous, an important requirement in this case being either that the fuel should be highly reactive, or that the melting point of the ash should be high, or both, in order that the fuel could be gasified at a temperature below that at which difficulty would be experienced owing to the fusion of its ash.

The sub-commercial Flesch-Winkler (single-generator) and BASF Flesch-Demag (twin-generator) processes are cyclic versions of the Winkler process designed to reduce fuel-dust carry-over by means of fuel-bed filtration.

## (c)  The Koppers-Totzek Process

The Koppers-Totzek process is designed to gasify pulverized fuel carried in suspension in oxygen at approximately atmospheric pressure in the presence of steam.

Plant operation is as follows. Coal dried to 2% moisture and pulverized to 0·1 mm is fed into twin hoppers and then conveyed to mixing heads where sufficient oxygen is added to each stream for its gasification. These two streams of coal dust in suspension in oxygen are fed through two groups of six independently fed nozzles into the opposite ends of a small cylindrical refractory-lined combustion chamber, thus producing considerable turbulence. This chamber could be spherical with a larger number of nozzle or tuyere groups arranged radially. Gasification proceeds rapidly owing to the very high temperature of the reaction chamber and some steam is injected around the nozzles to jacket the hot reaction zone and protect the burners and the chamber lining, and to enter into the reactions. The steam is preheated before use by direct firing.

The gas, at a temperature of 1 100 to 1 300°C, flows from the top of the reaction chamber up through a radiation boiler and downwards through a fire-tube boiler for waste-heat recovery. Approximately half of the fuel ash together with 10 to 15% of the fuel, most of which is recovered and used, is carried over in the gas, the remainder being deposited as a fluid slag on the walls of the reaction chamber, from which it flows through a slag tapping into a quenching bowl.

The absence of tar and hydrocarbons in the gas, resulting from the high reaction temperature, simplifies dust removal and renders the gas more suitable for industrial syntheses following carbon monoxide conversion, rather than for use in town gas.

A simplified diagram of the combustor is shown in Figure 6 and typical operating results are set out in Table 11.

This process is more flexible than the Lurgi process with regard to fuel quality, but suffers from the disadvantage of producing low-pressure gas. A pressurized version would be more competitive.

## (d)  Commercial Oxygen/Steam-fed Fixed-Bed Producers
## operated at Atmospheric Pressure

Fixed-bed, coke-fed producers, either of the slagging type such as Leuna, Leuna BASF and Thyssen Galoczy, or ashing-out types such as Kerpely, are uneconomical under present conditions for the following reasons:

1.  All use oxygen (some with steam) and coke, which is now a comparatively high-cost fuel in short supply. In order to offset the cost of

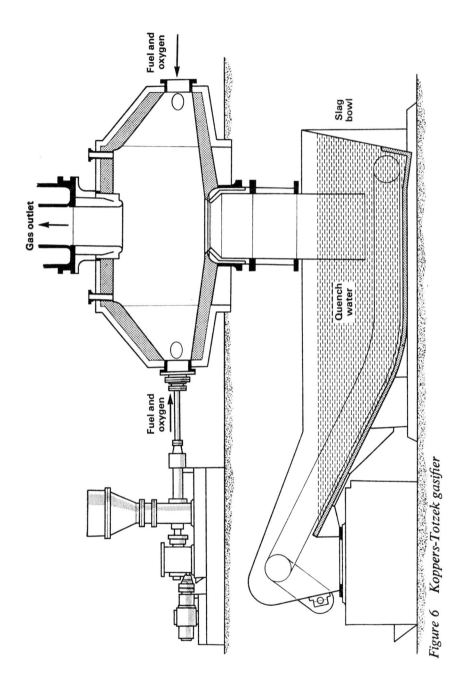

*Figure 6   Koppers-Totzek gasifier*

# Table 11 Typical operating results for the Koppers-Totzek process

| Type of fuel | | Powdered coal (High ash, medium coking) | Fuel oil |
|---|---|---|---|
| **Fuel analysis—dry** | | | |
| Composition | | | |
| C | % wt | 56·2 | 84·60 |
| $H_2$ | | 3·2 | 11·30 |
| $O_2$ | | 3·8 | 0·13 |
| $N_2$ | | 1·0 | 0·40 |
| S | | 0·8 | 3·50 |
| Ash | | 35·0 | 0·07 |
| Total | | 100·0 | 100·0 |
| Calorific value (gross) | Btu/lb | 9 820 | 18 770 |
| | therms/ton | 220 | 420·5 |
| | MJ/kg | 22·8 | 43·6 |
| **Analysis of gas** | | | |
| Composition | | | |
| $CO_2$ | % vol | 11·9 | 4·5 |
| CO | | 55·3 | 48·5 |
| $H_2$ | | 31·1 | 45·4 |
| $N_2$ | | 1·3 | 0·8 |
| $CH_4$ | | 0·1 | 0·1 |
| $H_2S$ | | 0·3 | 0·8 |
| Total | | 100·0 | 100·0 |
| Calorific value (gross) | Btu/ft³stp(sat) | 276·8 | 303·6 |
| | MJ/m³(st) | 10·5 | 11·5 |
| Specific gravity (air=1·0) | | 0·755 | 0·587 |
| NO | ppm | 4 to 5 | <1 |
| Organic sulphur | gr/100 ft³ | 21·9 | 43·7 |
| | g/m³ | 0·50 | 1·03 |

| Type of fuel | | Powdered coal (High ash, medium coking) | | Fuel oil | |
|---|---|---|---|---|---|
| Gas yield | ft³/ton | 56 600 | | 109 700 | |
| | m³/tonne | 1 547 | | 2 997 | |
| Steam generated | w/w of fuel | 1·06 | | 2·0 | |
| lb/1000 ft³stp(sat) of Totzek gas | | 41·93 | | 40·85 | |
| kg/1000 m³(st) of Totzek gas | | 683 | | 665 | |
| | | per 1000 ft³ gas | per 1000 m³ gas | per 1000 ft³ gas | per 1000 m³ gas |
| Consumptions | | | | | |
| Oxygen | ft³ | 360 | — | 277 | — |
| | m³ | — | 360 | — | 277 |
| Power (excluding oxygen) | kWh | 1·48 | 53·2 | 0·4 | 14·4 |
| Steam (low pressure) | lb | 12·5 | — | 16·0 | — |
| | kg | — | 204 | — | 261 |
| Water make-up | gal | 17·5 | — | 11·7 | — |
| | kg | — | 2850 | — | 1 905 |
| *Thermal efficiency | % | 71·3 | | 79·2 | |
| C conversion ratio | % | 96·0 | | 95·6 | |

*Gross heat in raw gas to gross heat in coal charged to gasifier. The efficiency of gas production would be slightly lower, since the process is not quite self-supporting for steam and power.

39

oxygen it is essential, in competing with processes based on hydrocarbon oils, to use low-grade fuels.

2. All operate at low pressure, resulting in substantially increased purification and compression costs relative to pressurized processes.

*(e)    The Rummel Slag-Bath Generator*
Fuel particles in suspension are gasified by injection, together with the preheated gasifying media (*ie* steam and air, or oxygen and air), into a slag bath maintained in the base of a producer shaft. The injection of the reactants is carried out in such a way as to produce turbulence in the slag bath (Figure 7). The fuel particles are further disintegrated by shock heating, and oxygen transfer also assists in promoting the

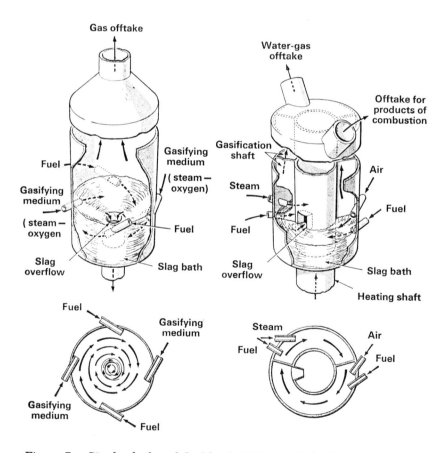

*Figure 7    Single-shaft and double-shaft Rummel slag-bath generators*

40

rapid high-temperature gasification of the fuel. The bulk of the fuel is gasified in the slag bath and the tall shaft above it. The remainder is carried forward in the gas and is recovered as a low-ash-content fraction, which is recycled, and a small high-ash-content fraction which is discarded.

A commercial-scale generator, approximately 6 feet (1·8 metres) in diameter, capable of producing 13 000 000 ft³ (370 000 m³) of water-gas per day, at approximately 1 bar, has operated for some years mainly on brown coal. It is claimed that a thermal yield of 81 % can be achieved with brown coal, although this might fall to 72% when gasifying a high-ash-content fuel of low reactivity. The efficiency of gas production (see page 282) would be approximately 10% lower.

The second device by means of which water-gas is manufactured by the use of air is the double-shaft generator shown in Figure 7. Here the exothermic blast phase and the endothermic water-gas phase are applied to separate sectors of a common slag-bath produced by means of a vertical division wall reaching down a short distance into the bath. This form of the slag bath is still in the experimental stage, and may be referred to as the Otto-Rummel double-shaft slag bath.

On the basis of operating experience with a pilot-scale Otto-Rummel double-shaft slag-bath plant, the view has been expressed by UK Gas Council research workers (19) that, if a sustained effort were made, a technically viable process using slag as a heat-transfer fluid could be developed; but such a process would certainly not be economic under present conditions in the UK.

*(f)   The Kellogg Molten-Salt Process*
This process (Figure 8), which is under development, is similar to the Otto-Rummel double-shaft slag-bath generator just described, in that the endothermic heat required for the manufacture of synthesis gas from solid fuel and steam is provided in the form of sensible heat derived from a molten-salt bath (20).

In both cases the heat input to the bath is achieved by the injection of finely ground coal and air at points separated by a diaphragm with openings below the level of the melt but closed above this level. The object of the design in both cases is to avoid the use of oxygen.

The difference between the two processes is that the Rummel bath is composed of fluid fuel-ash plus a small addition of flux, whereas the Kellogg bath is mainly flux (sodium carbonate) with a molten fuel-ash content limited to 8%. The Kellogg melt is constantly recycled for treatment. Its treatment comprises quenching, grinding, solution, filtration for ash removal and treatment with carbon dioxide (from

41

the purification system) at 38°C to precipitate the sodium as bicarbonate. Most of the fuel sulphur is retained by the salt bath and released as hydrogen sulphide during the treatment with carbon dioxide. The hydrogen sulphide is then reduced to sulphur, say by the Claus process.

The molten-salt bath is operated at 1 000°C and approximately 28 bars pressure. This results in a methane content in the synthesis gas of 7 to 8% by volume, an advantage if the final product is to be synthetic pipeline gas which is mainly methane. The overall efficiency of gas production claimed for the process is approximately 60%.

*(g)   The Texaco Solid-Fuel Gasification Process (Pilot Scale)*
This is a solid-fuel version of the process based on hydrocarbon oil described in Chapter 10 and operates at comparable pressures. The coal is fed to the combustor as a water-based slurry.

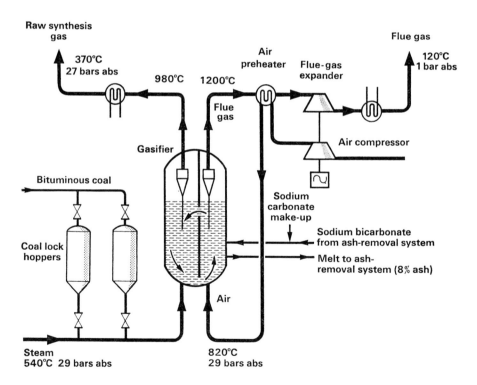

*Figure 8   The Kellogg molten-salt process*

42

*(h)    Underground Gasification of Coal*
Experimental work has been conducted with little success in the UK on the gasification of coal *in situ* both as a substitute for, or ancillary to, conventional mining. In Russia slightly better results were achieved with a special horizontal drilling technique developed to produce the long coal channels used for the purpose. Air and oxygen were the gasifying media and the small quantities of low-grade gas produced were used locally above ground for electricity generation.


## Processes Involving Hydrogasification

The hydrogasification of solid fuels, especially for the production of rich gases, appears attractive, being more direct than methods starting with the oxygenolysis of the whole of the solid process material.

Lignites and coals react rapidly with hydrogen at the start, but the reactions tail off leaving a hydrogen-resistant residue. This residue of roughly half the hydrogenated fuel approximates to the solid fuel requirement for the production of the process hydrogen, which would almost certainly involve oxygenolysis, *ie* reaction with air and/or steam.

No commercial solid-fuel hydrogasification processes have yet evolved, but several under development are described below.

On the basis of current predictions (21) of natural-gas resources in the USA, there is a high probability that prospective natural-gas supplies will appear inadequate in the mid 1970s. (It is feasible that a similar situation will arise in Europe a decade later.) As a result in the USA the development of pilot-scale plants designed to produce synthetic pipeline gas (*ie* methane) is now in progress.

A unique circumstance in the USA is the availability of coal and lignite, within economic gas-transmission range of major population centres, at 20 to 30% of the cost of petroleum feedstocks or imported liquefied natural gas. Hence most of the current synthetic pipeline gas studies in the USA are coal based.

The manufacture of a rich gas by upgrading the low-calorific-value gases made by the processes based entirely or mainly on oxygenolysis described in the previous section is wasteful thermally. The processes favoured, therefore, are those involving the production of the bulk of the methane by reacting hydrogen directly with the coal substance. This stage has to be combined in some way with the oxygenolysis of

43

part of the fuel, as a means of producing the excess hydrogen demand of the finished gas relative to the hydrogen content of the coal used in the process. These combined processes, described below, have been evaluated and costed by the American Gas Association and the Office of Coal Research (22). All the processes are claimed to be economically viable in the USA under the conditions envisaged for the late 1970s although, in view of the novelties involved in all of them, the investment and operation costs should be viewed with reserve until the results of at least sub-commercial-scale plants are available.

Analogous processes have been investigated in Europe, for example by the UK Gas Council's research stations, but the closer relativity of coal and oil prices in Europe should result in the use of hydrocarbon oils for the manufacture of natural gas replacements or supplements. Commercial processes described in Chapter 11 are already available for the purpose and are likely to be used in the USA, at least until one or other of the processes described below becomes technically and economically viable.

*(a)   IGT Hydrogasification Processes (HYGAS)*
An Institute of Gas Technology (Chicago) process design (23) for a plant to manufacture approximately 266 million ft³ (7·4 million m³) of synthetic pipeline-gas per day would operate as follows:

(i)   *Coal pretreatment*
The raw bituminous coal reduced to 2·4 to 0·07 mm by grinding is fed to a water/steam-cooled fluidized pretreatment bed (Figure 9) where it is contacted with approximately its own weight of air. The air pressure in the bed is slightly above atmospheric, and the temperature 400°C. The object of this mild pre-oxidation is to prevent agglomeration in the hydrogasifier.

The products of this stage are:

Loss of weight to pretreatment air*   15·7% w/w of raw coal
Solid fines for fuel use               2·6%     ,,
Char for hydrogasifier                81·7%     ,,
Total                                100·0%
*Mainly carbon dioxide and steam, plus sulphur dioxide equivalent to approximately 1 % w/w of raw coal.

(ii)   *Hydrogasification*
The char is then treated in two fluidized beds (Figure 10) in series, with steam/hydrogen at 740°C and 77 bars absolute

44

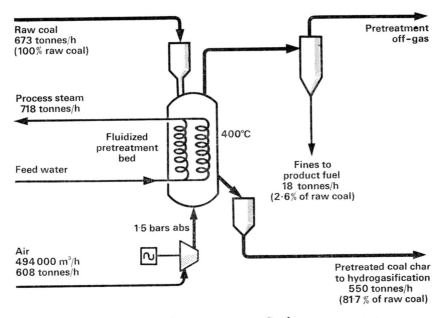

Raw coal
673 tonnes/h
(100% raw coal)

Pretreatment
off-gas

Process steam
718 tonnes/h

Fluidized
pretreatment
bed

400°C

Feed water

Fines to
product fuel
18 tonnes/h
(2·6% of raw coal)

1·5 bars abs

Air
494 000 m³/h
608 tonnes/h

Pretreated coal char
to hydrogasification
550 tonnes/h
(81·7 % of raw coal)

*Figure 9    IGT hydrogasification process: Coal pretreatment stage*

pressure. Slightly less than half of the char is gasified and the remainder is passed on to the gas producer as shown below:

| | | |
|---|---|---|
| Coal-char consumed | 36·9% | w/w of raw coal |
| Coal-char residue to producer | 44·8% | ,, |
| Total | 81·7% | ,, |

(iii)   *Purification and Methanation*
The effluent gas from the hydrogasifier contains large quantities of oxides of carbon and hydrogen. The carbon dioxide together with the bulk of the hydrogen sulphide present are removed by two stages of a hot potash process. The remaining traces of hydrogen sulphide and the organic sulphur present are then removed by solid absorbents, oxide of iron and active carbon respectively, to the low level required for the methanation stage. These purification processes are not illustrated.

In the methanation stages (Figure 11) the bulk of the carbon monoxide and hydrogen react to form methane, as follows:

$$CO + 3H_2 \rightleftharpoons CH_4 + H_2O$$

45

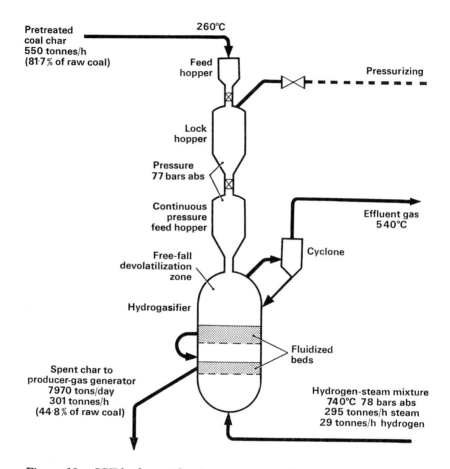

Figure 10    IGT hydrogasification process: Hydrogasification stage

Roughly 40% of the methane in the finished gas is derived from this reaction.

After dehydration the finished gas is estimated to have the following characteristics:

| | |
|---|---|
| Calorific value | 941 Btu/ft$^3$ |
| | 35 MJ/m$^3$ |
| Specific gravity | 0·534 |
| Methane content | 90% |
| Pressure absolute | 70 bars |

The overall efficiency of gas production is estimated at approximately 55%.

46

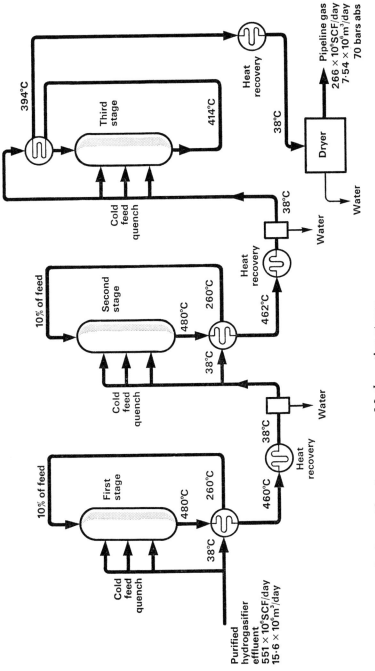

*Figure 11   IGT hydrogasification process: Methanation stages*

47

(iv)   *Hydrogen manufacture* (Figure 12)

The first stage in the production of hydrogen for the gasifier is the manufacture of producer gas from the hot coal-char residue. This is accomplished by means of a slagging cyclone combustor and a fluidized-bed producer in series, both operated at approximately 80 bars absolute.

The steam/iron section used for hydrogen production comprises an 'oxidizer' and a 'reductor' vessel, the iron oxide circulating from one to the other. In the former, roughly half the oxygen content of the steam fed is removed, producing the 50:50 (vol) mixture of steam and hydrogen required by the hydrogasifier. In the 'reductor' vessel this oxygen is removed from the iron oxide by the carbon monoxide and hydrogen in the producer gas.

All stages operate at pressures in the region 70 to 80 bars, and the pressure of the spent producer gas is used to provide the entire power requirements of the process.

Three other designs have been studied by IGT:

In one (24), the Texaco steam/oxygen process is used as the hydrogen source in place of the producer-gas/steam/iron process described above.

In the second (25) the hydrogen source is synthesis gas made from a reaction between steam and rejected fluidized char, the reaction heat being provided by electrically heated elements in the fuel bed.

The third system (26) also involves electrothermal gasification for the synthesis-gas production, but uses lignite as the base fuel and is planned to make approximately five hundred million ft³ (fourteen million m³) per day of pipeline gas, *ie* roughly twice that of the three projects based on bituminous coal. In this case a simple drying process is substituted for the mild air-oxidation pretreatment described above and is designed to prevent agglomeration in the fluidized gasifier when bituminous coal is used. The lignite is fed to the gasifier as a 65% lignite/ 35% light-oil slurry. This light oil is removed by the make-gas, condensed and recycled.

An unusual feature proposed for this project is the 870 MW magnetohydrodynamic (MHD) power and steam generation system fuelled by the spent electrogasifier char. Of this power 120 MW would be a by-product.

Of these three processes the first has a substantially higher estimated efficiency of gas production (65%) than the others, but

48

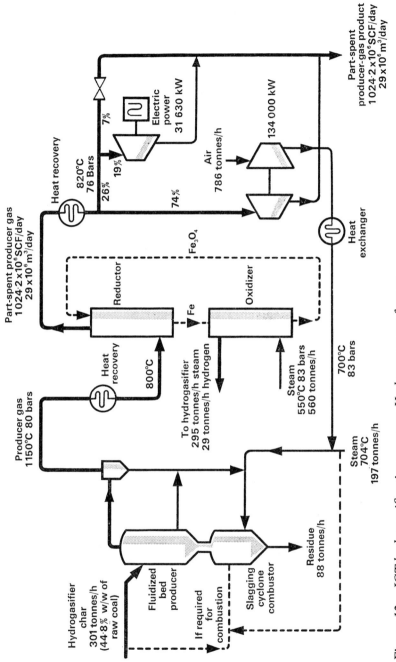

*Figure 12   IGT hydrogasification process: Hydrogen manufacture*

49

the resulting savings in low-cost fuel is more than offset by the cost of the oxygen used.

## (b)    The Carbon Dioxide Acceptor Process

The carbon dioxide acceptor process (27) at present under development on pilot scale in the USA would use powdered dried lignite. Gasification is achieved in two fluidized beds in series (Figure 13). In the first the dry lignite is devolatilized and partially hydrogenated by a lean gas produced in the gasifier. The gasifier is fed with the partially hydrogenated char from the devolatilizer.

The endothermic heat demand of the steam/carbon reactions occurring in the gasifier, and possibly in the lower sections of the devolatilizer, is provided by the exothermic reaction between the evolving carbon dioxide and powdered dolomite.

Incompletely gasified char plus the spent dolomite used as the acceptor for carbon dioxide pass from the gasifier into the regenerator vessel, where the dolomite is regenerated by the combustion in air of the residual combustible matter of the char.

It is proposed that the process should operate to produce a finished pipeline gas at 69 bars pressure with characteristics similar to those of the foregoing hydrogasification processes. In common with these processes, methanation stages will be required in the treatment of the gas, but the bulk of the methane in the finished gas should be obtained

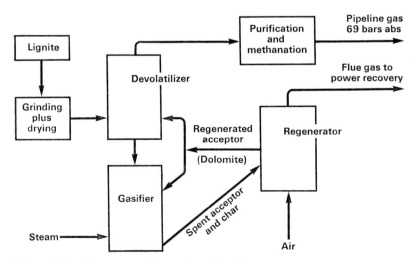

*Figure 13    Diagram of the carbon dioxide acceptor process*

from the hydrogasification stage. It should also be possible to provide all the steam and power requirements of the process from the high-pressure flue gases derived from the regenerator.

## Chapter 5    Carburetted-Water-Gas Process

Carburetted-water-gas manufacture is a combination of solid-fuel gasification, as in blue-water-gas manufacture, and oil gasification. The latter is effected by thermal cracking in the presence of steam and blue-water-gas when normal enrichment is carried out, and in the presence of steam, blue-water-gas and carbon when fuel-bed reforming is practised. The way in which this is accomplished is set out below.

The generator, normally coke fed, is blown alternately with steam to make blue water-gas (the endothermic phase) and with air to make producer gas (the counteracting exothermic phase). The producer gas made during the blow is burnt with secondary air in a second vessel, on the outlet of the generator, which serves as a combustion chamber but which is also the carburettor. The waste gas leaving the carburettor passes through a third vessel, the chequer-filled superheater, for heat exchange, before passing through a waste-heat boiler to atmosphere.

Following the blow, the plant is steam-purged if desired, the blast-stack valve is closed and the gas-making run commences with steam passing up through the generator –the up-run. Carburetting is accomplished by spraying feedstocks, which may range from light distillate to heavy oil, into the carburettor during this phase of the run. The mixture of blue-water-gas and thermally cracked oil-gas so produced passes into the superheater where the cracking operation is completed, the gas becoming stable before passing out of the plant through a wash box.

Following the up-run, more blue water-gas is made by passing steam in the reverse direction, ie from the top of the superheater through the carburettor and then down through the fuel bed. Some of the heat produced by the combustion of the blast gas is thus transferred back to the generator, and the effect of the up-run, which is to push the combustion zone away from the grate, is also counteracted. This phase is termed the back-run and is followed by a short up-run steam purge, so ending the cycle of operations.

If, during the back-run, a hydrocarbon feedstock is introduced into the system at any point from the superheater outlet to the top of the fuel bed, its vapour will be carried down with the steam through the fuel bed. There it will be subjected to severe thermal cracking, conventionally termed reforming, which distinguishes it from the less-rigorous cracking that takes place in the carburettor on the up-run. Provided the hydrocarbon feedstock is gaseous, or can be gasified in the up-run steam, fuel-bed reforming can also be carried out during the up-run phase of the cycle.

Modern carburetted-water-gas plants are fully automatic in operation and are therefore economical in the use of labour. Typical examples of modern plants are Humphreys & Glasgow's, with chequer-filled carburettor, and Power-Gas Corporation's with chequerless carburettor (Figure 14).

The thermal value of the blue-water-gas made when no oil gasification is practised is 60 to 65% of that of the coke fed. The thermal value of the oil-gas produced from enriching varies from 96% of the thermal value of the feedstock when the lightest distillates are used to 65% with heavy oil. There is no appreciable tar yield from the former, but 25 to 30% of tar on the volume of oil used is produced from heavy oil.

When enriching is carried out, the blue-water-gas efficiency calculated by conventional means (*ie* by the deduction of the oil-gas from the total gas produced) falls, for example, from 60 to 65% to 55 to 60% when gas of 500 Btu/ft$^3$ (18·98 MJ/m$^3$) is made. This arises from the fact that, in this process, the additional coke consumed during the blow to supply the heat demands of oil gasification is debited against the blue-water-gas efficiency. If the latter is assumed to remain unchanged at 60 to 65% (*ie* if the thermal value of the additional coke consumed during the blow as the result of oil gasification is debited against the oil-gas made) then the efficiencies of oil-gas manufacture by enriching and reforming become approximately 90% and 80% respectively.

The conventional role of the carburetted-water-gas process was that of meeting seasonal and peak gas loads, a function more economically effected by the use of the cheaper oil-gasification processes now available. The construction of new carburetted-water-gas plants has practically ceased. Those still in use mainly use light distillate feedstocks for enrichment and fuel-bed reforming, or are converted to cyclic hydrocarbon reforming. These techniques are described in the following pages.

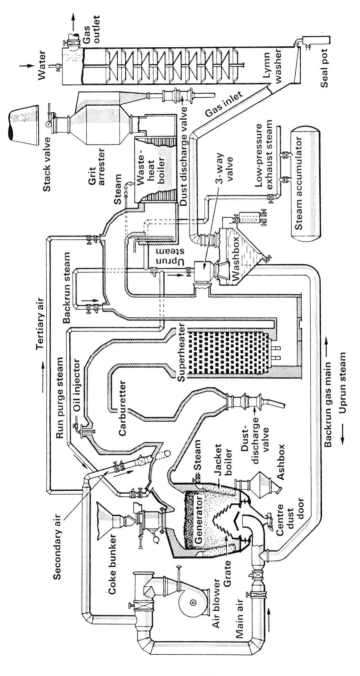

*Figure 14 Carburetted-water-gas plant, reverse-flow system, dry-base generator (Courtesy of Power-Gas Corporation)*

54

## Enriching Blue Water-Gas with Heavy Oil and Light Distillate Feedstocks

With minor adaptations, modern carburetted-water-gas plants can be made very flexible as to the type of enriching feedstock that may be used. Hydrocarbon materials from the lightest constituents to heavy oil (up to at least 12% Conradson carbon content) can be employed successfully.

Liquid feedstocks lighter than gas oil present no problem and may all be gasified more readily than the latter, resulting in a higher maximum obtainable degree of enrichment, and a slight increase in output at a given calorific value. Typical data relating to this are given in Table 12, from which it will be seen that the use of heavy oil involves a reduction in the degree of enrichment obtainable, and a loss of roughly 20% of output.

When heavy fuel oil is used, it is necessary to preheat to approximately 120°C and to apply sufficient pressure for good atomization at the spray. A value of 120 lb/in² (8·5 bars) should be regarded as the minimum, and 250 lb/in² (18 bars) is preferable.

Emulsion difficulties with the tar are solved by the use of surface-active agents such as 'Amine 220' and 'Fatchemco T.E.B.' at the rate of 1 part per 2 500 parts of dry heavy oil-tar made. This is added continuously to the wash box and scavenging spray liquor, the circulating rate of which is augmented. The moisture content of the tar is thereby reduced sufficiently for it to be used as boiler fuel without further dehydration.

Chequerless types of carburettor have mainly been used in the past for heavy oils of high Conradson carbon content, but the chequer-packed type is also effective. Carbon deposited in these vessels is removed either by maintaining an excess of oxygen during the combustion of the blast gas, or by means of a short blow with cold or preheated air into the carburettor following the main blast. In the case of the chequerless type of carburettor, any solid carbon residue can be removed by hand, say, every two days.

## Water-Gas Plant Fuel-Bed Reforming

The use of heavy oil for reforming, by spraying on top of the fuel in the water-gas plant generator during the back-run, has been used over a long period in the USA in order to substitute oil in part for the more

*Table 12   Comparative typical data for maximum output from the carburetted-water-gas plant described, with various feedstocks used for conventional enriching*

| | | | Conventional enriching only | | |
|---|---|---|---|---|---|
| | | Fuel oil | Distillate feedstocks | | |
| Enriching feedstock | | | Gas oil | Heavy naphtha | Light naphtha |
| Average time of operation | | 21 h 0 min | 23 h 4 min | 23 h 4 min | 23 h 4 min |
| Maximum daily output | 1 000 ft³ | 2 365 | 2 864 | 2 970 | 2 997 |
| | m³ | 65 702 | 79 567 | 82 509 | 83 262 |
| Oil gas | therms | 5 838 | 8 077 | 9 391 | 7 913 |
| | GJ | 616 | 852 | 991 | 835 |
| Coke gas | therms | 5 232 | 6 343 | 5 667 | 7 162 |
| | GJ | 552 | 669 | 598 | 755 |
| Total | therms | 11 070 | 14 420 | 15 058 | 15 075 |
| | GJ | 1 168 | 1 521 | 1 589 | 1 590 |
| Gas yield per UK gal feedstock | therms | 1·13 | 1·27 | 1·29 | 1·25 |
| Gas yield per kg feedstock | MJ | 27·4 | 34·7 | 40·0 | 44·7 |
| Calorific value of feedstock | therms/UK gal | 1·76 | 1·67 | 1·50 | 1·35 |
| | MJ/kg | 42·6 | 45·7 | 46·5 | 48·3 |
| Specific gravity of feedstock | | 0·96 | 0·85 | 0·75 | 0·65 |
| Tar produced | % vol of oil | 28·0 | 14·0 | trace | trace |
| Feedstock used | UK gal | 5 166 | 6 360 | 7 280 | 6 330 |
| | kg | 22 496 | 24 522 | 24 764 | 18 663 |
| Calorific value of gas made | Btu/ft³stp(sat) | 468* | 503 | 507 | 503 |
| | MJ/m³(st) | 17·73 | 19·06 | 19·21 | 19·06 |
| Specific gravity of gas made (air=1·0) | | 0·640 | 0·650 | 0·640 | 0·675 |
| Typical cycle (duration 3 minutes) | | | | | |
| Blow | % | 39·0 | 41·0 | 40·0 | 40·0 |
| Blow purge | % | 3·0 | 0·6 | nil | nil |
| Up-run oiling | % | 22·0 | 28·5 | 30·0 | 30·0 |
| Up-run total | % | 35·6 | 36·5 | 33·6 | 36·6 |
| Back-run oiling | % | nil | nil | nil | nil |
| Back-run total | % | 19·0 | 18·5 | 23·0 | 20·0 |
| Run-purge | % | 3·4 | 3·4 | 3·4 | 3·4 |

*Maximum calorific value obtained

56

expensive coke as generator fuel. In some cases the process was pressed to the extreme of excluding coke altogether, bringing out the point that it is not difficult technically to convert carburetted-water-gas plants into Hall-gas plants.

At the present time light petroleum distillates are being used for back-run reforming on conventional water-gas plants in England. The changes made in plant operation and process conditions in order to do this are slight, involving only the coke charging of the generator on the blow instead of the back-run, and an increase in the time allowed for the back-run and a reduction in the quantity of steam used during that phase of the cycle. Details of typical results obtained are given in Table 13, from which it will be seen that fuel-bed reforming with a light distillate produces an increase of 25 to 30% in gas output, and that the quality of the gas made is improved, the specific gravity being approximately 0·10 lower than that of carburetted-water-gas of equivalent calorific value made in the conventional manner. This improvement in the gas quality arises from the fact that the oil-gas element in the mixed gas derived from reforming has a calorific value of approximately 500 Btu/ft$^3$ (18·98 MJ/m$^3$) and a specific gravity of approximately 0·40, compared with a calorific value of 1 600 Btu/ft$^3$ (60·64 MJ/m$^3$) and a specific gravity of approximately 0·95 for the oil-gas element in the mixed gas made when conventional enriching only is practised.

The figures given in Table 13 are typical of those obtained when feedstock of 0·65 specific gravity is sprayed on top of the fuel bed during the back-run. The addition of feedstock to the carburettor enables a similar increase in output to be achieved, although when this vessel is used for enriching on the up-run it is necessary to add a small quantity of steam to the blast air. The factor limiting the extent of the reforming, and hence governing the gas output, is the possibility of delay in the ignition of the blast gas.

When the feedstock is applied to the superheater outlet, the efficiency of the process is improved, since the fuel is preheated and evaporated by the sensible heat in the superheater outlet chequers, and the temperatures of the up-run gas and blow gas leaving the plant are reduced.

Application of the feedstock for reforming to the carburettor and the superheater outlet simultaneously enables a peak gas output of 40% above the rated output to be obtained compared with the increase of 25 to 30% obtainable when the reforming feedstock is applied to the top of the fuel bed only. In this case, the heat transfer from the superheater outlet chequers counteracts the delaying effect of the feedstock supplied to the carburettor on ignition of the blast gas.

**Table 13** *Comparative results of LDF reforming only and LDF reforming and enriching, with gas oil enrichment. The second column shows the maximum fuel-bed reforming rate.*

| | | CWG with gas-oil enriching | Blue-water-gas plus light distillate reforming | CWG with gas-oil enriching | CWG enriching and reforming .with light distillate |
|---|---|---|---|---|---|
| Average time of operation | | 23 h 4 min | 23 h 4 min | 23 h 4 min | 23 h 4 min |
| Maximum make | 1000 ft³ | 2 500 | 3 283 | 2 864 | 3 607 |
| | m³ | 69 453 | 91 203 | 79 565 | 100 210 |
| Oil gas | therms | 3 542 | 8 173 | 8 077 | 14 455 |
| | GJ | 374 | 862 | 852 | 1 525 |
| Coke gas | therms | 6 158 | 4 597 | 6 343 | 3 688 |
| | GJ | 650 | 485 | 669 | 389 |
| Total | therms | 9 700 | 12 770 | 14 420 | 18 143 |
| | GJ | 1 024 | 1 347 | 1 521 | 1 914 |
| Yield | | | | | |
| per gal feedstock | therms | 1·30 | 1·13 | 1·27 | 1·18 |
| per kg feedstock | MJ | 35·6 | 40·4 | 34·7 | 42·2 |
| Calorific value of feedstock | therms/UK gal | 1·67 | 1·35 | 1·67 | 1·35 |
| | MJ/kg | 45·7 | 48·3 | 45·7 | 48·3 |
| Specific gravity of feedstock | | 0·85 | 0·65 | 0·85 | 0·65 |
| Tar produced per volume of feedstock | % | 14·0 | trace | 14·0 | trace |
| Feedstock used | UK gal | 2 725 | 7 233 | 6 360 | 12 250 |
| | kg | 10 506 | 21 325 | 24 521 | 36 117 |
| Product gas characteristics | | | | | |
| Composition | | | | | |
| $CO_2$ | % vol | 6·7 | 4·3 | 5·0 | 2·6 |
| $O_2$ | | 0·3 | 0·2 | 0·6 | 0·3 |
| $C_nH_m$ | | 4·9 | 2·8 | 9·0 | 7·7 |
| CO | | 32·7 | 27·0 | 30·5 | 24·3 |
| $CH_4$ | | 4·9 | 7·7 | 8·3 | 12·8 |
| $C_2H_6$ | | 1·1 | 0·1 | 1·6 | 1·0 |
| $H_2$ | | 42·7 | 52·6 | 36·4 | 44·2 |
| $N_2$ | | 6·7 | 5·3 | 8·6 | 7·1 |
| Calorific value | Btu/ft³ | 389 | 389 | 503 | 503 |
| | MJ/m³ | 14·77 | 14·77 | 19·09 | 19·09 |
| Specific gravity (air=1·0) | | 0·610 | 0·510 | 0·650 | 0·540 |
| Wobbe number (UK) | | 498 | 545 | 622 | 684 |
| | (SI) | 18·89 | 20·69 | 23·62 | 25·97 |

*Table 13* *(continued)*

| | | CWG with gas-oil enriching | Blue-water-gas plus light distillate reforming | CWG with gas-oil enriching | CWG enriching and reforming with light distillate |
|---|---|---|---|---|---|
| **Typical cycle (duration 3 min)** | | | | | |
| Blow | % | 33·0 | 35·0 | 41·0 | 42·0 |
| Blow purge | % | nil | nil | 0·6 | nil |
| Up-run oiling | % | 30·0 | nil | 28·5 | 24·0 |
| Up-run total | % | 38·6 | 28·6 | 36·5 | 30·1 |
| Back-run oiling | % | nil | 31·0 | nil | 23·5 |
| Back-run total | % | 25·0 | 32·0 | 18·5 | 23·5 |
| Run purge | % | 3·4 | 4·4 | 3·4 | 4·4 |
| Primary air rate | ft³/min | 8 500 | 8 415 | 8 300 | 8 300 |
| | m³/min | 236·1 | 234·3 | 231·0 | 231·0 |
| Up-run steam rate | lb/min | 110 | 170 | 130 | 150 |
| | kg/min | 49·9 | 77·1 | 59·0 | 68·0 |
| Back-run steam rate | lb/min | 230 | 100 | 260 | 130 |
| | kg/min | 104·3 | 45·4 | 118·0 | 60·0 |
| Primary air per cycle | ft³ | 8 420 | 8 840 | 10 210 | 10 450 |
| | m³ | 234·5 | 246·2 | 283·7 | 290·3 |
| Up-run steam per cycle | lb | 139 | 170 | 158 | 155 |
| | kg | 63·1 | 77·1 | 71·7 | 70·3 |
| Back-run steam per cycle | lb | 172 | 96 | 144 | 92 |
| | kg | 78·0 | 43·6 | 65·3 | 41·7 |
| Total steam per cycle | lb | 311 | 266 | 302 | 247 |
| | kg | 141·1 | 120·6 | 137·0 | 112·0 |
| Reformed light distillate per cycle | lb | — | 104·6 | — | 97·3 |
| | kg | — | 47·4 | — | 44·1 |
| Enriching feedstock per cycle | lb | 50·3 | — | 117·3 | 77·2 |
| | kg | 22·8 | — | 53·2 | 35·0 |

Although the figures shown result from the reforming of light distillate with a specific gravity of 0·65, heavier materials are normally used and the resulting increases in output are lower, possibly falling to approximately one half of the figures quoted if the specific gravity of the material used rises to 0·75. This reduction in output is attributable to restriction of air and gas flows resulting from carbonaceous deposits in the fuel bed, ash bed and grate louvres.

It will be useful to examine the main effects on the operation of ancillary plant of the use of light distillate feedstock for reforming in carburetted-water-gas practice. The principal general effect is that of overload arising from the increase in gas output obtainable. Where this cannot be tolerated, as may be the case with gas-exhausting plant, the modification, augmentation or replacement of plant will be necessary. On the other hand, for example in the case of the gas mains, condensers and detarrers, it may be practical and economical to tolerate the overload.

The second general effect is that which results from the loss of the scavenging action of gas-oil tar on the ancillary plant mains and vessels. This effect is tolerable when light distillates are used for enriching only, but when they are used for reforming it is exacerbated by a third effect, namely the presence of greater quantities of naphthalene in the gas.

The problem presented by the deposition of only a trace of tar together with the coke grit normally present in water gas, and the greatly increased naphthalene deposition in closed-surface condensers and other ancillary plant mains and vessels, is dealt with by operating water-gas plant condensers of this type at high outlet-gas temperatures and by the use of liquor, tar or creosote sprays at appropriate points prior to the naphthalene washing to which the gas at some stage must be subjected. Direct-contact condensers with closed cooling-water systems present no problem in this respect, and can be operated at as low a temperature as ambient conditions permit.

A very effective means of scavenging the gas mains and ancillary plant is to change over from light distillate feedstock to gas oil for enriching. The reforming light distillate feedstock can be retained during this period if desired. Where the price differential is small this could be carried out for one day each week and would largely remove the need for other precautions apart from the final naphthalene wash.


## Conversion of Carburetted-Water-Gas Plants to Hydrocarbon Reforming

The fuel-bed reforming technique in carburetted-water-gas manufacture that has been described is a means of increasing the content of the cheaper hydrocarbon-based gas component relative to the blue-water-gas element made from coke.

The process of the displacement of the coke-gas element can, however, be pressed to the limit by converting the plants into either continuous autothermic plants of the Distrigaz type to make a lean

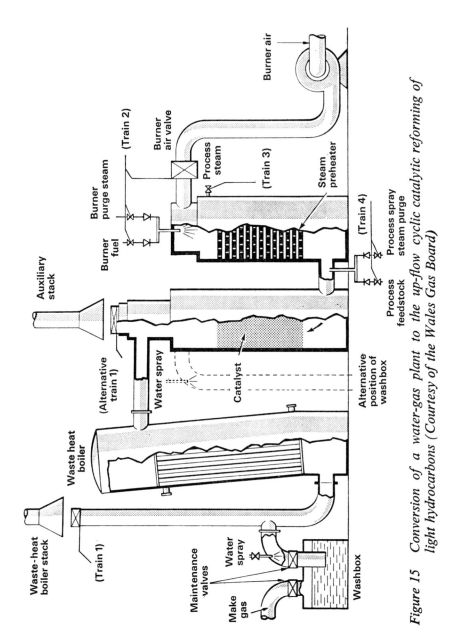

*Figure 15  Conversion of a water-gas plant to the up-flow cyclic catalytic reforming of light hydrocarbons (Courtesy of the Wales Gas Board)*

61

heavy gas, into cyclic Hall-gas plants for the manufacture of a rich oil-gas as has been done in America, or, more appropriately from the viewpoint of the quality of the gas made, into cyclic hydrocarbon-reforming plants manufacturing a high-flame-speed town gas in the range 450 to 550 Btu/ft$^3$ (17·1 to 20·9 MJ/m$^3$) direct from liquefied petroleum gases or light distillate. The gas made would be roughly equivalent in quality to the town gas, whereas carburetted-water-gas can be used only as a supplementary gas and is more toxic.

Figure 15 shows a diagram of the conversion in Wales of the carburettor and the superheater of a 1 to 1·5 million ft$^3$ (0·04 million m$^3$) per day carburetted-water-gas plant into a cyclic uniflow reforming plant in which the reactants flow upwards through the catalyst as in the CCR (UGI) reforming process. In this diagram the simplest possible arrangement of operating 'trains' is shown. It will be seen that four 'trains' only are required. Alternatively such a CWG plant could be converted into a cyclic uniflow reforming plant of the 'Onia Gegi' type with reactant flowing downwards through the catalyst bed.

The main object of such plant conversions is to exploit the roughly twofold increase in output obtainable when using a low-sulphur-content hydrocarbon feed such as liquefied petroleum gas in the converted plants, compared with the output of the original carburetted-water-gas plants. This is justified when the plants are to be used for extreme peak and stand-by purposes.

In conditions where load factors of the order of 50% or more are involved, it might be economical to forgo any increase in output in order to utilize a light distillate feedstock of appropriate quality in place of LPG, and exploit the conversion in terms of reduced process costs rather than in terms of reduced capital costs.

The quality of the gas made and the process efficiency of these converted plants, for a given feedstock, would correspond to those relative to similar types of plant described in Chapter 6.

# Chapter 6     Oil Gasification and Hydrocarbon-Gas
Reforming: Thermal-Cracking Processes

As stated in the Introduction, the manufacture of town gas or synthesis gas from solid or liquid mineral fuels may be regarded as a process
combining the cracking or breaking down of large molecules, and
the increasing of the proportion of hydrogen in the gaseous products
either by the removal of carbon or the addition of hydrogen, usually
derived directly or indirectly from steam.

From the following comparison of carbon/hydrogen ratios it will
be seen that, although the heaviest hydrocarbon oil has a considerable
advantage over coal as a starting point, its carbon/hydrogen ratio is
still much higher than that required in the finished gas.

**Carbon/Hydrogen ratio**
**[approximate]**

| | |
|---|---|
| Coking Coal | 15·5:1 |
| Heavy Fuel Oil | 7·8:1 |
| Light Distillate Feedstock | 5·6:1 |
| Natural Gas | 3·0:1 |
| Town Gas | |

From these ratios it can be seen that if town gas is manufactured by
simple thermal cracking without the addition of hydrogen, as in the
carbonization of coal, all the hydrogen gasified together with an
appropriate quantity of carbon amount to only 25% of the weight of
coal substance, leaving 75% mainly as coke and, to a small extent, as
high-carbon-content tar. A similar calculation applied to the heavy
oil would suggest that slightly less than half of it by weight could be
gasified, leaving 50% as either carbon or tar. This is what appears to
happen when heavy fuel oil is carbonized in admixture with coal,
although the thermal value of the gasified portion is approximately
60% of the total thermal value of the oil, owing to the fact that it
contains the bulk of the hydrogen of the heavy oil, which has a higher
calorific value than carbon.

The actual mechanism of the decomposition of hydrocarbons by
pyrolysis (*ie* thermal cracking) must vary according to the size and
type of the hydrocarbon molecules involved, and the temperature and
pressure at which the reactions take place. Low temperatures and high
pressures both favour the breaking of carbon-to-carbon bonds of

63

paraffins near the centre of the chain, whereas high temperatures and low pressures favour the breaking of the chain nearer the ends, and the breaking of carbon-to-hydrogen bonds, possibly with the production of carbon, particularly in the case of the smaller paraffin molecules.

The reaction sequence in the case of rigorous thermal cracking of large paraffin molecules is probably as follows:

*Phase 1* Production of lower paraffins and olefins by the breaking of the paraffin chain

*Phase 2* Cracking and polymerization of olefins to produce diolefins and still lower paraffins

*Phase 3* Further cracking, polymerization and 'condensation' of olefins and diolefins to produce ring compounds such as naphthenes and benzene

*Phase 4* Naphthenes and benzene further dehydrogenated to produce multi-ring aromatics, tar and, finally, carbon.

Following the first phase described, the remaining phases are of progressive dehydrogenation of the hydrocarbon molecules. Hydrogen and the relatively stable methane and ethylene appear from the second phase onwards, although as the condition becomes more rigorous these latter are to some extent further cracked to carbon and hydrogen. The final gaseous products normally consist mainly of hydrogen, methane, smaller amounts of ethane and propane, ethylene and still smaller amounts of its homologues, and benzene with small amounts of higher aromatics. The process also results in the production of some tar and/or carbon, which must inevitably rise in proportion to the extent to which the carbon/hydrogen ratio of the feedstock used exceeds that desired in the gaseous product. This accounts for the fact that the use of catalysts in purely thermal cracking, a common technique in the oil industry, has little significance in the manufacture of gas from hydrocarbon oils.

The reaction-heat demand arising from the production of a rich gas, say of 1 500 Btu/ft³ (56·94 MJ/m³), by the thermal cracking of liquid hydrocarbons is small since the degree of dehydrogenation involved is slight, but it rises to approximately 5-10% of the potential heat of the process material in the extreme case of methane cracked to carbon and hydrogen.

If the thermal cracking process is carried out in the presence of hydrogen at partial pressures in excess of 7 bars gauge, the results obtained suggest that the reactions follow a similar course, except that practically all the unsaturated hydrocarbon fragments produced are either hydrogenated, or 'condensed' to form parent aromatic hydro-

64

carbons such as benzene and naphthalene. Tar and/or carbon production is reduced in most cases, but the condensable saturated and aromatic hydrocarbon content of the gas is increased.

The reaction heat arising from hydrogen absorption from the carrier gas is considerable, even with a hydrogen partial pressure of 4 bars gauge, and permits autothermic enriching of hydrogen under certain conditions. At atmospheric pressure, however, reaction heat is negligible and the process would demand the application of external heat, or the use of process air, to offset any sensible and latent heat demand of the process material and heat losses of the system.

The application of this thermal cracking process to hydrocarbon feedstocks containing unsaturated, naphthenic or aromatic hydrocarbons would result in a decrease in gas yield, particularly of methane and ethylene, and in an increase in the tar and/or carbon produced.

Probably the first uses of petroleum oil for the manufacture of town gas were those in which crude oil was thermally cracked with steam at atmospheric pressure, and at temperatures in the range 1 000 to 1 100°C, to produce gas of 500 to 600 Btu/ft$^3$ (18·98 to 22·8 MJ/m$^3$) to replace the more costly coal gas. These techniques originated on the west coast of America and are usually termed 'Pacific Coast Oil-Gas' processes, exemplified by the Jones process. Under the severe cracking conditions employed to produce such a gas, the steam used entered into the reactions, and the resulting gas, a satisfactory substitute for coal-gas-based town gas, might have contained up to 40% of blue water-gas and have had a specific gravity of 0·45. The gas yield, however, was low at roughly 50% of the thermal value of the oil used, with a considerable production of carbon black, and possibly a smaller amount of viscous tar of high naphthalene and carbon content.

Subsequently the range of process materials used was extended to cover most liquid hydrocarbon feedstocks, and, in cases where increased carbon-black production was desired at the expense of the gas yield, the calorific value range was extended down to 350 Btu/ft$^3$ (13·2 MJ/m$^3$) at which point no fluid tar is produced. Natural gas has been reformed in this type of plant, with the production of carbon black and a methane/hydrogen mixture in the calorific value range 550 to 750 Btu/ft$^3$ (20·9 to 28·5 MJ/m$^3$).

This purely thermal cracking process for the manufacture of a high-flame-speed town gas from crude or residual oil may be regarded as superseded by the more efficient 'Segas' cyclic catalytic process, described later. For even more efficient processing of lighter materials a range of cyclic and continuous catalytic processes is now available.

65

Where the carbon black produced can be marketed at a price sufficient to offset the low gasification efficiency, the Jones type of process can be economical, and the description of a plant designed to operate in these conditions now follows.

## The Jones Process Modified for Carbon-Black Production

A Jones plant in which the emphasis in design and operation is on a high yield of dry carbon black, with gas yield and quality treated as secondary considerations, is illustrated diagrammatically in Figure 16. The economic basis of the process is the price obtained for the carbon black produced, and it is operated continuously under constant conditions. The gaseous by-product, which has a calorific value of 360 Btu/ft$^3$ (13·7 MJ/m$^3$) and specific gravity of 0·38, forms part of a base-load town-gas supply. The carbon yield, depending upon the feedstock used, may be 40% or more, the greater part of which is recovered dry (28).

It is a four-vessel plant in which the outer, smaller chequer-filled vessels are heat exchangers only, and the inner, larger, generator vessels are provided with heating and process-oil sprays and vaporizing spaces in the top, above large banks of chequers.

The cycle consists of a blow through the four vessels in one direction during which the plant temperatures are restored partly by the combustion of carbon left behind and partly by auxiliary oil-heating. This is followed by a gas-making run in the same direction, using steam which is preheated in the first vessel before meeting the process-oil spray in the top of the second vessel. As with the Hall plants, regeneration is achieved by operating the succeeding blow and run in the reverse direction. The time taken for one blow and run is approximately seven minutes.

The make-gas is partially quenched with water in the first of the four carbon-recovering vessels shown in the centre of the diagram, and 80 to 85% of the carbon produced is recovered in a dry state from this vessel and the three cyclones arranged in series to the right of it. The gas is then finally freed from carbon by various contacts with water, after which it passes to the relief holder prior to purification and naphthalene washing.

66

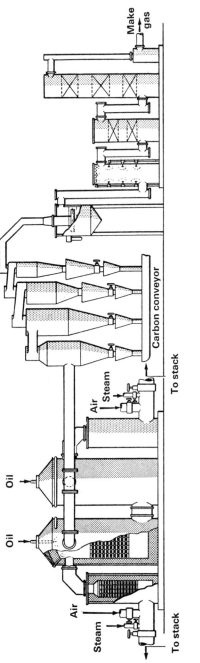

Air

Steam

Oil

Oil

Air

Steam

To stack

Carbon conveyor

To stack

Make
gas

Generator unit

Carbon recovery unit

Gas washing unit

*Figure 16   Jones plant*

67

## Hall-Type Processes

The cracking carried out in these processes is much less rigorous than that of the Jones process as normally operated. The object is to produce additives, or the closest possible substitutes, for natural gas. The process was originally carried out in adapted water-gas plants, but modern plants specifically designed for the purpose were constructed.

Distillate, crude or residual oils may be gasified, although, as would be expected, gasification efficiency and output fall away as heavier oils are used, especially those with high Conradson carbon contents. An attempt to make a low-inert-content gas of 1 000 Btu/ft$^3$ (37·96 MJ/m$^3$) from the latter oils usually results in operating difficulties owing to carbon and pitch deposition. As a result it is usual to make a richer gas of, say, 1 200 Btu/ft$^3$ (45·5 MJ/m$^3$) which is reduced by means of blow-running (ie passing the first blow gases into the make), which has the advantage of reducing smoke emission at the beginning of the blow.

Even with fuel oil of, say, 10 % Conradson carbon content it is usual to manufacture gas well above 1 000 Btu/ft$^3$ (37·96 MJ/m$^3$). However, the use of the blow-run on the latest plants is not essential for smoke reduction when oils with this level of Conradson carbon content are used, owing to improved design and control. The yield of unstripped gas in the calorific value range 950 to 1 250 Btu/ft$^3$ (36·0 to 47·4 MJ/m$^3$), resulting from thermal cracking in Hall-type plants, varies from 82 % of the thermal value of the feedstock in the case of light distillate feedstock of specific gravity 0·65, to as low as 50 % in the case of the heaviest fuel oils. In the latter case the yield of tar products would be equivalent to 20 to 30 % of the thermal value of the feedstock, whilst the yield from the light feedstock would be less than 5 %.

Although gases made in this way are, after stripping, sometimes fully substituted for natural gas, the substitution is not completely satisfactory. Furthermore, the gas is produced at low pressure, and if made from high-sulphur-content feedstock has an undesirably high organic-sulphur content. A more recent development when light distillate feedstock is being gasified is the introduction of a layer of catalyst above the oil-vaporizing space over the chequers. The characteristics of the gas made under these conditions are given in Table 14, Column 5, together with the characteristics of gas made by thermally cracking a variety of feedstocks.

For the manufacture of a rich gas from light distillate feedstock for use as a fuel-gas or town-gas component, the modern high-pressure continuous catalytic processes, such as the UK Gas Council's Rich-

Gas Process, are more economical than any of the variations of the Hall process. Purely thermal cracking processes, however, will continue to be used for the manufacture of gases rich in olefins for certain industrial syntheses.

A plant specifically designed for high-calorific-value gas manufacture by thermal cracking is the 'Semet-Solvay' (Hall-type) regenerative reverse-flow plant, which is cyclic, non-catalytic and which operates at

*Table 14*  *Characteristics of high-calorific-value gases made in Hall-type plants*

| Process | | | Normal, non-catalytic | | | | Catalytic |
|---|---|---|---|---|---|---|---|
| Feedstock | | | Heavy fuel oil | | | | |
| | | | 12% wt Conradson carbon | 6% wt Conradson carbon | Gas oil | LDF | LDF |
| Composition | | | | | | | |
| CO$_2$ | % vol | | 4·6 | 2·5 | 2·6 | 2·0 | 4·2 |
| O$_2$ | | | 1·4 | 0·4 | 0·8 | 0·8 | 0·8 |
| C$_n$H$_m$ | | | 26·4 | 32·6 | 24·9 | 29·4 | 29·2 |
| CO | | | 1·2 | 1·9 | 0·3 | 2·1 | 6·8 |
| CH$_4$ | | | 31·5 | 39·2 | 37·9 | 35·3 | 26·5 |
| H$_2$ | | | 13·9 | 17·2 | 11·2 | 19·4 | 26·1 |
| N$_2$ | | | 21·0 | 6·2 | 22·3 | 11·0 | 6·4 |
| Total | | | 100·0 | 100·0 | 100·0 | 100·0 | 100·0 |
| Specific gravity (air=1·0) | | | 0·83 | 0·79 | 0·80 | 0·72 | 0·71 |
| Calorific value | Btu/ft$^3$stp(sat) | | 1 000 | 1 140 | 1 000 | 1 050 | 1 050 |
| | MJ/m$^3$(st) | | 37·96 | 43·72 | 37·96 | 39·86 | 39·86 |
| Impurities | | | | | | | |
| H$_2$S | gr/100 scf | | 600 | 200 | | } 8 | } 3 |
| Organic S | ,, | | 40 | 15 | | | |
| C$_{10}$H$_8$ | ,, | | trace | trace | trace | trace |
| H$_2$S | g/m$^3$(st) | | 14·9 | 5 | | } 0·19 | } 0·07 |
| Organic S | ,, | | 0·9 | 0·4 | | | |
| C$_{10}$H$_8$ | ,, | | trace | trace | trace | trace |

Notes — The C$_n$H$_m$ is approximately 70% C$_2$H$_4$

The CH$_4$ includes higher paraffins

The Organic S is approximately 70% thiophen

69

approximately atmospheric pressure. This plant consists of two symmetrical vessels, each comprising an oil-vaporizing chamber above a chequer-filled base (Figure 17). The vessels are connected at the top, and each has a combined steam, air, run-gas and stack connection at the base. Process-oil sprays project vertically downwards into the vaporizing chambers and heating burners are provided below them. The method of operation is as follows:

The process steam enters the bottom of one of the vessels and is preheated by the chequers. It then ascends through the throat at the bottom of the vaporizing chamber of this vessel and meets the descending process-oil spray. The steam and oil vapour then pass downwards through the second vessel where the thermal cracking is completed, and thence through the wash-box to the condensers. Carbon is deposited in the vaporizing chambers and the chequers of the second vessel (*ie* the gas outlet) during this phase of the cycle.

The oil is then shut off with the steam left on in order to purge the plant, following which the appropriate steam-valve, gas-valve and stack-valve changes are made and the blast air is admitted counterflow to the direction of the gas during the preceding run. The blow restores the temperatures throughout the system by the combustion

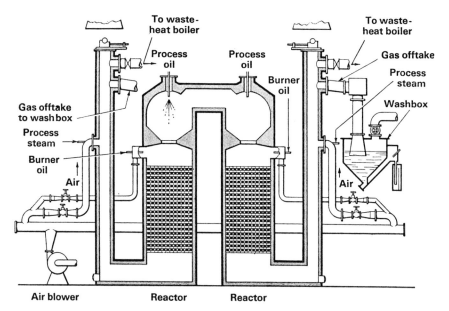

*Figure 17   Power Gas Semet-Solvay high-calorific-value oil-gas plant*

70

of the carbon left behind during the run, augmented if necessary by the use of the auxiliary burner sited below the throat of the appropriate vaporizing chamber. The waste gas, after transfer of some heat to the chequers that have been cooled by the process steam during the preceding run, passes up the stack to atmosphere, if desired by way of a waste-heat boiler. Following the blow, the plant is steam purged, and the second gas-making phase commences in the same direction as the preceding blow.

The complete cycle, therefore, comprises a blow and a run in one direction, followed by a blow and a run in the opposite direction for the purpose of regeneration. Thus, the blow always flows in the opposite direction to the run that precedes it and in the same direction as the run that follows it, *viz*:

$$
\begin{array}{ll}
\text{Blow} & \rightarrow \\
\text{Run} & \rightarrow \\
\leftarrow & \text{Blow} \\
\leftarrow & \text{Run} \\
\text{Blow} & \rightarrow \\
\text{Run} & \rightarrow
\end{array}
$$

The total time taken for a blow and run in one direction is three to four minutes. The total process steam requirement is approximately 0·6 kg per kg of feedstock, and 60% of this can be raised from the blast gases in waste-heat boilers.

*Chapter 7*    Oil Gasification and Hydrocarbon-Gas
Reforming: Catalytic Processes
–General Principles

As demonstrated by the Jones and Hall processes already described, the thermal cracking of oil in the presence of steam results in the production of a large quantity of carbon and/or tar, and a correspondingly low gas yield. The production of a lean gas or synthesis gas by this means results in even greater carbon production, since it involves more-rigorous cracking. This applies to the whole range of liquid and gaseous feedstocks, although carbon production from the latter would be relatively small owing to their lower carbon/hydrogen ratios.

The devices used to prevent or reduce the formation of tar or carbon and increase the gaseous yield are the addition of oxygen or air to the feedstock (the principal effect of which is to provide heat for the reactions) or the addition of hydrogen as such, or as reactant steam, or of a mixture of air or oxygen and steam. The resulting reactions, which are promoted at various temperatures, may also be facilitated by operation under pressure, or by the use of catalysts. These techniques superimpose on purely thermal cracking reactions those of partial combustion, or of hydrocarbon hydrolysis and water-gas reaction, or of hydrogenation, either singly or in combination. They usually result in considerably higher gasification and overall efficiencies than are obtainable by the gasification of solid fuels.

Because of the fluid state of hydrocarbon feedstocks and their low content of mineral impurities, oil-gas processes can more easily be fully mechanized and subjected to automatic control than solid-fuel gasification processes in general. The purification of oil-gas compared with coal-gas is simplified owing to the absence of ammonia and hydrocyanic acid. These factors increase the inherent advantage already conferred upon oil-gas processes by the relatively lower carbon/hydrogen ratios of the feedstocks. They generally result in relatively lower capital costs, in terms of both gas-making and ancillary plant and equipment for oil-gas processes, and also in lower operating labour costs.

The increasingly important role of hydrocarbon oils in the manufacture of town gas, synthesis gas and hydrogen following the Second World War resulted in the development of new processes adapted to the various purposes. Since 1962 the rate of change-over throughout the world from solid-fuel-based gas-making processes to certain of

72

these new processes based on hydrocarbon oils and gases has proceeded at such a pace as to justify its being termed a revolution in gas manufacture. Typical examples of these, together with examples of longer-established processes, are described briefly in Chapters 8 to 11.

## The Chemical and Thermodynamic Principles Involved in the Catalytic Steam Reforming of Hydrocarbons

The reactions between hydrocarbons and steam are brought about in the presence of a suitable catalyst, at temperatures in the range 300 to 1 000°C. If the mechanism of reforming is ignored, the general equation for the overall steam reforming of liquid hydrocarbons may be written as follows:

$$A(C_nH_m) + B(H_2O) \rightarrow C(H_2) + D(CO) + E(CO_2) + F(CH_4) + G(H_2O) \tag{a}$$

The final composition of the gas is controlled by the equilibrium of the secondary reactions

$$CH_4 + H_2O \rightleftharpoons CO + 3H_2 \qquad \textit{endothermic} \tag{b}$$
$$CO + H_2O \rightleftharpoons CO_2 + H_2 \qquad \textit{exothermic} \tag{c}$$

according to the following expressions, in which the gases are on a molar basis:

$$K_p = \frac{(H_2)^3 \, (CO)}{(CH_4) \, (H_2O)} \times p^2 \qquad \text{for reaction (b)}$$

$$K_p = \frac{(H_2) \, (CO_2)}{(CO) \, (H_2O)} \qquad \text{for reaction (c)}$$

From Table 15 it will be seen that $K_p$ for reaction (b) rises with increasing temperature whereas $K_p$ for reaction (c) falls.

Certain commercial activated-nickel catalysts used for the steam/hydrocarbon reactions are sufficiently active to produce fairly close approaches to thermodynamic equilibria. Table 16 shows the probable approach by the use of an alkalized nickel catalyst in the case of reaction (b); a slightly closer approach is claimed for nickel/uranium catalyst. Both catalysts give a close approach for the water-gas shift reaction (c). The equilibrium composition of the product gas will therefore depend upon the following factors or variables:

73

## 1 Feedstock Carbon/Hydrogen Ratio

An increase in the carbon/hydrogen ratio of the feedstock increases the steam requirements and the ratio of oxides of carbon to hydrogen in the product gas.

## 2 Steam/Carbon Ratio

Steam must be supplied substantially in excess of the stoichiometric requirements. An increase of steam in given conditions increases the carbon-dioxide/carbon-monoxide ratio through its effect on the water-gas shift reaction (equation (c)), and reduces the methane content through its effect on the steam/methane equilibrium (equation (b)).

## 3 Reaction Temperature

Increase in temperature reduces the carbon-dioxide/carbon-monoxide ratio and methane concentration by its effect on the equilibria of the shift reaction (equation (c)) and the steam/methane reaction (equation (b)).

## 4 Reaction Pressure

Increases in operating pressure have only a minor effect on the shift reaction, but have a pronounced effect on the methane reaction to give higher methane yields.

*Table 15   Equilibrium constants ($K_p$)*

| Temperature | | Reaction (b)<br>$CH_4 + H_2O \rightleftharpoons CO + 3H_2$ | Reaction (c)<br>$CO + H_2O \rightleftharpoons CO_2 + H_2$ |
|---|---|---|---|
| °C | K | $K_p$ | $K_p$ |
| 300 | 573 | $6.7 \times 10^{-8}$ | 39.1 |
| 400 | 673 | $6.1 \times 10^{-5}$ | 11.7 |
| 500 | 773 | $9.8 \times 10^{-3}$ | 4.90 |
| 600 | 873 | $5.2 \times 10^{-1}$ | 2.55 |
| 700 | 973 | $1.18 \times 10^{1}$ | 1.54 |
| 800 | 1 073 | $1.69 \times 10^{2}$ | 1.04 |
| 900 | 1 173 | $1.47 \times 10^{3}$ | 0.75 |
| 1 000 | 1 273 | $9.03 \times 10^{3}$ | 0.58 |

The effects of steam/carbon ratio and temperature variation at constant pressure (29) are given in Figure 18 and the effects of pressure and temperature variation at constant steam/carbon ratio are given in Table 16.

An important factor is the need to prevent the formation of carbon on the catalyst, which would cause reduced activity and possible disintegration. Catalysts that are active for reforming also promote the decomposition of carbon monoxide to carbon and carbon dioxide according to the Boudouard reaction

$$2CO \rightarrow CO_2 + C \qquad \text{(d)}$$

Carbon formation becomes thermodynamically possible at any temperature when

$$\frac{(p_{CO})^2}{p_{CO2}} \geqslant K_p \text{ at this temperature} \qquad \text{(e)}$$

Table 16 Variations in calculated equilibrium gas compositions with temperature and pressure, for the steam reforming of light distillate (carbon/hydrogen ratio 5·6:1) at a steam/carbon ratio of 3:1

| | Temperature | °C | 705 | 760 | 870 |
|---|---|---|---|---|---|
| | | K | 978 | 1033 | 1143 |
| | Gas analysis | | | | |
| | $H_2$ | mol % | 71·5 | 71·3 | 70·8 |
| | CO | | 14·6 | 16·3 | 19·0 |
| Pressure: | $CO_2$ | | 13·5 | 12·3 | 10·2 |
| 1 bar absolute | $CH_4$ | | 0·4 | 0·1 | trace |
| | Total | | 100·0 | 100·0 | 100·0 |
| | (Probable $CH_4$) | | (0·9) | (0·2) | (0·02) |
| | Undecomposed steam* | | 43·4 | 44·6 | 47·6 |
| | Gas analysis | | | | |
| | $H_2$ | mol % | 57·5 | 63·0 | 68·8 |
| | CO | | 8·3 | 12·0 | 17·9 |
| Pressure. | $CO_2$ | | 18·0 | 15·3 | 11·0 |
| 20 bars absolute | $CH_4$ | | 16·2 | 9·7 | 2·3 |
| | Total | | 100·0 | 100·0 | 100·0 |
| | (Probable $CH_4$) | | (20·0) | (13·3) | (3·3) |
| | Undecomposed steam* | | 82·2 | 67·4 | 53·1 |

* per 100 moles of dry gas

75

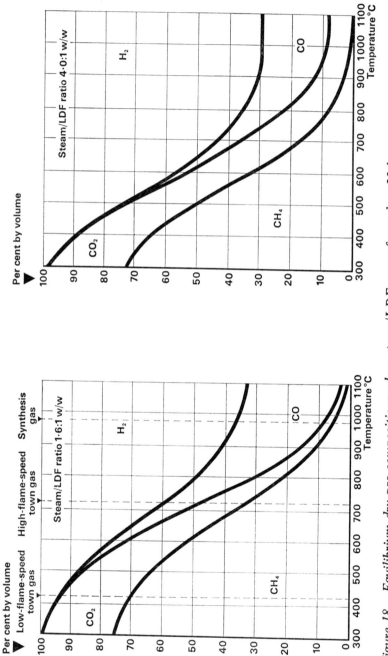

Figure 18  *Equilibrium dry-gas compositions when steam/LDF are reformed at 25 bars*

76

In order to control the carbon-dioxide/carbon-monoxide ratio, steam must be in excess of that required for the water-gas shift reaction (reaction (c)). Dent has stated that the steam in excess of that required for the shift reaction can be calculated from the equilibrium constants, but his experimental results show that the deposition of carbon on catalysts is not governed by the constants for graphitic carbon (29). Special measurements over a nickel catalyst and graphite give the curves shown in Figure 19 in which the deviation of the equilibrium constants at low temperature is large.

A further possibility is gum formation and hence carbon deposition. If the rate of decomposition of hydrocarbon molecules exceeds the rate at which the fragments can react with steam, or with any hydrogen present, free radicals may form polymers on the catalyst surface at temperatures below 500°C. At higher temperatures these radicals may decompose to produce carbon. Dent has called this 'kinetic carbon'.

No clear picture emerges from research work carried out to date of the detailed mechanism of catalytic steam-reforming. There is evidence that the first products appearing in the presence of undecomposed hydrocarbon at low temperatures are carbon oxides resulting from such overall reactions as:

$$C_nH_{2n+2} + 2nH_2O \rightarrow nCO_2 + (3n+1)H_2 \qquad endothermic \ (f)$$
$$C_nH_{2n+2} + 2H_2O \rightarrow CO_2 + 3H_2 + C_{n-1}H_{2n} \qquad endothermic \ (g)$$
$$C_nH_{2n+2} + nH_2O \rightarrow nCO + (2n+1)H_2 \qquad endothermic \ (h)$$

This is followed by the appearance of methane, the source of which involves three possibilities:

formation from the steam/hydrocarbon reaction

$$C_nH_{2n+2} + \frac{n-1}{2}H_2O \rightarrow \left[\frac{3(n-1)}{4} + 1\right]CH_4 + \frac{n-1}{4}CO_2$$
$$exothermic \ (j)$$

synthesis from the carbon oxides and hydrogen produced in the reactions (f), (g) and (h).

$$3H_2 + CO \rightleftharpoons CH_4 + H_2O \qquad exothermic \ (k)$$
$$4H_2 + CO_2 \rightleftharpoons CH_4 + 2H_2O \qquad exothermic \ (l)$$

and the hydrogenation of hydrocarbons by the hydrogen produced from the earlier reactions

$$C_nH_{2n+2} + (n-1)H_2 \rightarrow nCH_4 \qquad exothermic \ (m)$$

77

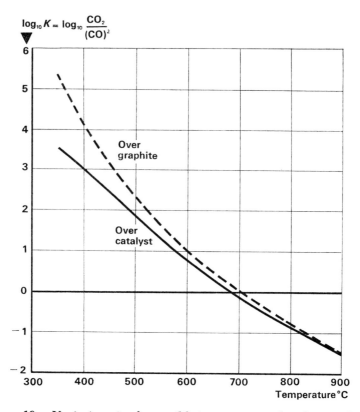

$$\log_{10} K = \log_{10} \frac{CO_2}{(CO)^2}$$

*Figure 19    Variations in the equilibrium constant for the Boudouard reaction* $2\,CO \rightleftharpoons CO_2 + C$

Figure 20 shows a temperature profile in the catalyst bed observed in the UK Gas Council's Catalytic Rich-Gas Process. This supports the view that endothermic reactions (equations (f), (g) and (h)) occur initially. Shpolyanskii and Leibush (30) and Rozhdestvenskii and Yerofeyeva (31) have produced experimental evidence of hydrogen deficiency in the product gas (from reaction equations (f), (g) and (h)) indicating that methane is produced by the hydrogenation reaction (equation (m)). Other workers have found methane present in excess of the thermodynamic equilibrium of reaction (equations (k) and (l)). This also supports the view that reactions of this type are predominant and that synthesis reactions (equations (k) and (l)) operate to reduce the methane content to equilibrium. However, later researches by the ICI and the Gas Council's Research Station in the UK support the view that the methane equilibrium is reached from the low

78

side by means of reactions (k) and (l) and that reactions (j) and (m) assist in the process.

Light distillates normally contain naphthenic and aromatic hydrocarbons. Andrew showed that benzene reacts with steam more slowly than hexane (32). Maslyanskii *et al* indicate that alkylbenzenes, which have first to be de-alkylated by the catalyst, are reformed even more slowly (33).

The conditions described above are applicable to such processes as the Gas Council's Catalytic Rich-Gas Process and the early stages of the continuous catalytic reformers to be described later. When the temperature of these gases is raised, as in a continuous reformer following the CRG process, or lower down the tube of the continuous catalytic reformer, the methane reacts with steam to form oxides of carbon and hydrogen (reactions (f) and (h)) and from this stage methane will be present more or less in excess of the equilibrium according to the effectiveness of the catalyst employed.

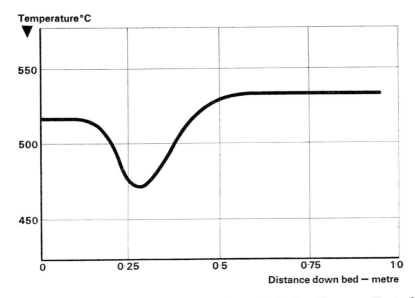

*Figure 20    UK Gas Council's Catalytic Rich-Gas Process. Typical temperature profile in the catalyst bed*

79

# The Theoretical Scope of the Steam Reforming Reactions and their Current Practical Limitations

The theoretical possibilities of LDF/steam reforming are demonstrated in Figure 18, which shows that with appropriate steam ratios it should be possible, aided by carbon monoxide conversion and carbon dioxide adjustment, to manufacture under pressure gases ranging from almost pure methane to high-flame-speed town gas and commercial hydrogen, in a single stage, continuously, and without the production of non-gaseous material. Subject to provisos concerning the composition and purity of the LDF used, detailed later under the heads of the various commercial processes, this can be achieved in the most highly developed processes available, over the approximate temperature range 500 to 950°C. In order to operate below 400°C without kinetic gum or carbon formation it is necessary to use feedstocks in the range $C_4$ or lower; the limitations above 950°C are metallurgical.

One of the ancillaries of such processes is a feedstock hydrodesulphurization stage. This is expensive if scaled down below the requirement of plant with a capacity of 200 000 m³ of gas per day. As a result small-scale continuous reforming plants, usually operated at lower pressures, have been developed which do not demand feedstock hydrodesulphurization. Where in addition the relative costs of feedstocks render economical the use of heavier undesulphurized materials, cyclic processes are available which permit the cyclic scavanging of the catalyst during an air-blast phase, the other purpose of which is to provide the reaction heat.

The reforming processes referred to above are dealt with in detail in the following two chapters.

# Chapter 8 Oil Gasification and Hydrocarbon-Gas Reforming: Cyclic Catalytic Processes

Cyclic catalytic plants operate at low pressure, plant design and the choice of catalyst to be used being influenced by the type of feedstock to be processed. When materials in the range gas oil to medium fuel oil are gasified, lime catalysts produce a similar gasification efficiency, but in some cases a less viscous tar, than nickel catalysts. For these feedstocks the regenerative design of plant, in which the blast air and reactants are counterflowing, has considerable advantages over the 'uniflow' design. No difficulty is experienced with regard to the replacement of the reaction heat in the catalyst bed, since this process is greatly assisted by combustion of carbon deposited in the system during the run.

Process materials in the range of light distillate to gases are best reformed by the use of nickel catalysts which, compared with lime catalysts, produce higher gasification efficiency, reduced carbon deposition on the catalyst, and less non-gaseous material in the gas stream. However, when these light feedstocks are used in conjunction with nickel catalysts in the regenerative type of plant, the low level of carbon deposition on the catalyst contributes little to the restoration of temperature in the reaction zone. Therefore the 'uniflow' plant designs (ie non-regenerative designs in which the heating gas and reactants flow in the same direction) are preferable. In these plants the heating gases are applied with the least impediment to that part of the catalyst bed which suffers the greatest loss of heat. A further advantage stemming from the 'uniflow' principle is that the air used can be restricted to that required for the combustion of heating feedstock and deposited carbon, plus a small excess. This has the effect of maintaining the catalyst in a more reduced, and therefore more active, state than is possible in a regenerative plant in which air additional to that required for combustion is used in the process of heat transfer.

Cyclic processes are much less sensitive than continuous tubular reformers to the sulphur content of feedstocks and, provided that the gas-treatment plant is designed to deal with any non-gaseous materials that may appear in the gas stream, and the specific output of the plant is sufficiently reduced, materials containing certainly as much as 3% by weight of sulphur can be reformed. Subject to these provisos, feedstocks having high contents of unsaturated, naphthenic and aromatic

81

hydrocarbons can be processed. Necessary items of equipment for operation under these conditions are naphthalene washers and continuously irrigated electrostatic detarrers.

In order to manufacture cyclically a gas sufficiently free of non-gaseous material to allow its passage in the raw state through a carbon-monoxide conversion plant and/or a waste-heat boiler, it is necessary with most catalysts to restrict the feedstock reformed to straight-run light distillate having the following approximate characteristics:

| | |
|---|---|
| Specific gravity | 0·70 |
| Sulphur content | 0·03% wt |
| 95% distilling at | 120°C |
| Aromatics content | 5% vol |
| Olefins content | 1% vol |

Improved nickel catalysts are now being brought into use which, it is claimed, will produce clean gas from light distillate feedstocks containing up to 0·15% of sulphur and with distillation end-points lying between 140°C and 250°C. The gas yields obtainable from materials of relatively high carbon/hydrogen ratio (*ie* at the upper limits of the specific gravity and boiling range), are roughly 5% less than from the lightest materials used.

When 500 Btu/ft$^3$ (18·98 MJ/m$^3$) gas is made from heavy fuel oil the catalyst is so poisoned cyclically with sulphur and carbon deposits that the process may be regarded as one combining thermal cracking with hydrocarbon reforming.

At the other extreme, when uranium/nickel catalyst is used to reform cyclically a low-sulphur-content LDF or LPG, the process is comparable with that of a low-pressure continuous reformer.

By reforming gaseous feedstocks in cyclic plants, it is possible to manufacture gas conforming to the whole range of UK gas groups from G4 to G7 inclusive (7), Wobbe Number range 530 to 760 UK units (20·1 to 28·8 SI units). When liquid hydrocarbons are used, however, it is not possible to make gas conforming to Group 4, Wobbe Number range 700 to 760 UK units (26·5 to 28·8 SI units). The margin of failure is small in the case of light distillate feedstock, but substantial when heavy fuel oil is used. Similar gas-making efficiencies are produced by all the 'uniflow' cyclic processes when operated under similar conditions regarding scale, make-gas and feedstock quality and loading.

When 500 Btu/ft³ (18·98 MJ/m³) town gas is made directly, the yield may vary as follows according to the feedstock used

| | |
|---|---|
| Liquefied petroleum gas | 86 to 87% |
| Light distillate feedstock of specific gravity 0·65 | 85% |
| Light distillate feedstock of specific gravity 0·73 | 80% |

With a given feedstock the gas yield falls away by approximately 5% when the calorific value of the make-gas is reduced from 500 to 320 Btu/ft³ (18·98 to 12·14 MJ/m³), eg the 85% yield shown in the preceding paragraph for gas made from light distillate feedstock of specific gravity 0·65 would fall to 80% for 320 Btu/ft³ (12·14 MJ/m³) make-gas.

The effect of standby heating on efficiency is small, eg a loss of approximately 2% is normal for a reduction in plant loading from 100% to 25%.

In the following sections of this chapter a number of the better-known cyclic processes are described.

## The Segas Process: Regenerative, Cyclic and Catalytic

The special features of the Segas process (34) are the regenerative design of the plant, and the catalyst. The latter is in the form of hollow cylindrical pellets of magnesia with a diameter of 1¼ inch (3·2 cm) and with 1% of free lime as the active agent. It is robust, has a life of three years, and the results obtained indicate a considerable degree of effectiveness, eg a gasification efficiency of 70% is achieved in the manufacture of a 500 Btu/ft³ (18·98 MJ/m³) gas from 950 seconds fuel oil compared with 50% obtainable without a catalyst in the Jones process.

This process is one of the most economical means of gasifying residual oils, which was its original purpose. Higher space velocities, gasification efficiencies and a cleaner gas are obtainable when treating light distillates and gaseous feedstocks, by the use of nickel catalysts in place of lime catalysts. The normal regenerative method of operation of a three-vessel Segas plant (Figure 21) with lime catalyst, is as follows.

The counterflowing blast air enters the top of the air preheater at a point near the make-gas outlet. After being preheated in this vessel with sensible heat left behind by the make-gas, it passes up through the

83

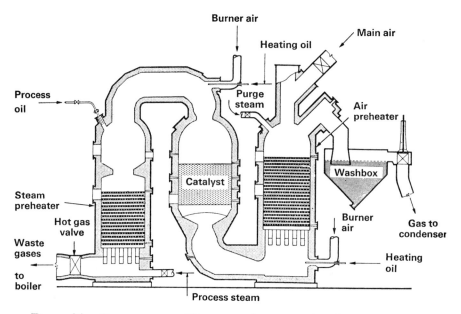

*Figure 21    Segas process: Three-vessel regenerative plant*

catalyst vessel, where its temperature is raised by the burner shown, and down through the vaporizing chamber, where it consumes the carbon deposited during the run and restores the temperatures throughout the plant. The blast then passes down through the steam preheater for heat transfer and, finally, through the waste-heat boiler to atmosphere.

At the end of the blow, the air is shut off and the plant is steam purged in the direction of the blast. Following this, the steam is shut off, the hot-gas valve is closed, the gas valve on the outlet of the wash-box is opened, and the gas-making run commences by the addition of steam, counterflow to the blast, into the bottom of the steam preheater. The preheated steam then meets the feedstock spray in the vaporizing chamber and the mixture of steam and hydrocarbon vapour passes down through the 6 ft (1·8 m) deep catalyst bed where the reactions occur. The gas, which for practical purposes is stable by the time it reaches the bottom of the catalyst vessel, then passes up through the air preheater for heat transfer, through the wash-box, the direct-contact cooler (Lymn washer), electrostatic detarrer and into the relief holder.

84

At the end of the oiling period, the run-steam is left on to purge the rich gas from the plant through to the wash-box, following which it is shut off, the gas valve on the wash-box outlet is closed, the stack valve is opened, and, following a very brief steam purge in the direction of the blast, the next cycle commences with the re-opening of the blast-air valve.

Carbon is deposited during the run, mainly in the vaporizing chamber and catalyst bed when heavy oil is being gasified, and in the catalyst bed alone when lighter feedstocks are being gasified. The heat liberated by the combustion of this carbon during the blow, after allowing for that which passes into the waste-heat boiler, is not adequate to fully restore the temperatures throughout the system to the desired levels. Some auxiliary heating has therefore to be applied during the blow. When a 500 Btu/ft$^3$ (18·98 MJ/m$^3$) gas is made from heavy oil, the amount of heat used is equivalent to approximately 5% of the total feedstock and is applied to the vaporizing chamber. When lighter feedstocks are used it will increase to 10% and be applied mainly between the air preheater and the catalyst vessel.

The total duration of the cycle can be varied between three and four minutes according to the feedstock used and the purge losses involved. The tar produced readily separates with the aid of surface-active agents, such as 'Amine 220' and 'Fatchemco T.E.B.', which are added in small quantities to the wash-box circulating liquor. Calorific value is controlled mainly by varying the operating temperature, normally achieved by slight adjustments to the auxiliary heating.

The plant is extremely flexible and output can readily be controlled, either by maintaining the plant in a stand-by condition, which can be done with very little heat loss or, alternatively, under continuous operation by varying the steam, air and feedstock rates.

Operating results including gas characteristics and thermal balances obtained by the use of medium/heavy fuel oil feedstock are set out in Table 17.


## The Onia-Gegi Oil-Gas Process: Cyclic and Catalytic

The object of this process, as with Segas, is to manufacture a gas similar to coal-gas-based town gas by the use of a catalyst (in this case nickel) to promote reactions between steam, carbon and hydrocarbons, at atmospheric pressure and at approximately 900°C, in order to produce a higher gas yield and lower carbon and/or tar yields

85

*Table 17* *Outputs, thermal balances and characteristics of gas produced by the Segas process operated regeneratively with lime catalyst and medium/heavy fuel oil feedstock*

| Feedstock | | |
|---|---|---|
| Specific gravity | | 0·963 |
| Viscosity at 122°F          cSt | | 122 |
| Capacity of 6ft (1·8m) diameter plant : 1000 ft³/day | | 950 |
| m³/day | | 26 456 |
| Heat input | | |
| Process oil Potential heat          heat units | | 100·0 |
| Sensible heat | | 0·3 |
| Process steam Total heat | | 11·1 |
| Air Total heat | | nil |
| Heating gas or oil Potential heat | | 3·7 |
| Purge steam Total heat | | 2·9 |
| Total | | 118·0 |
| Heat output | | |
| Gas made | | |
| Potential heat          heat units | | 71·9 |
| Sensible heat | | 1·7 |
| Undecomposed steam Total heat | | 9·4 |
| 'Tar' Potential heat | | 11·9 |
| Sensible heat | | 0·3 |
| Waste gases Total heat | | 14·8 |
| Purge steam discharge Total heat | | 4·0 |
| Total heat accounted for | | 114·0 |
| Radiation, convection losses and errors | | 4·0 |
| Total | | 118·0 |

| Thermal efficiencies | |
|---|---|
| Gas made heat units per 100 heat units of process feedstock | 71·9 |
| Gas made heat units per 100 heat units of total feedstock | 69·4 |

| Gas characteristics | | |
|---|---|---|
| Calorific value Btu/ft³stp(sat) | | 473 |
| MJ/m³(st) | | 17·95 |
| Specific gravity (air=1·0) | | 0·52 |
| Composition $CO_2$ | % vol | 12·1 |
| $O_2$ | | 0·6 |
| $C_nH_m$ | | 5·2 |
| CO | | 16·7 |
| $H_2$ | | 48·2 |
| $C_2H_6$ | | 0·6 |
| $CH_4$ | | 12·9 |
| $N_2$ | | 3·7 |
| Total | | 100·0 |
| Hydrogen sulphide gr/100 ft³ | | 50 to 250 |
| g/m³ | | 1·16 to 5·82 |
| Total organic sulphur gr/100 ft³ | | 30 to 40 |
| g/m³ | | 0·70 to 0·93 |
| Carbon disulphide gr/100 ft³ | | 15 to 20 |
| g/m³ | | 0·35 to 0·46 |
| Ammonia | | nil |
| Hydrogen cyanide | | nil |

86

than would result from thermal cracking in the absence of a catalyst, as for example in the Jones process.

For operation with heavy oil as the feedstock, three-vessel regenerative plants similar in design and method of operation to the Segas plant shown in Figure 21 have been constructed. The main points of difference are that in the Onia-Gegi plant a nickel catalyst is employed and the process feedstock is sprayed on top of the chequers of the steam preheater, whereas the Segas process uses a lime catalyst and incorporates a chequerless feedstock vaporizing chamber sited above the steam preheater. The gas yield, gas quality and tar yield obtained by operation of the regenerative Onia-Gegi plant in this way are practically the same as those given for the Segas process in Table 17.

For operation with hydrocarbons in the range methane to light distillate as the feedstock, a number of two-vessel 'uniflow' plants have been constructed (Figure 22). These non-regenerative plants are self-supporting for steam owing to the high temperature of the waste gases at the waste-heat boiler inlet, and are sometimes referred to as 'self-steaming' plants. The method of operation is as follows.

Following the blow or heating phase, steam is admitted to the steam-preheater base and the residual blast-gas is purged out of the plant vessels through the waste-heat boiler to the desired extent. The stack valve is then closed and the reactor-outlet stream is diverted

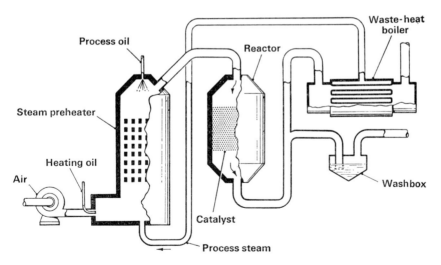

*Figure 22    Onia-Gegi self-steaming non-regenerative plant*

87

through the wash-box. Simultaneously the process-feedstock valve opens, and the gas-making phase then proceeds for about 40% of the cycle time when light distillate feedstock is being reformed, and 50% or more when methane is the feed. The process-feedstock valve then closes and the residual make-gas is steam purged through the wash-box, after which the steam valve closes. The blast-air and heating-feedstock valves then open, followed rapidly by the opening of the stack, and the heating phase commences. The total duration of the cycle may vary between 4 and 5 minutes.

For small-scale to medium-scale operation a simplified single-vessel 'uniflow' version has been developed (35) (Figure 23). Process data relating to this plant when reforming light distillate feedstock of specific gravity 0·65 and a sulphur content of 0·05% are given in Table 18. This table also shows process data and characteristics of lean gas and a finished town gas made directly from refinery-gas feedstock. The lean gas may be subsequently enriched to town gas quality,

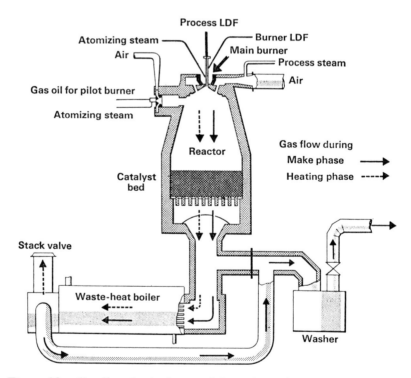

*Figure 23    Small-scale single-vessel Onia-Gegi plant*

preceded if desired by carbon monoxide conversion. For improved catalyst temperature control in large-scale operations under these conditions, designs are used in which the catalyst bed is divided into two layers with a secondary-heating burner sited between them.

*Table 18    Process data relating to 'uniflow' Onia-Gegi plants*

| Feedstock | | Light distillate (Sp gr 0·65  Sulph 0·05%wt) | Refinery gas (Sulph 0·01%wt) | |
|---|---|---|---|---|
| Product | | Finished gas | Lean gas | Finished gas |
| Gas characteristics | | | | |
| Composition | | | | |
| CO₂ | % vol | 6·5 | 8·8 | 7·3 |
| O₂ | | 0·2 | 0·5 | 0·4 |
| $C_nH_m$ | | 7·5 | nil | 2·0 |
| CO | | 22·2 | 16·8 | 13·9 |
| H₂ | | 47·0 | 64·7 | 57·5 |
| CH₄* | | 11·9 | 3·5 | 14·0† |
| N₂ | | 4·7 | 5·7 | 4·9 |
| Total | | 100·0 | 100·0 | 100·0 |
| Calorific value | Btu/ft³stp(sat) | 507 | 294 | 500 |
| | MJ/m³(st) | 19·24 | 11·16 | 18·98 |
| Specific gravity (air=1·0) | | 0·53 | 0·43 | 0·51 |
| Impurities | | | | |
| C₁₀H₈ | gr/100 ft³ | 8 | nil | nil |
| | g/m³ | 0·19 | | |
| H₂S | gr/100 ft³ | 4 | trace | trace |
| | g/m³ | 0·09 | | |
| Organic S | gr/100 ft³ | 2 | trace | trace |
| | g/m³ | 0·05 | | |
| Process steam used | | | | |
| Instantaneous ratio w/w feedstock | | 1·34 | 1·68 | — |
| Total | | 1·69 | 1·92 | — |
| Air used | w/w feedstock | 6·9 | not stated | — |
| Gas made | heat units per 100 heat units of total feedstock | 85 | 83 | 91 |

*Includes higher paraffins                    † Mainly higher paraffins

89

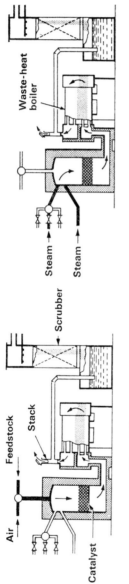

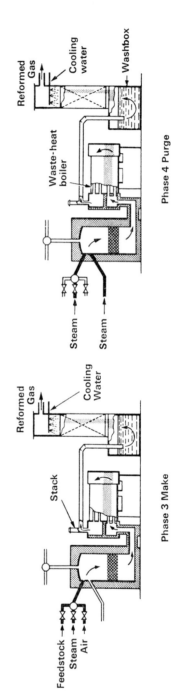

*Figure 24   Diagrams showing flow during phases of operation of W-D/MS plant
(Courtesy of Woodall-Duckham Construction Company Limited)*

90

# The MS Process

The MS process, initially termed *Micro-Simplex*, was developed jointly by Gaz de France and Stein & Roubaix for the reforming of hydrocarbon gases and liquefied petroleum gases by the use of a nickel catalyst. Later installations have been operated on light distillates of specific gravity 0·66 to 0·72, sulphur content of 0·01% to 0·07% and containing up to 20% hydrocarbons other than paraffins. The plant is a simple single-vessel version of the uniflow, cyclic, catalytic gas-making process as shown in Figure 24. Both make-gas and waste-gas go the same route through the double-pass waste-heat boiler which renders the process self-supporting for steam. Plants in the capacity range 0·3 to 4·0 million ft³ (10 000 to 100 000 m³) per day have so far been constructed. The controller relays impulses to the electrically controlled, pneumatically powered valves.

The special feature of this version is that the timing of the change from the blast-phase to the make-phase, and *vice versa*, is controlled by the catalyst-bed temperature, thus reducing the possibility of accidental overheating of the catalyst. The electrical mechanism promoting these changes is set to operate at the desired maximum and minimum temperatures indicated by a thermocouple in the catalyst bed. This arrangement is more practicable on a single plant than on two plants operating together, since the cycle durations inevitably diverge, and this involves cyclic waiting time on the plant with the shorter cycle if the ancillary plant is designed to deal with one plant only. With skilled operation, however, two plants can be maintained operating in harmony.

When operated on gaseous feedstocks, a lean gas of approximately 320 Btu/ft³ (12·15 MJ/m³) is made and subsequently cold-enriched to the desired calorific value. By the use of light distillate, a gas of the desired calorific value can be produced directly in the reformer with some slight loss of overall efficiency and output. A variation of the latter technique, which assists control and may also reduce the production of tar traces in the gas stream when light distillate at the upper limit of the distillation range is being used, is to manufacture gas at, say, 450 Btu/ft³ (17·08 MJ/m³) and to enrich with liquefied petroleum gases in order to raise this to the required level. If desired a lean gas can also be made from light distillate feedstock.

The heat requirements of the process are supplied mainly by a burner sited above the catalyst bed, and in part by the partial combustion of air added during the gas-making phase. Two tangential burners are provided on the larger sets. Combustion air is controlled

Table 19 Typical process data for MS (Micro-Simplex) plants

| Product | | Town gas | Lean gas for enrichment |
|---|---|---|---|
| Feedstock: LDF | | | |
| Specific gravity | | 0·66 | 0·70 |
| Calorific value | Btu/lb | 20 600 | 20 400 |
| | MJ/kg | 47·9 | 47·4 |
| Instantaneous flows | | | |
| Heating LDF | UKgal/min | 4·0 | 2·9 |
| | kg/min | 12·0 | 9·2 |
| Heating air | ft³/min | 6 167 | 4 800 |
| | m³/min | 172 | 133 |
| Process LDF | UKgal/min | 16·5 | 7·9 |
| | kg/min | 49·4 | 25·1 |
| Process steam | lb/h | 10 000 | 5 000 |
| | kg/min | 75·6 | 37·7 |
| Reactant air | | nil | nil |
| Cycle | | | |
| Heat phase | % | 46·2 | 56·0 |
| Make phase | % | 37·1 | 30·1 |
| Total duration | seconds | 204 | 212 |
| Temperatures | | | |
| Catalyst top | °C | 885 to 910 | 910 |
| Catalyst bottom | °C | 825 to 835 | 870 |

| Product | | Town gas | Lean gas for enrichment |
|---|---|---|---|
| Gas production | | | |
| Volume | 1000 ft³/day | 2 426 | 2 570 |
| | 1000 m³/day | 67·5 | 71·4 |
| Total thermal value | therms/day | 12 033 | 8 040 |
| | 1000 MJ/day | 1 269 | 848 |
| Gas yield  heat units per 100 heat units total feedstock | | 83 | 78 |
| Gas characteristics | | | |
| Specific gravity (air=1·0) | | 0·55 | 0·47 |
| Calorific value | Btu/ft³stp(sat) | 496 | 313 |
| | MJ/m³(st) | 18·82 | 11·88 |
| Composition | % vol | | |
| $CO_2$ | | 5·0 | 7·0 |
| $O_2$ | | 0·4 | 0·2 |
| $C_nH_{2n}$ | | 7·4 | 2·2 |
| CO | | 20·3 | 26·7 |
| $H_2$ | | 50·3 | 58·4 |
| $CH_4$* | | 11·0 | 5·0 |
| $N_2$ | | 5·6 | 0·5 |
| Total | | 100·0 | 100·0 |

* Includes higher paraffins.

at 15 to 20% above the level required for complete combustion of the heating feedstock.

When it is desired to ballast the finished gas, the use of reactant air is an advantage, but in cases where a low-density finished gas is required, it is a disadvantage and its use can be dispensed with.

The low hydrogen-sulphide content of the gas made from the feedstocks used in this type of process renders the use of a wet process for its removal more economical than conventional dry purifiers. However, if dry purifiers are dispensed with it is prudent when using the heavier light distillates to install an electrical precipitator to perform the tar and carbon trace removal, which is the secondary function of dry purifiers.

Various catalysts, a selection of which is now commercially available, have been used in this process. Typical process data are given in Table 19 and characteristics of typical light distillate feedstocks in Table 20.

*Table 20    Typical light distillate feedstocks gasified in MS plants*

| Specific gravity at 60°F | | 0·64 | 0·70 | 0·71 |
|---|---|---|---|---|
| Initial boiling point | °C | 28 | 33 | 30 |
| Final boiling point | °C | 86 | 186 | 170 |
| Paraffins | % vol | 99·6 | 79·5 | 82·2 |
| Naphthenes | % vol | nil | 16·7 | 15·6 |
| Aromatics | % vol | 0·4 | 3·8 | 2·2 |

## The CCR (UGI) Process (Licensed Versions: W-D/CCR and IBEG/CCR Processes)

The UGI cyclic catalytic reforming process was one of the earliest cyclic reforming processes to be devised. It was developed originally by the United Engineers & Constructors, and the United Gas Improvement Company of America, to manufacture the lean-gas element of high-flame-speed town gas. The largest cyclic reforming plants in use are of this type.

First used to reform gaseous feedstocks to produce lean gases in the calorific value range 300 to 350 Btu/ft³ (11·39 to 13·29 MJ/m³) in plants ranging from 5 to 15 million ft³ (150 000 to 450 000 m³) per day of lean gas, it was later adapted to the use of light distillate feedstock and kerosine. Enrichment is normally by natural gas or liquefied petroleum gas. In recent years smaller versions down to 0·5 million ft³ (15 000 m³) per day capacity have been built. These smaller plants, it is claimed, can be used to produce either a lean gas or town gas direct from light distillate by the use of the same catalyst. The process consists of a two-vessel uniflow arrangement (Figure 25) in which the reactants and heating gases in turn flow upwards through the catalyst bed and, thence, through the waste-heat boiler to the wash-box or stack respectively. Carbon monoxide conversion can be applied either to the hot gas at the waste-heat boiler outlet or to the quenched gas.

The special features of this process are set out below.

Both blast-air and heating-feedstock are fed into the combustion chamber above the steam-preheater chequers. At this point a swirling motion is imparted to the air, by means of adjustable vanes, in order to achieve uniform heating of the chequers. Process air can be used if desired by the device of restricting the rate of the burner feedstock and air during the run instead of shutting them off.

Some control of the temperature gradient of the catalyst bed can be achieved by delaying the admission, or initially reducing the rate of admission, of the heating-feedstock. The process-feedstock is injected on both sides of the cross-under flue at right angles to the flow and at different levels. The resulting turbulence assists the mixing of the reactants.

The cycle is of short duration (only two minutes) divided in roughly equal proportions between the make and heating phases. The cyclic variation of catalyst temperature is claimed to be only 20 to 25 degC.

The process efficiency and characteristics of the gas made from a given feedstock, when the CCR (UGI) process is operated to produce lean gas or town gas of a given calorific value, are similar to those shown in Table 19 for the MS process.


## The Silamit P3 Process

The P3 plant, built by Silamit Indugas of Düsseldorf, was developed by Gaz de France from their continuous catalytic autothermic P2 process. It is a single-vessel uniflow cyclic catalytic process with an 'up-flow' bed of nickel catalyst. Several commercial catalysts have been used. One, used to good effect when town gas is made direct from light distillate feedstock, is supplied by Stickstoffwerke of Linz, Austria and is designated 'M1'.

94

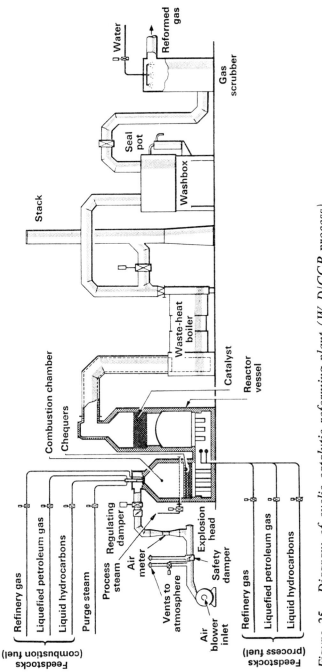

*Figure 25   Diagram of cyclic catalytic reforming plant (W-D/CCR process)*

95

The P3 process was originally used to produce a lean gas from liquefied petroleum gas for subsequent enrichment. A typical composition of such a gas is:

| | |
|---|---|
| $CO_2$ | 8·0% |
| CO | 16·5% |
| $H_2$ | 52·5% |
| $CH_4$ | 8·5% |
| $C_nH_m$ | 1·0% |
| $N_2$ | 13·5% |
| Total | 100·0% at cal val 330 Btu/ft$^3$ (12·53 MJ/m$^3$) |

This would produce a town gas of approximately 0·55 specific gravity when enriched. Process air could be eliminated if desired and this would produce a finished gas of approximately 0·52 specific gravity.

Currently this process is being used to produce town gas direct from light distillate feedstock (Figure 26). Particular features are as follows.

The unique feature is that the blast, and the process air and steam, are preheated in turn in a steel pipe in the annulus surrounding the catalyst bed. The blast and make-gases pass in turn through this annulus after leaving the bed. As a result the gas-making efficiency at 81 to 86%, according to the feedstock used, is very slightly higher than that of uniflow plants without heat exchange. A common waste-heat boiler is used successively by the blast and make gases.

Gas quality corresponds to those of similar processes already described, such as the MS and Onia-Gegi. It is recommended that the sulphur content of the feedstock should be limited to 300 parts per million.

The timing of the change of cycle phase is controlled by the catalyst-bed temperature as in the MS and SSC processes. Units of as low a capacity as 200 000 ft$^3$ (5 600 m$^3$) per day can be supplied.

## The SSC Reforming Plant

This uniflow cyclic reforming plant developed by the Stazione Sperimentale per i Combustibili, of Milan, employs a downflow reactor vessel similar to that used in the MS and P9 processes.

It is claimed that the type of nickel catalyst used can deal satisfactorily with light distillate containing as much as 0·15% wt of sulphur.

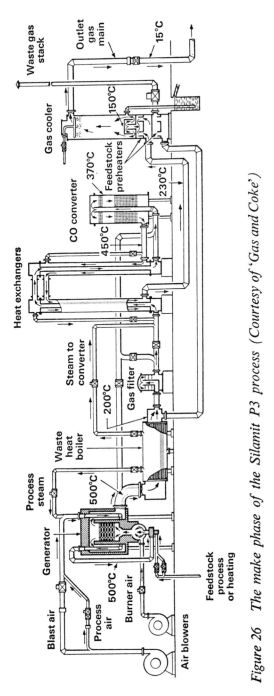

Figure 26 *The make phase of the Silamit P3 process* (*Courtesy of 'Gas and Coke'*)

The largest plant constructed so far is of 2·75 million ft³ (77 000 m³) per day capacity. The feedstock range is from gas to light distillate. The calorific value of gas made may be varied from 380 to 525 Btu/ft³ (14·43 to 19·93 MJ/m³) yielding gasification efficiencies of approximately 80 and 85 % respectively.

The cyclic controller is electro-pneumatic and either time or catalyst-bed temperature can be used to control the duration of the cycle phases. If failure of temperature control occurs, the time control will take over automatically.

A dual-passage waste-heat boiler is used, with separate sections for the make-gas and waste-gas.

# Chapter 9    Oil Gasification and Hydrocarbon-Gas Reforming: Continuous Catalytic Steam Reforming

The cyclic catalytic processes described in Chapter 8 show to considerable advantage compared with the thermal cracking processes referred to earlier. Furthermore, when gas quantities up to 10 million ft³ (300 000 m³) per day have to be made from high-sulphur-content feedstocks, or are required at low pressure, or both, the cyclic processes may be competitive with continuous processes. However, for larger outputs of high-pressure desulphurized gas, made from light distillate or gaseous feedstocks of sulphur contents below 800 ppm, whether for use as town gas, synthesis gas or hydrogen, the more complex high-pressure (10 to 35 bars) continuous reformers, described in this chapter, are currently substantially more economical.

Less complex, smaller-scale, continuous, low to medium pressure (1-5 bars) reformers are also available as alternatives to cyclic reformers, but these are more restrictive with regard to the untreated feedstock quality than are the large high-pressure reformers, since they do not incorporate a desulphurization stage. Several of these also are described.

The thermodynamic and chemical principles involved in these processes have already been detailed in Chapter 7. Comments on other aspects of the continuous reforming processes of general application are set out below.

## Types of Product Gas

With the aid of the addition to the reactants of carbon dioxide derived from the waste gas on the one hand, and carbon monoxide shift conversion on the other, synthesis gases or reducing gases with carbon monoxide/hydrogen ratios ranging, for example, from 4·0:1·0 to 0·5:1·0 can readily be produced. Alternatively, with steam only as the gasifying medium, hydrogen of greater than 99 % purity can be made by carbon monoxide conversion of the reformed gas followed by carbon dioxide washing and, if necessary, by methanation or washing for reduction of residual carbon monoxide. In this latter application

99

it is normal to operate at as high a reaction temperature as the catalyst tubes can withstand, at a high steam/carbon ratio, and at an appropriately low operating pressure.

Another variation of the process, where ammonia synthesis gas is the objective, is for the first stage of tubular reforming to be carried out at a low temperature, yielding gas with a high methane content, followed by a second-stage autothermic catalytic reformer of the single-vessel type in order to dispose of the bulk of the residual methane. In this second stage, the air added to the reactants provides the nitrogen necessary for the synthesis.

The process may be used for the manufacture of the lean-gas component of town gas. When used for this purpose, control of the toxicity of the final town-gas is achieved by a carbon monoxide shift conversion stage after reforming. The Wobbe Number of the gas made can be controlled by the addition of air to the reactants if the final mixed gas needs ballasting, as it may if methane is used for enriching, or by washing part of the carbon dioxide from the gas if ballast reduction is necessary, as it may be if butane, for example, is used as the enricher. If, however, it is desired to use process air for ballast when light distillate is being reformed, its addition to the reactants might give rise to carbon formation on the catalyst in the top of the tubes. It is therefore best added at the reformer outlet.

When the feedstock is to be methane or ethane, there is no incentive to attempt to modify the tubular reforming process (or for that matter any other continuous reforming process that may be introduced) in order to manufacture a town gas directly in the reformer, since any hydrocarbon passing through the process in excess of the optimum required to minimize the cost of production of the essential lean-gas element would be heated to no purpose, and loss of efficiency would result. Where heavier process materials are concerned, however, there are incentives to produce a gas of town-gas quality in a single stage, and commercial catalysts capable of doing this in tubular reformers are now available.

## Types of Feedstock Reformed

The feedstocks used comprise natural, refinery and liquefied petroleum gases and light distillates of low sulphur content and usually, but not invariably, of low unsaturated-hydrocarbon content.

100

## 1   Heating Feedstock

Any gaseous or liquid hydrocarbon may be used as heating feedstock provided that the products of combustion do not corrode the alloy tubes. This proviso normally eliminates medium and heavy fuel oils, the sodium and vanadium contents of which are corrosive under the conditions of this process.

## 2   Pretreatment of Process Feedstocks

Certain low-sulphur-content (*ie* up to 20 ppm) gaseous and liquefied petroleum gas feedstocks of relatively high unsaturated-hydrocarbon content can be reformed without pretreatment, especially if this is carried out at low pressure, with a high steam ratio, and with a low efficiency for the conversion of methane. Periodic regeneration of the catalyst with steam is required in these circumstances, and the scale of operation is usually low.

Distillate feedstocks of substantially higher sulphur content (*ie* up to 800 ppm) are subjected to a vapour-phase catalytic hydrodesulphurization, at approximately 400°C, prior to the addition of the reaction steam. For this treatment a stream of hydrogen-rich gas is added to the vaporized or gaseous feedstock.

These hydrodesulphurization processes may also be applied, wholly or in part, to gaseous feedstocks where the nature of the sulphur compounds present, the degree of desulphurization required, or the unsaturated hydrocarbon content of the gas warrant it. Alternatively, the desulphurization of gaseous feedstocks can be effected by adsorption on active carbon, or, where the 'hard' (*eg* thiophenic) sulphur content is sufficiently low, by absorption using zinc oxide.

## 3   Main Catalysts Used

For many years nickel-on-alumina catalysts were used to reform continuously $C_4$ and lower-molecular-weight hydrocarbons. When light distillates became economical as gas-making feedstocks, a commercial potassium-alkali-activated form of the nickel catalyst was produced, first by Imperial Chemical Industries and subsequently by others. The object of the alkali was to suppress the deposition of coke, which otherwise would result from the use of the earlier catalysts, so preventing continuous operation and possibly also damaging the catalyst. This was completely effective, with the minor drawback that, under certain conditions, traces of potassium hydroxide volatilize and condense as carbonate in the gas-treatment train, sometimes with embarrassing effect.

More recently it has been found that urania enhances the activity of nickel catalyst to such an extent that an extremely refractory low-surface-area corundum support can be used. It is claimed that this nickel/urania/α-alumina catalyst is less subject than nickel alone to coke formation and requires less alkali. In its latest form a non-volatile alkali has been substituted for the potassium base (36).

**4    Process Yields**
The thermal efficiency of a reforming process depends upon four main factors, namely the carbon/hydrogen ratio of the feedstock, the degree of reduction of methane demanded in the reformed gas, the addition or otherwise of air to the reactants, and the efficiency with which the sensible heat of the make-gases and waste-gases are returned to the reactants.

With large-scale operation under pressure, efficient heat exchange, and with a methane slip of 5 to 14%, lean-gas yields expressed as heat units of reformed gas per 100 heat units of process and heating feedstock can be obtained ranging from 80 to 88%. These efficiencies are roughly 10% better than those obtained on the smallest continuous reformers not equipped with the elaborate heat-exchange arrangements used on the larger installations.

**5    Utilities**

*(a)  Power*
The major power demand would arise from the need for the processing at high pressure of gaseous feedstocks available at low pressure (*ie* for the process-gas compression) and, if the lean gas is subsequently enriched, the enriching-gas compression. Apart from this, the power required would be of the order of 0·5 kW per 1 000 ft³ (30 m³) of lean gas made. This could be generated, by the use of pass-out turbines, from waste-heat steam which would then pass on to process use, where the relative steam-raising and process-steam pressures permitted this course.

*(b)  Steam*
The process-steam demand, for a given catalyst, increases with increasing feedstock carbon/hydrogen ratios. The steam or power required for ancillaries also tends to increase as a result of this effect. By giving priority in waste-heat recovery to steam-raising from the sensible heat of both waste-gas and make-gas, the process can be made self-supporting for steam with all feedstocks. The steam must be free

from sulphur and is usually produced from condensate and demineralized water.

*(c)  Flexibility on Starting Up*
New continuous reformer installations require up to six days for the process of drying out the brickwork, raising temperatures to working level, and reducing the catalysts. Subsequent start-up from cold takes up to sixteen hours, and from stand-by hot not more than six hours.

A stand-by hydrogenation gas side-stream, including carbon monoxide conversion and carbon dioxide removal stages, will take up to twenty-four hours to start up from cold.

The process is extremely flexible. The output of a given furnace can be reduced to 30 to 40%. Alternatively, control can be achieved by placing a furnace on stand-by. Down-time for repairs is estimated to be approximately two weeks per annum.

*(d)  Ground Space Required*
The ground space required will be of the order of 0·5 acre (0·2 hectare) per 50 million ft³ (1·42 million m³) of finished gas per day for the plant and its ancillaries, or approximately 1 acre (0·4 hectare) when office buildings are included.


## The ICI Continuous Reforming Processes

### 1  Lean-Gas Process
This was the first of the commercial continuous naptha solidus steam-reforming processes. A simplified flow diagram of the process as applied to making the lean-gas element of town gas is shown in Figure 27. The method of operation, the operating conditions and the results obtained are as follows:

*(a)  Hydrodesulphurization Stage*
The light distillate feedstock for reforming is preheated by heat exchange with the outgoing make-gas. It is then mixed with recycled hydrogen-rich gas containing hydrogen equivalent to approximately 0·06 to 0·12 cubic metres per kilogramme of feedstock. The preheated light distillate is then vaporized in the presence of the hydrogen either by heat exchange as shown, or in a direct-fired heater.

The feedstock/hydrogen mixture is then contacted with zinc oxide at approximately 400°C. This is a mild hydrogenation catalyst and an

103

absorbent of such sulphur compounds as mercaptans, carbon oxy-sulphide, carbon disulphide and hydrogen sulphide, sometimes termed 'soft' or 'reactive' sulphur compounds. This first desulphurization stage is followed by a hydrogenation stage starting at approximately the same temperature and with the use of a cobalt/molybdenum-based catalyst. In this the 'hard' or 'unreactive' sulphur compounds such as thiophen ($C_4H_4S$) are reduced to hydrogen sulphide. At the same time any unsaturated hydrocarbons present are hydrogenated, and aromatics are stripped of side-chain hydrocarbons. The hydrogenated gas is then passed through a second bed of zinc oxide, the function of which at this stage is solely that of a solid absorbent by chemical reaction of the hydrogen sulphide produced in the hydrogenation stage. The sulphur content of the treated gas is less than 1 ppm.

The zinc oxide can be retained in use until the sulphur content is 25% w/w; the cobalt/molybdenum (Comox) catalyst has an anticipated life of four years.

The recycled gas is taken from the reformed gas stream after the reduction of oxides of carbon to which the main stream is subjected. If, at this stage, the carbon oxides content does not exceed a prescribed level, with not more than one third in the form of carbon dioxide, the gas is suitable for recycle; otherwise ancillary treatment must be undertaken to reduce the carbon oxides to the appropriate level. This may vary from a total of 7% to 12%, the lower level being associated with a high ratio of recycle gas to feedstock. The purpose of this restriction is to avoid overheating the pretreatment system through the highly exothermic methanation reactions between carbon oxides and hydrogen, especially during periods when, for any reason, recycle gas rates are high relative to feedstock rates, *eg* on start-up.

*(b)   Reformer Stage*
Superheated process steam is added to the desulphurized feedstock in the ratio 3 molecules per molecule of feedstock carbon and the mixed reactants enter the reactor tubes at a temperature of approximately 450°C.

The catalyst employed is nickel oxide, with added alkali mainly in the form of a potassium salt, on a robust, hydraulic-cement-bonded, ceramic-ring base. The nickel oxide is reduced to metal *in situ* under carefully controlled conditions prior to gas making.

The reformer furnace shown in Figure 27 is provided with three rows of vertical tubes made of a nickel-chrome-steel alloy, each having an internal diameter of 5 inches (127 mm) and measuring 28 feet (8·5 m) in length. Each is charged with ICI nickel catalyst. The tubes

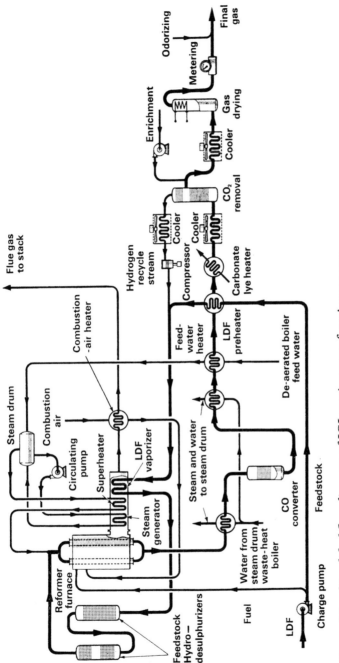

*Figure 27   Simplified flow diagram of ICI continuous reforming process*

are heated by five rows of top burners. The burners are air-atomizing and the combustion air is preheated by heat exchange with the flue gases. The flue gases leaving the furnace after being used to raise steam at 20 bars are used to preheat the reactor steam before passing on to the air preheater. An induced-draught fan is used to withdraw the flue gases from the air preheater and discharge them to atmosphere through a stack 35 metres high.

The make-gas exit temperature anticipated is normally in the range 720 to 850°C. Examples of exit gas temperatures and pressures and the resultant gas compositions are given in Table 21.

*(c)  Heat Transfer from Lean Gas, and Shift Conversion*
The lean gas passes first through the waste-heat boiler, raising steam at 20 bars, and then through the shift converter, where the carbon monoxide is reduced to 3% by shift conversion with ICI brown-oxide catalyst (chromia-promoted iron oxide).

Table 21    *Approximate characteristics of gases made by reforming LDF in the ICI continuous tubular reformer*

| | | Typical lean gases | | Typical ammonia synthesis gas after secondary reforming and CO conversion |
|---|---|---|---|---|
| Plant conditions | | | | |
| Maximum tube-exit pressure | bars | 27 | 12 | — |
| Tube-exit temperature | °C | 775 | 815 | — |
| Gas characteristics | | | | |
| Composition | | | | |
| $CO$ | % vol | 9·1 | 14·0 | 1·3 |
| $CO_2$ | | 17·1 | 13·6 | 21·1 |
| $H_2$ | | 64·4 | 70·8 | 57·7 |
| $CH_4$ | | 9·4 | 1·6 | 0·3 |
| $C_2H_6$ | | nil | nil | nil |
| $N_2$ | | nil | nil | 19·6* |
| Total | | 100·0 | 100·0 | 100·0 |
| Specific gravity (air=1·0) | | 0·445 | 0·400 | 0·565 |
| Calorific value | Btu/ft³stp(sat) | 327 | 285 | 191 |
| | MJ/m³(st) | 12·4 | 10·8 | 7·2 |

*Includes Argon

106

The shift-converted gas then passes through a secondary waste-heat boiler, the boiler-water preheater, the naphtha preheater already referred to, and, if desired, other heat-exchange items such as the carbonate lye reboiler and the low-pressure boiler shown on the diagram.

*(d)   Gas Treatment*
Following the various stages of cooling by heat exchange, the make-gas temperature is adjusted by air-cooling to that required for carbon dioxide removal. Density control of the finished gas can be achieved by varying the main-stream carbon dioxide removal. Final trimming can be effected by the addition of part of the carbon dioxide released from the regeneration of the carbonate lye, by the addition of air or, if available, nitrogen.

After carbon dioxide removal and further air-cooling the gas can be automatically enriched with natural gas, refinery gas, rich gas made by the Gas Council's Rich-Gas Process, or liquefied petroleum gas. The enriched gas is then cooled to the desired dewpoint, by the use of glycol cooled in a refrigeration plant using F-22 refrigerant, and, after heat exchange with the ingoing gas, it leaves at approximately ambient temperature.

After metering and odorization, for example with 20 to 40 ppm w/w of tetrahydrothiophene, the gas is delivered for use at 12 bars. Alkyl sulphides and mercaptans are also used alone or in mixtures as odorants (see Chapter 15).

*(e)   Reformer Feedstock Quality*
Limiting characteristics for the straight-run distillate feed to the process are as follows:

| | |
|---|---|
| Final boiling point | 215°C max |
| Aromatics | 12% vol max |
| Naphthenes | 25% vol max |
| Unreactive sulphur | 0·01% wt max |
| Total sulphur | 0·08% wt max (approx) |

Sulphur contents above this level can be dealt with more economically by employing a preliminary treatment, *eg* with sulphuric acid in the Howe-Baker process.

*(f)   Gas Yield*
The yield of converted lean gas per 100 heat units of heating and process feedstocks used will vary between 80% and 88% according to

the extent to which, by heat exchange, the sensible heat of the make gas and waste gas and the latent heat of the undecomposed steam are transferred to the incoming reactants and burner fuel and air. In the example described the gas yield approximates to the upper limit.

*(g)   Lean-Gas Quality*
The process can be designed for a methane slip at the reformer outlet of 7 to 14%, as may be economical in town gas or first-stage ammonia synthesis manufacture, down to 0·4%, for example, for hydrogen manufacture. In the latter case the tubes would be operated under the maximum permissible temperature stress and this would involve limiting the operating pressure; a higher steam to feedstock ratio also would be used.

Typical gas compositions obtainable are given in Table 21. With the aid of carbon monoxide conversion and carbon dioxide reduction, most desirable ratios of hydrogen to carbon oxides can be achieved.

## 2   Town-Gas Process: the ICI '500' Process
In this application of the ICI continuous reforming process to town gas manufacture, the ICI tubular reformer is operated under optimum conditions for the production of a lean gas. This gas, together with a quantity of steam and desulphurized light distillate vapour, passes into a secondary reforming stage. This demands a minimum pressure of approximately 27 bars, and operates within the range 600 to 700°C and with a lower steam ratio than the main reformer. The lean gas is autothermically enriched, mainly with methane (42).

As with the Gas Council's Catalytic Rich-Gas Process, the heat of formation of the methane is utilized largely for the endothermic production of hydrogen by hydrocarbon hydrolysis.

A gas with a calorific value of 500 Btu/ft$^3$ (18·98 MJ/m$^3$) can be produced that satisfies all the requirements of UK G4 group gases, with an estimated overall thermal yield of 93·5%.

## 3   Power Gas/ICI Reformer followed by the UK Gas Council's Gas Recycle Hydrogenator
Where operating scale and conditions justify the use of the ICI continuous reformer operating at 12 bars or more for the manufacture of the lean-gas element of town gas, and the feedstock price and/or other considerations justify the use of light distillate for the manufacture of the enriching element also, two of the most promising means of manufacturing the latter are the UK Gas Council's Gas-Recycle Hydrogenator and the Catalytic Rich-Gas Process. Figure 28 is a

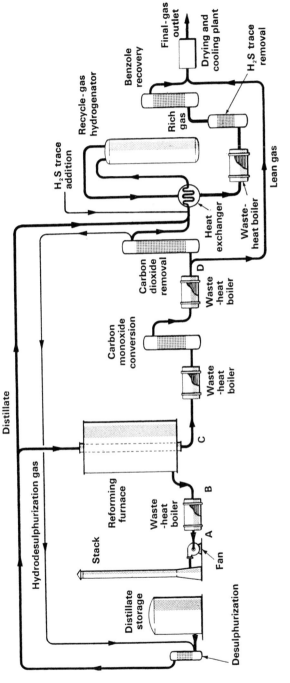

*Figure 28   Simplified flow diagram of Power-Gas/ICI continuous reformer with enrichment by the gas-recycle hydrogenator (Courtesy of Power-Gas Corporation Limited)*

109

simplified flow diagram showing the application of the Gas Recycle Hydrogenator to this purpose.

From the diagram it will be seen that after carbon monoxide conversion and two heat-recovery stages, the converted gas stream divides. Roughly half the gas passes to the hydrogenator stream where, after the addition of the enrichment light distillate vapour, it is preheated to 500 to 600°C by heat exchange with the hydrogenator exit gases. In the hydrogenator the light distillate vapour is subjected to pyrolysis under pressure in the presence of the lean gas which is allowed to retain, at this stage, undecomposed steam to the extent of 5 to 8 % by volume. The reactions are slightly exothermic and the gas leaves at a temperature of approximately 750°C with a calorific value of 750 to 800 Btu/ft³ (28·5 to 30·4 MJ/m³). The main products from the hydrogenation of the light distillate are methane and ethane.

The rich gas, after heat exchange with the ingoing lean gas or, if desired, the mixed ingoing reactants, passes through a waste-heat boiler and thence to benzole recovery stages, first by cooling and finally by oil washing. The lean-gas and enriched-gas streams are then brought together and the mixture is subjected to a final stage of cooling and drying.

The crude aromatics produced are equivalent approximately to the aromatics content of the hydrogenator feedstock and can be used as a source of benzene, their principal constituent, or mixed with the fuel used to heat the reformer.

The carbon dioxide washing stage shown on the hydrogenator stream serves two purposes:

the removal of excess ballast to meet the desired Wobbe Number in the finished mixed gas;
the reduction of the carbon dioxide content of the shift-converted gas, in order to reduce the total of carbon oxides to the level required in the side stream of hydrogenating gas for protection of the desulphurization catalyst.

The demand for carbon dioxide reduction for the first reason stated is usually more rigorous than that for the second. In Figure 28, ballast control is achieved by applying carbon dioxide reduction only to the lean-gas stream passing on to the hydrogenator. If desired, however, it could be applied to all or any part of the total lean gas.

The upper limit of the operating pressure for this process is the same as that of other versions of the ICI continuous reformer described in this Section. However, with this process there is a lower limit of approximately 12 bars required to permit the operation of the recycle hydrogenator without excessive slip of unsaturated hydrocarbons. As will be seen in Table 22, the overall thermal yield and output of town gas, based on a reformer of given capacity, is lower when the hydrogenator is used than it is with cold enrichment. These

Table 22  *Comparison of town-gas characteristics, yields and outputs from a tubular reformer when enriching by recycle hydrogenator, cold butane and Saharan methane (primary feedstock is LDF 170°C)*

| | | Enrichment by gas recycle hydrogenator | Cold enrichment with Butane | Cold enrichment with Saharan Methane |
|---|---|---|---|---|
| Gas characteristics | | | | |
| Composition | | | | |
| $CO_2$ | % vol | 16·4 | 16·9 | 15·7 |
| CO | | 4·1 | 3·9 | 3·0 |
| $H_2$ | | 55·1 | 66·4 | 51·1 |
| $CH_4$ | | 15·8 | 6·1 | 27·5 |
| $C_2H_6$ | | 7·7 | nil | 2·0 |
| $C_3H_8$ | | nil | nil | 0·5 |
| $C_4H_{10}$ | | nil | 6·7 | 0·2 |
| $C_2H_4$ | | 0·2 | nil | nil |
| $C_3H_6$ | | 0·7 | nil | nil |
| Total | | 100·0 | 100·0 | 100·0 |
| Wobbe number (UK) | | 702 | 700 | 715 |
| (SI) | | 26·7 | 26·6 | 27·1 |
| Weaver flame-speed ($H_2$=100) | | 38·9 | 43·8 | 36·1 |
| Calorific value | Btu/ft³stp(sat) | 500 | 500 | 500 |
| | MJ/m³(st) | 18·98 | 18·98 | 18·98 |
| Specific gravity (air=1·0) | | 0·508 | 0·510 | 0·490 |
| Output | ft³/day | $19·77 \times 10^6$ | $20·64 \times 10^6$ | $26·85 \times 10^6$ |
| | m³/day | $0·55 \times 10^6$ | $0·57 \times 10^6$ | $0·75 \times 10^6$ |
| Gas yield | heat units per 100 heat units of total feedstock | 88·8 | 90·4 | 92·3 |

differences result from the consumption of lean gas hydrogen for hydrogenation of the light distillate and require a price differential of approximately £1·50 per tonne in favour of light distillate relative to the alternative cold-enrichment materials for it to be the more economical proposition.

In the simplified flow diagram, the only heat-recovery units shown are the waste-heat boilers. In practice further stages of heat recovery are normally provided, such as burner-air preheat by the waste gas leaving the waste-heat boiler at point A, process-steam and/or process-feedstock-vapour preheat at points B or C, boiler-feed water and possible carbon dioxide extraction-plant lye preheat at point D. Some detail of the gas recycle hydrogenator is shown in Figure 49 in Chapter 11.

If, as is normally the case, hydrodesulphurized feedstock is used in the hydrogenator, it is necessary to add sulphur in order to inhibit the formation of carbon by various mechanisms, which have been investigated and described (37, 38). The quantity of sulphur required is approximately 20 ppm of the hydrogenator reactants.


## The Haldor-Topsøe, Onia-GI and Koppers Kontalyt Processes

From Figure 18 in Chapter 7 it can be seen that, provided the steam/ LDF ratio is 1·6:1 w/w, a high-flame-speed town gas can theoretically be made in a single stage of steam reforming at 25 bars and at approximately 720°C, followed by appropriate shift reforming and carbon dioxide removal. In practice, operating in the pressure range 28 to 40 bars with a steam/carbon molar ratio of 2·0:1, Haldor Topsøe have produced such a process.

The features that distinguish this process from lean-gas-producing reformers are a higher minimum operating pressure of 28 bars, the provision for quenching the outlet reformer gas in case it is necessary in order to avoid carbon formation by the Boudouard reaction (see page 75), and a feedstock final boiling point restricted to 160°C maximum. A side-burner heating system is used and outlet reformer gas temperature is 680°C.

The hydrodesulphurization catalyst used is Nimox followed by zinc oxide for sulphur absorbtion. Gas quality and yield per unit of total feedstock are similar to those achieved on a similar scale by the alternative routes based on LDF described in this chapter. This pro-

112

cess is therefore a simpler means of producing town gas than the two-stage processes described, but it is more delicate to control, being more sensitive to changes in conditions compared with the lean-gas reformer. Analogous processes have been developed, *eg* the Onia-GI and Koppers Kontalyt, the latter process being available in the form of relatively smaller units operating at lower pressure with either BASF or nickel/urania catalyst.

## The Vickers-Zimmer Continuous Catalytic Reformer

The VZ process manufactures a lean gas, in a tubular reformer of an unusual design, from gaseous, LPG and light distillate feedstocks, at pressures from 1·3 to 3·3 bars absolute. After carbon monoxide shift conversion for detoxification, high-flame-speed town gas is then produced by cold enrichment.

When LDF is used as process material a simple distillation column is provided, as shown in Figure 29, which separates this feedstock into a light fraction for reforming and cold enrichment, and a heavier fraction for heating. The fractionation serves a second purpose in that feedstock sulphur tends to be concentrated in the heavier ends.

When LDF is used for enrichment the dew point of the finished gas is significant since hydrocarbon condensation must be avoided. In temperate zones, limitation on the enrichment to below 500 Btu/ft$^3$ (18·98 MJ/m$^3$) is unlikely to arise unless gas distribution pressures exceeding 3 bars absolute are required.

The particular features of the VZ plants are as follows:

### 1   Design and Arrangement of Reactor Tubes
The design originates from the so-called 'Field' tubes, which are a pair of co-axial tubes forming an annulus which is packed with catalyst. Straight inner tubes (A) can be used for normal three-shift operated plants, whereas a special helical inner tube design (B) has been developed and tested in practical operation for almost three years to suit the extreme requirements of two-shift-operated peak-shaving plants without heating during stand-by periods. An advantage of the annular tube is the low-temperature profile across the minor axis of the catalyst layer. The vertical reforming-tubes are freely suspended and can be arranged in a circle within a refractory-lined cylindrical radiation furnace for smaller unit sizes, heated by a single burner at the centre of the furnace lid. For larger furnace capacities the tubes

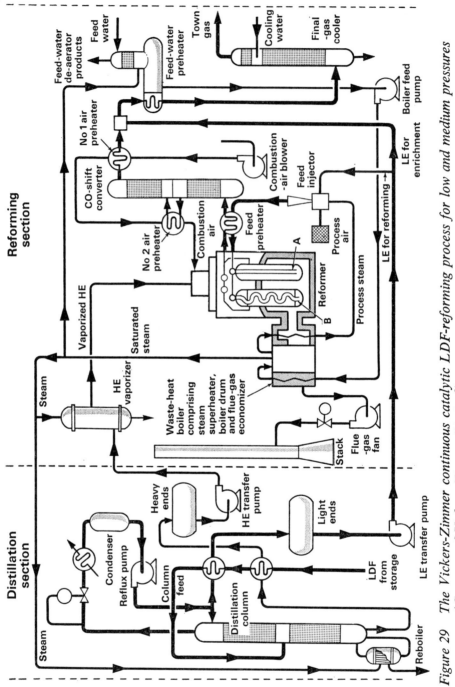

Figure 29  The Vickers-Zimmer continuous catalytic LDF-reforming process for low and medium pressures (Courtesy of Vickers-Zimmer Limited)

114

are arranged in rows in a rectangular box-type furnace. Each pair of tubes is provided with one burner firing horizontally near the top of the furnace on one side, and a similar burner roughly half-way down the length of the tubes on the opposite side of the furnace. The waste gases leave the bottom of the furnace at outlets between each pair of tubes on the side provided with the high-level burners.

## 2 Catalyst and Feedstock Quality
The reforming catalyst used has a low nickel content of approximately 6·5% and hence a low sensitivity to sulphur, in order to allow the reforming of undesulphurized reformer feedstocks to a limit not exceeding 50 ppm w/w. This normally means that LDF containing up to a maximum sulphur content of 100 ppm w/w can be fed to the fractionating column since most of the sulphur present becomes concentrated in the heavy ends used for heating.

Periodic regeneration of the catalyst by steaming for two hours is necessary at intervals which may be of two weeks when using LDF, or as long as two months when using low-sulphur-content LPG. In this process of catalyst regeneration, feedstock sulphur retained by the catalyst is removed from the system. The finished gas therefore normally conforms to Continental hydrogen sulphide standards without treatment.

Furthermore the absence of the hydrodesulphurization stage, employed in larger-scale reformers, permits the use of relatively more-olefinic refinery gas and LPG feedstocks, up to a maximum of 20% w/w. Aromatics are limited to 5% maximum. Naphthene contents up to 35% w/w have been found to have no significant influence on operation. The LDF feedstock should be straight run, should have a final boiling point of 125°C maximum, and contain adequate light ends for cold enrichment.

## 3 Process Air
When the finished-gas quality requirement permits the ballasting of the product gas, this can be achieved by the use of process air, which results in an improvement in the overall thermal efficiency of the process.

## 4 Plant-Capacity Range and Flexibility
Current plant capacities range from 246 000 to 3 670 000 ft³ (7 000 to 104 000 m³) per day of town gas of 500 Btu/ft³ (18·98 MJ/m³) calorific value. A larger unit with an output of 7 340 000 ft³ (208 000 m³) per day should be available by the end of 1971.

115

The outputs just expressed relate to high-calorific-value enrichment with LDF vapour. As the calorific value of the enrichment falls, the finished-gas output increases, to a level of 30% if natural gas is used. Unit output can be reduced to 25% if desired. This, together with the possibility of two-shift operation, without heating on standby, gives more flexibility than is normally demanded. Start-up time from standing-by cold is six hours and from standing-by hot is one hour.

Details of operating results obtained with LDF and LPG feeds are given in Table 23.


## The Otto Continuous Catalytic Reformer

The Otto process was originally introduced for the manufacture of the lean-gas element of town gas by the continuous reforming of liquefied petroleum gas at low pressures. It is equally suitable for the reforming of methane or refinery gas, and versions capable of reforming light distillate feedstocks at low or medium pressures are now available. A large number of these reformers are operating in Europe, mainly processing LPG.

A typical diagram of one of these low-pressure gas reformers is given in Figure 30. Although this example does not show a carbon monoxide conversion stage, this could readily be provided if required. The particular features of the Otto plants of small to medium capacity are as follows:

### 1 Arrangement of Tubes
The vertical reaction tubes are arranged in a circle within a refractory-lined cylindrical radiation furnace, heated by a single burner arranged centrally at the base of the furnace. Heating control, restricted to one burner, is simple but limited.

### 2 Process Air
The use of some process air is normal and preferable, although it can be dispensed with if the product-gas quality cannot tolerate it.

### 3 Catalyst
A catalyst is used of relatively high density and low nickel content (5 to 7%) compared with that used in the high-pressure light-distillate reformers. Loss of catalyst activity, due to its requiring either regen-

116

eration or replacement, results in the appearance of up to 1% by volume of olefins in the reformed gas. Occasional regeneration of the catalyst with steam is necessary when liquefied petroleum gas is used, and more frequent, possibly daily, regeneration is required when

Table 23    Process data relating to town-gas production by the Vickers-
Zimmer continuous reformer

| | | LDF to distillation column | LDF light fraction for reforming | LDF heavy ends for heating | LPG* |
|---|---|---|---|---|---|
| Feedstock | % vol | 100 | 80 | 20 | 100 |
| Mean empirical formula | | $C_{5.3}H_{12.3}$ | $C_{5.1}H_{12.0}$ | $C_{6.5}H_{13.7}$ | $C_{3.2}H_{8.0}$ |
| Sulphur content | ppm w/w | 72 | 32 | 235 | 10 |
| Calorific value | Btu/lb | 20 800 | 21 000 | 20 200 | 21 500 |
| | MJ/kg | 48·4 | 48·8 | 47·0 | 50·0 |
| Gas characteristics | | | | | |
| Composition | | | | | |
| $CO_2$ | % vol | | 18·4 | | 16·1 |
| CO | | | 5·0 | | 5·0 |
| $H_2$ | | | 62·9 | | 55·2 |
| $CH_4$ | | | 7·8 | | 5·5 |
| $N_2$ | | | 0·8 | | 8·3 |
| $C_nH_m$ | | | 5·1 | | 9·9 |
| Total | | | 100·0 | | 100·0 |
| Calorific value | Btu/ft³stp(sat) | | 500 | | 500 |
| | MJ/m³(st) | | 18·98 | | 18·98 |
| Specific gravity (air=1·0) | | | 0·55 | | 0·60 |
| Wobbe number (UK) | | | 673 | | 645 |
| (SI) | | | 25·5 | | 24·5 |
| Flame-speed factor | | | 45 | | 34·6 |
| Outlet pressure | bars gauge | | 1·6 | | 1·6 |
| Hydrocarbon dew point | °C | | −0·6 | | −43 |
| Gas yield | heat units per 100 heat units of total feedstock | | 88·5 | | 93·5 |

* Footnote to Table 23: The propylene content of this LPG was 5% and the butylenes content 15% approximately. The low Wobbe number and flame-speed factor of the gas produced resulted from the use of air at the reformer inlet, which had the effect of increasing the thermal efficiency of the process. Without the use of this air the Wobbe number of the finished gas would be slightly higher and the specific gravity slightly lower than that of the gas made from LDF.

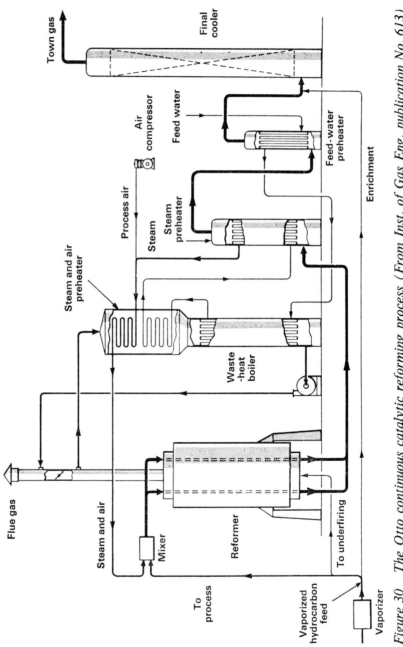

*Figure 30   The Otto continuous catalytic reforming process (From Inst. of Gas Eng. publication No. 613)*

light distillate is being gasified. This is a characteristic of reformers employing low-nickel-content catalysts and reforming undesulphurized feedstocks.

## 4  Plant-Capacity Range
The plant-unit capacity range is from 0·1 to 7·0 million ft³ (3 000 to 200 000 m³) per day expressed as town gas.

## 5  Heat-Recovery and Cost
The heat-recovery arrangements are slightly less elaborate than is normal for the large high-pressure units now being constructed. This, together with the absence of hydrogenation equipment, renders it less costly with regard to capital, although the thermal efficiency of lean gas production is slightly lower, especially on the smallest units.

## 6  Feedstock Quality

*(a)*   *Liquefied Petroleum Gas*
Sulphur content is restricted to 30 ppm.

*(b)*   *Light Distillate Feedstock*

| | |
|---|---|
| Final boiling point | 205°C max |
| Sulphur | 20 ppm max |
| Unsaturated hydrocarbons | 1·0% vol max |
| Aromatics | 5·0% vol max |
| Naphthenes | 15% vol max |
| Carbon/hydrogen ratio | 5·8:1 max |

(It is assumed this will be fractionated — yielding a lighter fraction boiling up to 150°C for reforming and a heavier fraction for feed to the burners.)

Other features of this process and the thermal efficiency and gas characteristics related to a given feedstock are similar to those of the Vickers-Zimmer process already described.

# The Didier Continuous Reformer

A considerable number of small-capacity and medium-capacity reformers have been built by the German firm Didier for use with liquefied petroleum gas. The special feature of these plants is the annular reactor-tube design, the catalyst being charged into the annulus down which the reactants pass. (Figure 31.) These plants can tolerate 20 ppm of sulphur in the feedstock and achieve similar performance and results to those described for the Vickers-Zimmer process.

Annular tube installations can be supplied for outputs as low as 100 000 ft³ (3 000 m³) per day up to 5 million ft³ (150 000 m³) per day.

For larger-capacity units, rectangular furnaces with side-burner systems and single reactor tubes are used. One interesting example in this range uses refinery gases with compositions as set out in Table 24. These show very high olefin contents. In these applications the Gas Council nickel/urania catalyst was found to give excellent results.

The desulphurization of these highly unsaturated feedstocks was simplified since the total sulphur content was only 30 to 40 ppm, and

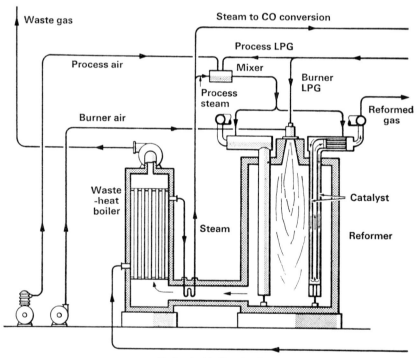

*Figure 31*    *Didier continuous catalytic reformer (Courtesy of Didier-Werke AG)*

120

this was successfully dealt with by absorption by zinc oxide. Had it been higher, a preliminary treatment involving active carbon absorption would have been necessary, since conventional single-stage hydrodesulphurization would be ruled out by the overheating of the catalyst owing to the highly exothermic nature of the hydrogenation resulting from the high olefin contents.

## Application of the High-Pressure Continuous Reformer to Synthesis Gas, Reducing Gas and Hydrogen Manufacture

Most of the applications of continuous reformers dealt with so far in this chapter are concerned with the production of the lean-gas element of town gas. This will become less important as the development of natural-gas resources becomes more widespread. Concurrently, increased quantities of lean gas will be required for ammonia, methanol and other sytheses, as a source of hydrogen for oil refining and other purposes, and possibly for ore reduction.

The technique adopted for the main reforming process, whatever the feedstock, is varied according to the type of gas to be produced.

Table 24   Feedstocks used in Didier large-scale continuous reformer with nickel/urania catalyst

| | | Refinery gases | | LPG |
|---|---|---|---|---|
| Composition | | | | |
| $H_2$ | %vol | 33·53 | 9·80 | |
| $CH_4$ | | 24·68 | 30·20 | |
| $C_2H_6$ | | 19·32 | 17·60 | |
| $C_3H_8$ | | 7·92 | 6·40 | 12·86 |
| $C_4H_{10}$ | | 2·71 | 2·50 | 33·17 |
| $C_5H_{12}$ | | 0·50 | 0·50 | |
| $C_2H_4$ | | 5·07 | 15·90 | |
| $C_3H_6$ | | 4·64 | 14·50 | 28·34 |
| $C_4H_8$ | | 0·63 | 1·60 | 25·63 |
| $N_2$ | | 1·00 | 1·00 | |

## 1 Synthesis Gas Production

When ammonia synthesis gas is required the tubular reformer can be operated with the optimum economic methane slip. This demands a reformer such as is required for the manufacture of the lean-gas element of town gas. This would be followed by a secondary reformer consisting of a simple vessel containing a bed of nickel catalyst, in which the reformed gas, undecomposed steam and some added air would react autothermically to reduce the methane content of the reformed gas to the desired low level. The air used provides the nitrogen for ammonia synthesis. It can be preheated by the residual heat in the waste gases from the furnace, and thereby contribute to an overall gas yield from the process of up to approximately 90% of the thermal value of the total feedstock used. The gas leaving the secondary reformer, containing less than 0·4% by volume of methane, is then further processed for the removal of oxides of carbon, either at reformer outlet pressure, which may reach 30 bars, or following a further degree of compression. Figure 32 is a simplified flow diagram showing the arrangement of a main and secondary reformer as described.

Other syntheses, for example that of methanol, demand a carbon monoxide/hydrogen ratio of 1:2. To achieve this it is necessary to add carbon dioxide from the purification plant to the reactants.

## 2 Hydrogen and Reducing Gas Production

The technique of the secondary adiabatic reformer cannot be used for the production of hydrogen, synthesis gas or reducing gas, when the presence of nitrogen cannot be tolerated in these gases. Further, the methane content acceptable from the reformer for town gas or ammonia production cannot normally be tolerated, either because it is wasteful or chemically unacceptable. The manufacture of these gases therefore usually involves operation closer to the maximum permissible tube-skin temperature of 950°C, with relatively high steam/carbon feed ratios (see Chapter 7). Less commonly a reducing gas may be required at low pressure, in which case less change in regard to reaction temperature and steam ratio would be demanded.

Where reformed gas of low methane content is demanded the importance of reformer-catalyst activity increases. Experiences have been quoted (39) claiming an improved approach to thermodynamic equilibrium when nickel/urania catalyst is used.

When it is required to operate close to the maximum permissible reactor-tube-skin temperature, burner systems that give better control over the tube-wall temperature throughout its length are often used.

122

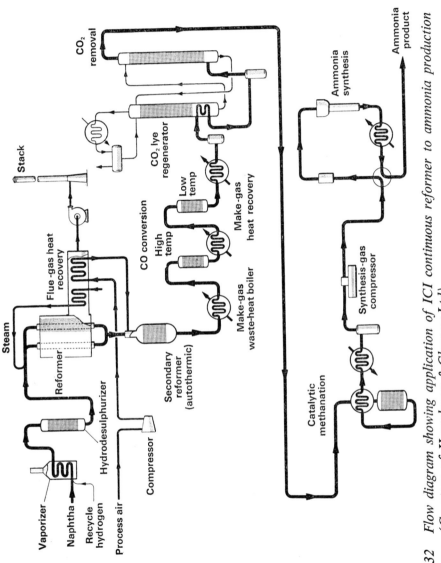

*Figure 32   Flow diagram showing application of ICI continuous reformer to ammonia production (Courtesy of Humphreys & Glasgow Ltd)*

123

One system of wall burners, which gives satisfactory control under these rigorous conditions, is that by SELAS shown in Figure 33. This furnace is heated by seven rows of SELAS 'Duradient' radiant cup-burners fired with gas or feedstock vapour. These individually adjustable rows of burners permit a controlled heat flux density, which can be varied along the length of the reactor tubes as required by the reaction kinetics.

Another burner system, which it is also claimed gives greater control over the tube temperature than can be achieved by the use of top or bottom burners only, is the Foster Wheeler terraced burner system. In this design, illustrated in Figure 34, a series of upward-pointing burners are arranged on a terrace, and two or more such terraces are provided at appropriate levels in the furnace. The burners are fired with either gaseous or liquid fuel.

## 3  Small-Scale Hydrogen Production

The capacity of the continuous reformer using nickel catalyst can be scaled down to as low as 40 $m^3$ hydrogen per hour. Before reaching this level, however, it becomes economical to employ a low-sulphur-content feedstock such as LPG or natural gas in order to avoid the need for hydrodesulphurization. The precise scale at which this change becomes economical is determined by the relativity of feedstock prices.

Within the output range 1 to 40 $m^3$ of hydrogen per hour the choice is between the following processes:

Catalytic splitting of ammonia at 650 to 800°C by the use of nickel or iron catalyst.

Catalytic reforming of methanol by the use of, for example, a chromium-oxide/zinc-oxide catalyst at 350 to 450°C.

The electrolysis of solutions of caustic soda or caustic potash to produce hydrogen and oxygen.

Ammonia splitting may compete with continuous reforming to the output level of 150 $m^3$ hydrogen per hour. Electrolytic hydrogen can compete up to the large-scale level of 5 000 $m^3$ per hour if associated with oxygen production and low-cost electricity.

If extremely high purity is demanded of the hydrogen, this is best achieved on the small scale using the product of ammonia splitting or electrolysis subjected to diffusion through palladium. This can yield 99·9999% volume hydrogen. Where only 98% purity is demanded this can be achieved without difficulty from all the processes described.

Under present conditions the long-established steam/iron process, in which iron oxide is cyclically reduced to a sub-oxide by means of,

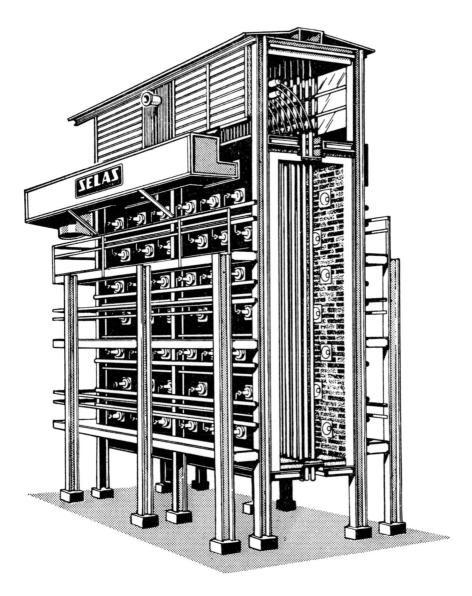

*Figure 33    Typical SELAS reformer furnace*

125

say, producer gas, and reoxidized with steam, thus producing hydrogen, is rarely economical on any scale. One large-scale project is, however, under consideration (23).

## The UK Gas Council's Catalytic Rich-Gas Process

The various applications of the CRG process (40) are now described. Analogous processes have subsequently been developed –namely Lurgi Gasynthan, BASF Lurgi and Japan Gasoline Osaka MRG.

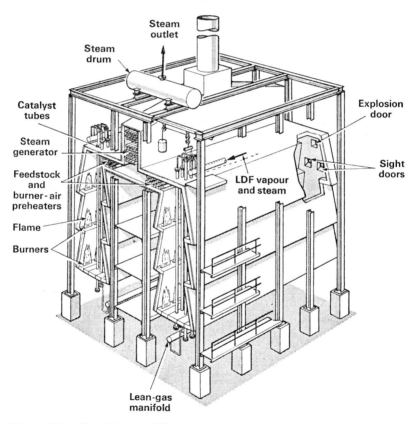

*Figure 34    The Foster Wheeler heating system for the continuous tubular reformer (Courtesy of Foster Wheeler Ltd)*

# 1 Untreated Rich-Gas Production

*(a) Feedstock quality*
The feedstock-quality requirements for this process are similar to those described for the foregoing ICI continuous reformer except for a current (1971) limitation of the final boiling point to 185°C in the case of LDF. It has been indicated that higher-boiling-range material may be used subject to a substantial increase in the hydrogen-rich gas added prior to the reactor (41).

*(b) Method of operation* (Figure 35)
When LDF is used as feedstock, make-gas equivalent to roughly 1 ft³ of hydrogen per pound of feedstock (0·06 m³/kg) is recycled into the feedstock stream. When lighter feedstocks are used, recycle hydrogen can be reduced, to a minimum of 0·2 ft³/lb (0·01 m³/kg) for propane.

A minimum operating pressure of approximately 10 bars is required in order to give satisfactory hydrodesulphurization and to avoid a high hydrogen content in the product gas.

The LDF is vaporized in the presence of the recycle gas, preheated to 350°C and passed to the nickel/molybdenum hydrogenation catalyst vessel where all sulphur is converted to hydrogen sulphide. This hydrogen sulphide is then removed by treatment with reduced Luxmasse pellets in two vessels provided with series/parallel connections to achieve a high level of sulphur absorption in the Luxmasse before replacement. The Luxmasse is followed by a zinc oxide catch in order to ensure sulphur reduction to a level of approximately 0·2 ppm. The advantage arising from the use of Luxmasse is solely economic and is limited to feedstocks of high sulphur content. Zinc oxide alone is likely to prove more economical for concentrations below 100 ppm.

The Nimox hydrogenation catalyst, when first taker as in this case, is relatively inactive for the methanation reaction, compared with the Comox used as second taker in the ICI process. Nevertheless a restriction has to be maintained on the carbon oxides content of the recycle gas similar to that proposed for the ICI process when Luxmasse is used as a sulphur absorbent; otherwise methanation and other undesirable effects would result through reaction with the Luxmasse. If zinc oxide alone is used as the absorbent following the Nimox, treatment of the recycle gas for carbon oxides reduction would be unnecessary.

Steam in the weight ratio of 2:1 of feedstock is then added and the mixed reactants are preheated to approximately 450°C in order to yield a minimum temperature of 440°C in the main reactor vessel.

127

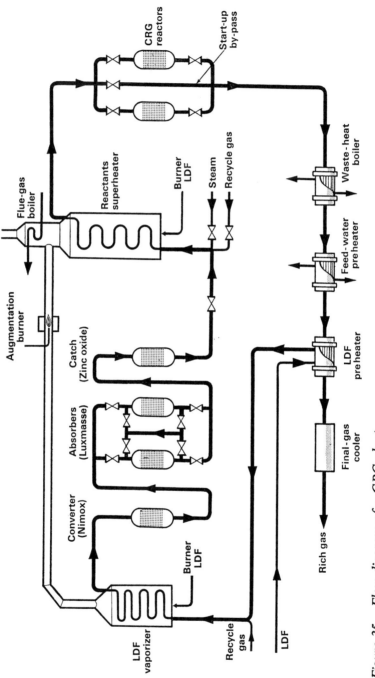

*Figure 35   Flow diagram of a CRG plant*

128

This is charged with a highly active alkalized nickel catalyst, and is sometimes arranged in parallel with a stand-by unit.

After an initial slightly endothermic stage the reaction becomes exothermic as shown in Figure 36, and the product gas leaves the reactor at 490°C, with the characteristics listed in Table 25. These show a close approach to the thermodynamic equilibrium, and a gaseous thermal yield equivalent to 94% of the thermal value of the process and heating feedstock.

The main catalyst life is about one year. The residual life is accurately predictable from the progress of the temperature peak downwards through the bed, shown in Figure 36, which is determined at intervals by means of an adjustable thermocouple and plotted against an operating time scale.

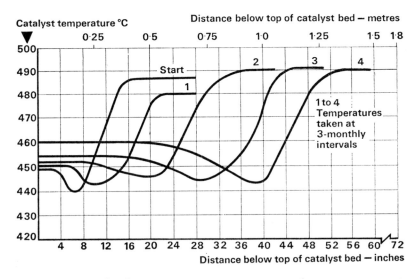

*Figure 36   Graph showing movement in time of reaction zone in CRG process catalyst bed*

## 2   Application of the CRG Process in High-Flame-Speed Town-Gas Manufacture

The CRG process can be applied to high-flame-speed gas manufacture in the following ways:

*(a)   UK Gas Council's Series (A) Arrangement*

The capacity of the CRG stage can be designed to produce all the

129

*Table 25  Typical characteristics of gases produced from LDF by the CRG-based processes*

| | | Rich gas | | High-flame-speed town-gas made by combined CRG and tubular reforming processes |
| --- | --- | --- | --- | --- |
| | | Raw | After methanation and $CO_2$ removal | |
| Composition | | | | |
| $CO_2$ | % vol | 20·0 | 1·0 | 15·4 |
| CO | | 1·0 | nil | 2·4 |
| $CH_4$ | | 61·0 | 98·3 | 34·2 |
| $H_2$ | | 18·0 | 0·7 | 48·0 |
| Total | | 100·0 | 100·0 | 100·0 |
| Calorific value | Btu/ft³stp(sat) | 668 | 978 | 500 |
| | MJ/m³(st) | 25·44 | 37·09 | 18·98 |
| Specific gravity (air=1·0) | | 0·66 | 0·56 | 0·482 |
| Wobbe number (UK) | | — | 1312 | 735 |
| (SI) | | — | 49·80 | 27·90 |
| Weaver flame speed factor (hydrogen=100) | | — | 14·2 | 34·4 |
| Gas yield | heat units per 100 heat units of total feedstock | 94 | 92 | 91 |

enrichment required and sufficient rich gas to provide, after treatment in a tubular reformer, the necessary lean-gas element. This is the UK Gas Council's Series (A) arrangement, Figure 37. The characteristics of the finished gas after carbon monoxide conversion and carbon dioxide adjustment are very satisfactory (see Table 25), although the flame speed of the gas is close to the lower limit acceptable in the UK. If a higher flame speed is required of the finished gas, LPG or LDF vapour can be used for enrichment in place of a part of the rich gas.

*(b)  UK Gas Council's Series (B) Arrangement*
An alternative arrangement is to process the whole of the rich gas in a continuous reformer operated in the temperature range 650°C to 700°C, followed by the desired degree of detoxification by shift conversion and ballast adjustment by carbon dioxide removal. This is the UK Gas Council's Series (B) arrangement and is less favoured than the Series (A) described above.

130

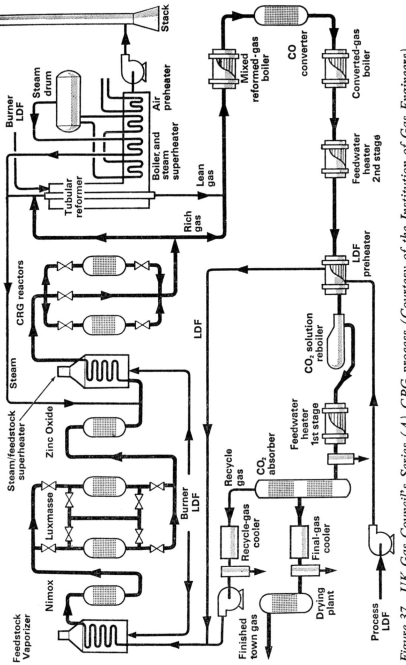

*Figure 37  UK Gas Council's Series (A) CRG process (Courtesy of the Institution of Gas Engineers)*

*(c)    The Preheat/Reheat Process*

An alternative to the continuous reformers used to produce the lean-gas element in the UK Gas Council's Series (A) and (B) processes is the preheat/reheat process (42). In this the rich gas, plus steam equivalent to 1·5 parts by weight per 1·0 part of LDF additional to that used in the CRG stage, is preheated in two stages in order to provide the endothermic heat for two successive stages of reaction with steam in fixed-bed adiabatic reformers at approximately 600°C and 640°C respectively. Final-gas characteristics are identical with those achieved by the Series (A) and (B) routes.

On the only commercial plant at present installed, the preheat/reheat process costs are similar to those for the Series (A) process except for the effect of a 7% lower gas-making efficiency. It is doubtful whether this can be offset by the increased flexibility of the process and the substitution of adiabatic beds for the tubular reformer.

*(d)    Using the CRG Plant for Enrichment*

A fourth route is to use the CRG plant as a source of enrichment for lean gas made by any means, *eg* by a continuous tubular reformer operated on LDF. On an existing installation this entails only the substitution of catalytic rich gas for the existing source of enrichment where it is economical to do so, or, in rare cases, where it is desired to exploit the higher pressure at which the finished gas can be distributed when so enriched compared, say, with LPG enrichment.

Of these routes the Series (A) is the most favoured for high-flame-speed town-gas manufacture and a considerable number of commercial Series (A) plants are now in operation with finished gas pressures up to 35 bars. The thermal value of the high-flame-speed gas produced by the processes just described under (a), (b) and (d) is equivalent to approximately 91% of the thermal value of the process and heating feedstock (Table 25).

### 3   The CRG Process used to Supplement or Replace Natural Gas

Natural gas supplies can be augmented by gases of non-standard characteristics to an amount limited by the extent of the departure from standard of such gases, and subject also to limitation on the hydrocarbon dew point of the mixed gas imposed by the temperature and pressure at which it is distributed. For example the use of untreated rich gas from the CRG process (see Chapter 1, Table 5, line 6), enriched with propane to raise the calorific value to that of natural gas, would be limited, mainly owing to its low Wobbe Number and relatively high propane dew point. If the propane enrichment is

132

increased in order to raise the Wobbe Number to that of natural gas, the propane dew point would be raised further and the calorific value would be roughly 30% higher than that of North Sea natural gas.

This low Wobbe Number of the raw-rich-gas/propane mixture derives from its carbon dioxide content, and lines 4 and 5 of Table 5 show the improvement produced by progressively eliminating it. With complete carbon dioxide removal the propane requirement for enrichment to natural-gas standard is halved and the Wobbe Number is raised to standard. The effect of the presence of hydrogen in the rich gas on its flame speed, masked by the carbon dioxide, now becomes apparent, but judging from Figure 2 (Chapter 1) it appears to be acceptable. It is probable, therefore, that the only limitation on the use of rich-gas/propane mixtures with carbon dioxide content reduced to 0 to 5% would be that imposed by the propane dew point.

The restriction imposed by the propane dew point of the gases so far considered can be eliminated if the calorific value of the rich gas is raised by methanation (43), *ie* by reacting the carbon oxides and the hydrogen present over a highly active nickel catalyst to produce methane as follows:

$$CO + 3H_2 \rightarrow CH_4 + H_2O$$
$$CO_2 + 4H_2 \rightarrow CH_4 + 2H_2O$$

Two stages are required owing to the highly exothermic nature of the methanation reactions. A simple flow diagram for the process is shown in Figure 38 and the results obtained from pilot-scale operation are given in Table 25. The product is almost entirely methane, and requires approximately 1% by volume of propane to raise its calorific value to 1 000 Btu/ft$^3$ (37·96 MJ/m$^3$).

An alternative to the first of the two stages of methanation is to produce a higher-calorific-value rich gas by placing two CRG reactors in series. In the second of these the presence of the products from the first stage would permit operation at a lower temperature than is possible with normal LDF/steam/recycle-gas. This in turn results in a higher methane content in the rich gas which eliminates the need for a second methanation stage. A simplified flow diagram for this proposal is shown in Figure 39.

Another method of reducing the hydrogen content of the product gas is to air-cool or water-cool the CRG catalyst bed in order to remove the reaction heat. This has not yet (1971) been applied on a commercial scale.

The CRG process reacts more favourably than other gas-making processes to the substitution of LPG for LDF as the feedstock. The space velocities in the reactor can be increased and the temperature lowered. A richer gas results, and if a natural-gas substitute is the objective, there is less carbon dioxide to remove and a single stage of methanation would suffice.

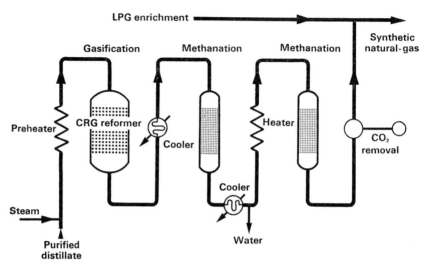

*Figure 38*   *Flow diagram for the production of synthetic natural-gas by two stages of methanation (Courtesy of the Institution of Gas Engineers)*

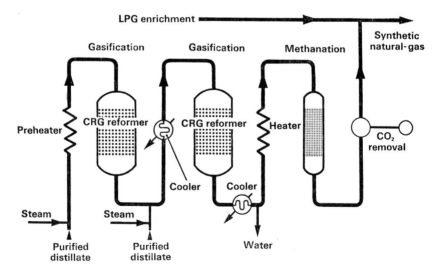

*Figure 39*   *Flow diagram for the production of synthetic natural-gas by two reforming stages and one stage of methanation*

134

# Chapter 10    Oil Gasification and Hydrocarbon Gas Reforming: Partial-Combustion Processes

In these processes the hydrocarbon feedstock is brought together with a limited amount of air and/or oxygen in a reaction tube or vessel. In those cases where oxygen is used, steam also is usually employed. The resultant partial combustion of the feedstock is a very efficient means of supplying the heat required for the processes, sometimes referred to as 'autocaloric' or 'autothermic', which are continuous in operation.

A further advantage of the introduction of oxygen into the reactions, relative to purely thermal cracking, is a reduction in the quantity of carbon or tar produced from a given degree of cracking of a given feedstock. This arises from the gasification of carbon in the form of oxides, and also, where the partial combustion proceeds at a sufficiently high temperature, from endothermic reaction between carbon and the steam, which may be used to help to control the temperature of the reaction in this case.

According to the choice of process, the feedstock may vary from natural or refinery gas to heavy fuel oil or tar. The cracking can be light, in which case gases or distillate oils are normally used with air as the gasifying medium. Then the product is usually a gas in the calorific value range 500 to 1 100 Btu/ft$^3$ (18·98 to 41·76 MJ/m$^3$), together with some tar when distillates are used and carbon when gaseous feedstocks are used. Alternatively reactions can proceed to the point where hydrogen, carbon monoxide, carbon dioxide and a small quantity of carbon are the final products, in which case oxygen is used as the gasifying medium either alone or under pressure in combination with steam. In this case, the hydrocarbon feedstock range is practically unlimited.

When air is used, the capital costs are at the lowest level for oil gasification plants, and the process is extremely flexible in operation. Unfortunately, however, the characteristics of the gas produced severely limit its use as an additive for natural gas or high-flame-speed town gas to meet peak loads.

When oxygen is used, capital costs are greatly increased and the plants must be used on base load. Subject to adjustment, where necessary, of the carbon monoxide and carbon dioxide contents by appropriate treatments, synthesis gas, hydrogen or a lean-gas component of town gas can be made.

The limitations on the use of gases made by partial combustion as additives or substitutes for town gas or natural gas are inherent, since little is done to reduce the carbon/hydrogen ratio of the feedstock to the level of approximately 3:1 which is desired in these gases, and the introduction of large quantities of nitrogen when air is used as the gasifying medium excessively ballasts the gas. When cracking is light, the carbon/hydrogen ratio of the feedstock is maintained in the gas or even slightly increased as a result of the combustion of hydrogen to steam. Even when cracking is sufficiently rigorous to decompose added steam, only a small reduction is achieved. For example, when oxygen and steam under pressure are used, a gas with a carbon/hydrogen ratio of 6·5:1 may be produced from an oil with a ratio of 7·5:1.

The term 'autothermic' was originally restricted to the type of process sometimes referred to as homogeneous partial combustion. Here the exothermic partial combustion of part of the feedstock effected almost simultaneously the endothermic cracking of the remainder, without a catalyst as in the Dayton processes, or in the presence of a catalyst as in the Distrigaz process. However, the term is now tending to be applied to any continuous oil gasification or reforming process–including even catalytic carbon monoxide conversion–that is self-supporting for its heat requirement. The term, when used in this broad sense, would be equally applicable to solid-fuel producers. In fact the Shell and Texaco oil gasification processes are more closely akin to the oxygen-fed solid-fuel producer-gas process than to the homogeneous partial combustion processes named.

Examples of autothermic processes based on air and oxygen, both catalytic and non-catalytic, are described in this chapter.

## Dayton Oil-Gas, GEIM (Gegi) and Sun/Thermal Processes: Continuous, Autothermic, Non-Catalytic and Low Pressure

In these processes LPG or a distillate fuel is partially combusted with air at pressures up to 0·7 bars, and in the temperature range 700 to 850°C to produce gases of 300 to 1 000 Btu/ft³ (11·39 to 37·96 MJ/m³). The tar yield varies from 15% when gas oil is the feedstock to a trace or nil when LDF and LPG respectively are used; gas yields are approximately 75%, 89% and 90% respectively.

The air used for partial combustion is about 10% of the stoichiometric requirement, and the reactions involved take place in a fraction of a second. Most of the sulphur content of the feedstock is oxidized and removed by washing. The hydrogen sulphide and organic sulphur content of the cooled gas is therefore very low, and this simplifies purification.

These are the most flexible, and the cheapest and simplest of gas-making processes to install and operate. The gas characteristics however limit their use even for peak shaving, and the low pressure of the product-gas limits their application to low-pressure gas-supply systems or to low-pressure gas-storage centres supplied from high-pressure systems.

The Howe-Baker Sun/Thermal plant shown in Figure 40 can be supplied in packaged form, skid-mounted, pre-piped and pre-wired. The 0·5 to 2·5 million ft³ per day (15 000 to 75 000 m³ per day) capacity units are compact, and require minimal installation and start-up time. This plant is designed to operate on naphtha feedstock. Examples of the results obtained from the process are given in Table 26.

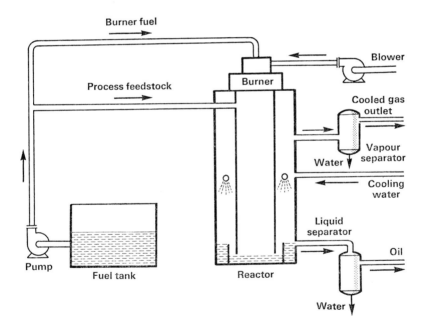

*Figure 40    The Howe-Baker Sun/Thermal partial combustion process*

137

# The Shell and Texaco Gasification Processes: Continuous, Autothermic, Non-Catalytic and Medium- and High-Pressure

The American Texaco process, and the very similar Dutch Shell process, have been developed in recent years for the manufacture of synthesis gas by the partial oxidation of any gaseous or liquid hydrocarbon feedstock. Even heavy oils having the highest sulphur contents normally encountered, and with vandium and nickel contents up to 500 ppm and 100 ppm respectively, have been used successfully. Analogous processes have been developed by Montecatini in Italy and Didier in Germany, amongst others.

*Table 26*  *Typical gas properties and process data for the Howe-Baker Sun/Thermal process*

| Gas characteristics | | | | |
|---|---|---|---|---|
| Calorific value | Btu/ft³stp(sat) | 450 | 550 | 1000 |
| | MJ/m³(st) | 17·08 | 20·88 | 37·96 |
| Specific gravity (air=1·0) | | 1·0 | 0·98 | 0·92 |
| Composition | | | | |
| $CO_2$ | % vol | 8 | 6 | 3 |
| CO | | 4 | 4 | 4 |
| $C_2H_6$ and lighter | | 21 | 28 | 54 |
| $C_3$ and heavier | | 6 | 10 | 12 |
| $N_2$ | | 61 | 52 | 27 |
| Total | | 100 | 100 | 100 |
| Gas yield | heat units per 100 heat units of total feedstock | 80 to 90 | 80 to 90 | 80 to 90 |
| Gas delivery pressure | bars | 1 to 2 | 1 to 2 | 1 to 2 |
| Utilities | | | | |
| Low-pressure steam | kg/100m³ | 130 | nil | 57 |
| Cooling water | kg/100m³ | 13 000 | 13 000 | 16 000 |
| Electricity | MJ/100m³ | 2·5 | 4·0 | 4·0 |
| Labour | | | | |
| Manpower per shift (not including supervision and maintenance) | | 1 | 1 | 1 |

138

Oxygen and steam are used as gasifying media, and the processes normally operate under pressures of from 10 to 40 bars, and in the temperature range 1 100 to 1 500°C, although Texaco now offer plants operating at 80 bars or more. In all these conditions, the products consist mainly of hydrogen and the oxides of carbon, together with a small quantity of methane and solid carbon. Nitrogen introduced as an impurity in the oxygen remains mainly unchanged. Thus only traces of nitrogenous impurities in the form of hydrocyanic acid are present in the gas, an advantage that most oil gases have relative to coal gas, and which simplifies oil-gas purification. Oxygen of 90 to 95% purity is normally used, but this can be economically reduced in some circumstances when ammonia synthesis gas is the final product.

The carbon produced is less than 0·05% by weight when methane is gasified and 2 to 3% by weight when liquid hydrocarbon feedstocks are used. It can be removed from the gas by washing with water, the resulting carbon slurry being reduced to a convenient form for handling by means of vacuum filtration. The disposal of this filter cake containing 80% water is costly. Preferred alternatives are the Shell process of removing the carbon from the slurry by the use of distillate or fuel oil and pelletizing the product for use as boiler fuel, or the Texaco technique of incorporating the carbon/oil mixture in either the steam-raising fuel or the process fuel. In this latter technique most of the oil ash is removed by the cooling water and the build-up of ash in the feedstock or in the plant is slight.

Ninety per cent of the sulphur content of the feedstock appears in the gas as hydrogen sulphide and the remainder as carbonyl sulphide, the latter being hydrolyzed to hydrogen sulphide if the gas is subjected to carbon monoxide conversion ($COS + H_2O \rightarrow CO_2 + H_2S$).

The thermal value of the gas made is approximately 84% of the potential heat of the feedstock, and, as the bulk of the remainder of this heat is recoverable as waste-heat steam, the losses involved in the gasification process are very small. When allowance is made for the oxygen plant and other ancillary plant, and the process steam and energy requirements, the resulting estimated efficiency of gas production is 70%, and compares favourably with the estimate of 67% for the Lurgi process (a comparable solid-fuel gasification process).

The capital costs, including those of the oxygen equipment, are such as to place the plants in the large-scale base-load category. Their application to base-load town gas manufacture is limited by the gas characteristics, such as its high carbon/hydrogen ratio and low calorific value. The former can be reduced to any desired level by stages of carbon monoxide conversion and carbon dioxide removal, leaving hydrogen or a hydrogen-rich gas, which can be used as a low-density diluent for a rich gas. This may be natural gas, refinery gas, rich gas made from light distillate by the UK Gas Council's catalytic process or recycle hydrogenator or the product of a carburettor installed on the combustor outlet.

Combustor design, burner adjustment and the oxidant proportioning are far more critical in oxygen-using processes than when air is used (44). A 5% increase in air dosage would produce an increase in flame temperature of only 40 degC; a similar increase in oxygen dosage would give an increase of 140 degC. A simplified diagram of the combustor of the Shell process is given in Figure 41. This indicates the double-vortex mixing pattern which ensures that the endo-

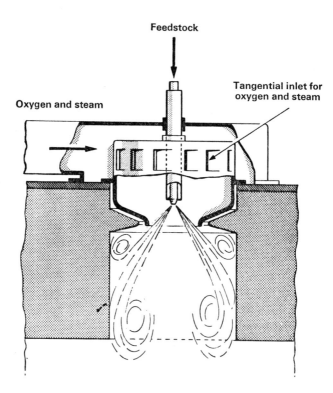

*Figure 41    Simplified diagram of the combustor in the Shell gasification process (Courtesy of Bataafse Internationale Petroleum Maatschappij NV)*

140

thermic steam reactions take place as close as possible to the exothermic combustion reactions. This is also effectively achieved in the Texaco combustor. Owing to the extreme sensitivity of the process to the proportioning of the reactants, extreme care is taken with regard to proportioning gear, control devices, safety or warning devices and other instrumentation.

The generators are cylindrical steel vessels, lined for their protection with layers of highly refractory material, such as silimanite or alundum and insulating material.

The adaptation of the continuous tubular reformer to the use of light distillate feedstock under pressure is likely to have the effect of limiting the application of these partial combustion processes to such materials as heavy distillates and residual oils.

For applications in which hydrogen or synthesis gas is required at high pressure, the continuous reformer is at a disadvantage, since the limiting design pressure is approximately 40 bars, whilst the corresponding pressure for the Shell and Texaco processes is roughly two to three times as high, but it is questionable whether operation above 40 bars is on balance economical.

Diagrams of the Shell and Texaco processes are given in Figures 42 and 43, and a set of typical results obtained from the Shell process is given in Table 27. Similar results are obtainable from the Texaco process.

Full details with regard to the burners, combustors and main ancillary equipment of these processes are not generally available. The method of operation is as follows.

The reactants, which are usually the hydrocarbon feedstock, oxygen and steam (the latter may be dispensed with when the feedstock is methane) are separately pre-heated to, say, 300°C in order to economize on oxygen. They are then brought together at carefully controlled pressures and flow rates in the burner, under conditions that ensure thorough and rapid mixing of the steam and oxygen immediately before partial combustion, and turbulence immediately after. This enables the heat released to be used as effectively as possible to promote secondary reactions between steam and carbon or hydrocarbons.

The gases leaving the generator at a temperature of 1 200°C to 1 400°C may either be quenched, in which case some low-pressure steam may be raised from the circulating condensate, or they may be passed through a waste-heat boiler.

The thermal and gasification efficiencies quoted in Table 27 take no account of the fuel-equivalent of the steam and power required by ancillaries, the principal of which are the oxygen plant and, if installed,

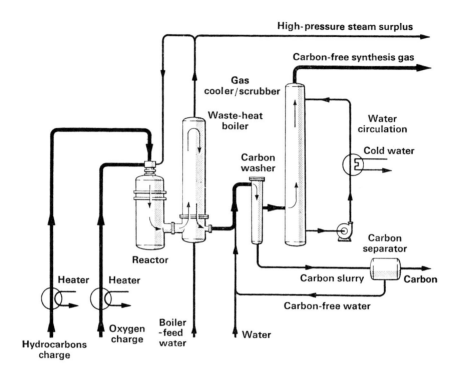

*Figure 42  Diagram of the Shell partial oxidation process (Courtesy of Bataafse Internationale Petroleum Maatschappij NV)*

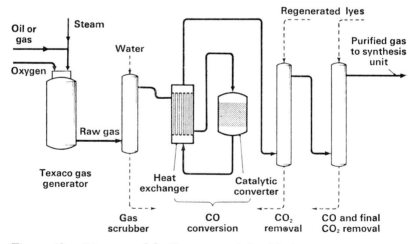

*Figure 43  Diagram of the Texaco partial oxidation process*

142

*Table 27 Typical data for the Shell process operated on various feedstocks*

| Gasification feedstock | | Natural gas | Liquid naphtha | Heavy fuel oil |
|---|---|---|---|---|
| Feedstock to reactor | kg | 1 | 1 | 1 |
| Preheat temperatures: | | | | |
| Feedstock | °C | 425 | 25 | 236 |
| Oxygen | °C | 236 | 236 | 236 |
| Steam | °C | 246 | 246 | 246 |
| Operating pressure | bars | 31·5 | 31·5 | 31·5 |
| Oxygen (36 bars) to reactor (as 100% at 95% purity) | $m^3$(st) | 1·02 | 0·93 | 0·79 |
| Steam to reactor (sat 246°C) | kg | 0·05 | 0·35 | 0·40 |
| Crude dry gas produced | $m^3$(st) | 3·97 | 3·45 | 3·11 |
| $(CO+H_2)$ produced | $m^3$(st) | 3·81 | 3·17 | 2·89 |
| $(CO+H_2)/O_2$ | vol/vol | 3·72 | 3·41 | 3·66 |
| Composition of product gas | % vol | | | |
| $CO_2$ | | 2·6 | 4·8 | 4·3 |
| CO | | 34·5 | 41·8 | 46·9 |
| $H_2$ | | 61·2 | 51·7 | 46·2 |
| $CH_4$ | | 0·3 | 0·3 | 0·3 |
| $N_2$ and Ar | | 1·4 | 1·4 | 1·4 |
| $H_2S$ (COS) | | — | 70 (ppm) | 0·9 |
| Total | | 100·0 | 100·0 | 100·0 |
| Delivery pressure of product gas | bars | 29·0 | 29·0 | 29·0 |

| Gasification feedstock | | Natural gas | Liquid naphtha | Heavy fuel oil |
|---|---|---|---|---|
| Carbon content of product gas | | | | |
| Before treatment | kg/kg feedstock | negligible | 0·03 | 0·03 |
| After treatment | ppm | approx 1 | approx 1 | approx 1 |
| Thermal efficiency* | % | 93·7 | 94·1 | 94·6 |
| Steam produced in waste-heat boiler (sat 246°C) | kg | 3·10 | 2·52 | 2·30 |
| Steam to preheaters (sat 246°C) | kg | 0·16 | 0·15 | 0·35 |
| Net steam production (sat 246°C) | kg | 2·94 | 2·02 | 1·55 |
| Boiler feed-water consumption (41 bars, 90°C) | kg | 3·10 | 2·52 | 2·30 |
| Cooling water consumption | kg | 1·2 | 32·1 | 33·6 |
| Fresh water consumption | kg | 0·25 | — | — |
| Condensate production | kg | 0·16 | 0·15 | 0·35 |
| Electricity consumption | kJ | 60 | 91 | 91 |
| Heating fuel | kg | 0·04 | — | — |
| $(CO+H_2)$ yield $\dfrac{\text{heat units per 100}}{\text{heat units total feedstock}}$ | | 84·1 | 81·7 | 81·0 |

$$*\text{Thermal efficiency} = \frac{\text{heat units produced [gas heating value (excluding sensible heat) + net steam + residual carbon]}}{\text{heat units consumed (hydrocarbon feed to process + preheat fuel)}} \times 100$$

143

the carbon dioxide removal system. These could demand fuel equivalent to 50% or more of the process feedstock, thus reducing the thermal efficiency of approximately 94% as expressed in Table 27 to an overall efficiency of gas production of approximately 60% to 70% according to the ancillaries involved.

The small amount of carbon produced is then washed from the gas and the resulting carbon slurry is treated in one or other of the manners already described.

Subsequent carbon monoxide conversion followed by carbon dioxide removal is desirable if the gas is to be used in town gas mixtures; firstly to improve the combustion characteristics of the mixed gas, secondly to reduce toxicity and, finally, to reduce to hydrogen sulphide the carbonyl sulphide present, since this compound would otherwise be difficult to deal with.

These processes are readily adaptable to the production of hydrogen-rich or carbon-monoxide-rich gases for the reduction of ores, by the use of oxygen at pressures above 7 to 10 bars, or air at pressures below this.


## The Distrigaz, Onia Autothermic and P2 (Gaz de France) Processes: Continuous, Autothermic, Catalytic and Low- to Medium-Pressure

In these processes, as usually operated, the heat required for the catalytic reforming of undesulphurized methane, refinery gas or liquefied petroleum gases at atmospheric pressure is provided by partial combustion with air. A small quantity of steam is added to the reactants to prevent the formation of carbon, which would choke the catalyst. The plant is made self-supporting for steam.

The reformed gas of high inert content made in this way has a calorific value of 160 to 180 Btu/ft$^3$ (6·08 to 6·84 MJ/m$^3$) and a specific gravity of 0·66 to 0·68. Cold enrichment would produce a gas of 500 Btu/ft$^3$ (18·98 MJ/m$^3$) with a specific gravity of 0·7 to 0·8.

Efficiencies of these processes are higher than are those of the air-using, non-catalytic, autothermic processes described and the specific gravity of the gas produced for a given calorific value is slightly lower. It is still sufficiently high, however, to place severe limitations on its use in town-gas mixtures.

A flow diagram of the Onia process is shown in Figure 44. Typical results obtained from this plant are given in Table 28.

144

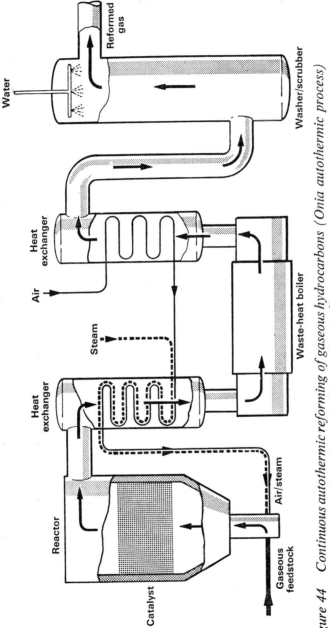

*Figure 44  Continuous autothermic reforming of gaseous hydrocarbons (Onia autothermic process) (Courtesy of Humphreys & Glasgow Limited)*

145

*Table 28  Typical results from the continuous reforming of gaseous hydrocarbons by the Onia autothermic process*

| Feedstock | | Operated with air | | |
|---|---|---|---|---|
| | | Mine gas | Commercial propane | Commercial butane |
| Feedstock characteristics | | | | |
| Composition | | | | |
| $CO_2$ | % vol | 2·4 | nil | nil |
| $C_3H_6$ | | nil | 45·5 | 1·0 |
| $C_nH_m$ | | nil | nil | 4·0 |
| $O_2$ | | 7·9 | nil | nil |
| $CH_4$ | | 48·3 | nil | nil |
| $C_3H_8$ | | nil | 54·5 | 6·0 |
| $C_4H_8$ | | nil | nil | 22·0 |
| $C_4H_{10}$ | | nil | nil | 67·0 |
| $N_2$ | | 41·4 | nil | nil |
| Total | | 100·0 | 100·0 | 100·0 |
| Calorific value | Btu/ft³stp(sat) | 480 | 2 460 | 3 140 |
| | MJ/m³(st) | 18·22 | 93·36 | 119·22 |
| Reformed gas characteristics | | | | |
| Composition | | | | |
| $CO_2$ | % vol | 4·7 | 6·2 | 7·6 |
| $C_nH_m$ | | nil | nil | nil |
| $O_2$ | | 0·1 | 0·6 | 0·5 |
| CO | | 13·3 | 16·6 | 15·5 |
| $H_2$ | | 35·4 | 36·8 | 36·1 |
| $C_nH_{2n+2}$ | | 1·1 | 0·8 | 1·7 |
| $N_2$ | | 45·4 | 39·0 | 38·6 |
| Total | | 100·0 | 100·0 | 100·0 |
| Calorific value | Btu/ft³stp(sat) | 166 | 182 | 181 |
| | MJ/m³(st) | 6·29 | 6·90 | 6·86 |
| Specific gravity (air=1·0) | | 0·675 | 0·67 | 0·68 |
| Gas yield | heat units per 100 heat units of total feedstock | 89 | 92 | 92 |

146

## The Topsøe-SBA and Didier Catalytic Partial-Oxidation Processes: Continuous, Autothermic and High-Pressure

In the first of these processes, developed jointly by Haldor Topsøe of Denmark and the Société Belge de l'Azote (SBA) of Liège for the manufacture of synthesis gas, partial oxidation is followed by catalytic reforming carried out at pressures between 15 and 30 bars. It may be regarded as a pressurized version of the Distrigaz and Onia-Gegi autothermic processes. For the manufacture of gas for ammonia synthesis the process air is enriched with oxygen, and for the manufacture of methanol-synthesis-gas or hydrogen it is replaced by oxygen. Carbon monoxide conversion of the make-gas can readily and efficiently be effected, and carbon dioxide can be recycled if desired.

Up to 20% of unsaturated hydrocarbons and 50 ppm of sulphur can be tolerated in the feedstock which, on full commercial scale, has so far been restricted to $C_1$ to $C_4$ hydrocarbons, but a pilot-stage plant has operated successfully on light distillate feedstock with a distillation end-point of 150°C.

Didier have built an analogous plant. The advantage of these processes compared with non-catalytic partial oxidation under pressure is that no carbon is produced. The disadvantage, however, is that they are less flexible with regard to feedstocks than the non-catalytic processes such as Shell and Texaco, which can use residual oils. Because of this restriction in feedstock range the Topsøe-SBA process may be regarded more as competing with the continuous tubular reformer and, in this context, it is at a disadvantage with regard to both capital and process costs, and overall efficiency of gas making.

A diagram of the Didier process is shown in Figure 45.

## Endothermic Generators

The term *endothermic generators* is used to describe the small-scale (200 to 1 000 m³/day) catalytic tubular reformers used for the production of reducing gases for use in the heat treatment of metals. They are made by heat-treatment-furnace manufacturers such as Wild Barfield, British Furnaces, Birlec and Efco Furnaces.

The reactants are air and town gas or $C_1$ to $C_4$ hydrocarbons at approximately ambient temperature and pressure. Usually a single, short, heat-resisting alloy-steel catalyst tube is used.

In spite of the exothermic nature of the partial combustion of the reactants, external heat is applied, for example by means of tangential

147

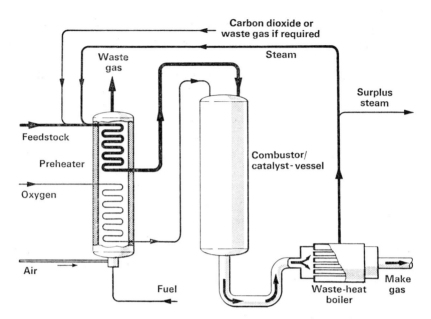

*Figure 45    Diagram of the Didier catalytic partial oxidation process (Courtesy of Didier-Werke AG)*

LPG side-burners as shown in Figure 46, to give a product-gas temperature of 1 000 to 1 100 °C. The object of the application of this heat is, with the aid of the catalyst, to shift the equilibrium composition of the product gas to the point where carbon dioxide and water vapour are almost eliminated, as shown below with propane as an example:

$C_3H_8 + 1.5 O_2 + 5.7N_2 \rightarrow 3CO + 4H_2 + 5.7N_2$
1 volume propane + 7.2 volumes air → 12.7 volumes of product gas.

In practice, product gas of the following composition was obtained from propane:

CO$_2$    Trace
CO      23.4% vol
H$_2$      31.1   ,,
CH$_4$    0.2   ,,
N$_2$      45.3   ,,

Total 100.0   ,,   (water dew point —5°C).

148

Extremely close control of the carbon dioxide and water contents of the product gas is normally required by the metal-treatment processes for which the gas is used. This demands constant monitoring, *eg* by dew-point determination. On the larger plants an automatic control relay, impulsed by an infra-red analyser continuously monitoring the carbon dioxide content of the gas, may be used to adjust automatically either the feedstock supply or the air supply. In Figure 46 the relay is shown controlling part of the air supply.

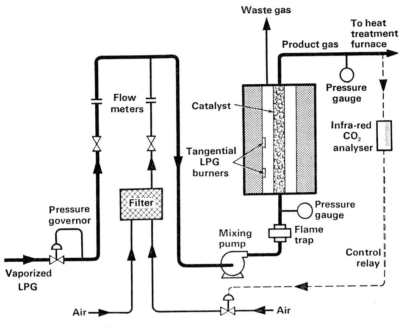

*Figure 46*    *Endothermic generator*

It has been demonstrated that up to the level of $C_3$ hydrocarbons, satisfactory operation can be achieved with high unsaturated hydrocarbon contents in the feedstock (45). However, high-purity grades of LPG are commonly specified for this purpose, mainly in order to avoid the possible risk, in spite of the controls, of feedstock quality variations affecting either product-gas quality or the continuous operation of the reformer.

Carbon formation on the catalyst is indicated by a rise in the reactor differential pressure. Continuous operation for a year has been

149

claimed, but more commonly the catalyst is regenerated monthly, by the use of 20% of the normal air rate and a reactor temperature of 700 to 750°C. A robust nickel catalyst is used which is tolerant to the sulphur content of LPG.

The small scale of these gasifiers renders it uneconomical to apply heat exchange or recovery processes either to the process gas or combustion products, with the result that the thermal efficiency expressed as a percentage of the process and heating feedstock is approximately 50 to 60%.

*Chapter 11*    Oil Gasification and Hydrocarbon-Gas
Reforming: The Non-Catalytic
Hydrogasification of Hydrocarbon Oils

The high-pressure processes described in this chapter are of interest as alternatives to the solid-fuel processes described in Chapter 4 and the CRG process described in Chapter 10, for the production of synthetic natural gas, or gas to supplement natural-gas supplies.

## The UK Gas Council's Fluidized-Bed Hydrogenator (37)

The sulphur and non-volatile constituents in crude oil and heavy fuel oils restrict their direct use in catalytic processes. However, they can be hydrogenated, and the rich gas produced after purification can then be reformed into a synthesis gas, or the lean-gas component of town gas, or synthetic natural gas. Simplified flow diagrams showing possible arrangements of plant to produce town gas and synthetic natural gas by this means is shown in Figure 47.

The method of operation of the process is as follows. The hydrogenator shown in Figure 48 contains a circulating bed of coke particles of 0·1 to 0·4 mm diameter. Heavy oil is atomized into these particles at the base of the riser tube with part of the hydrogenating gas and the remainder of the reactant hydrogen is added at the points shown.

The oil and hydrogen react under a pressure of 50 to 70 bars at a temperature of 750°C. The aliphatic constituents of the oil are converted to gaseous hydrocarbons, the aromatic constituents being stripped of side chains to give benzene, naphthalene and higher aromatics.

The process is exothermic, 3 to 5% of the potential heat of the feedstock being liberated. The temperature level is controlled by the degree of preheat of the oil and hydrogen, and is rendered uniform throughout the bed by the movement of the fluidized particles.

Some carbon is deposited, equivalent roughly to one third of the Conradson carbon content of the feedstock oil, and is dealt with by the withdrawal and replacement of a proportion of the bed without interruption of the process. Agglomeration of the coke particles at the point of entry into the hydrogenator is prevented by the recirculation

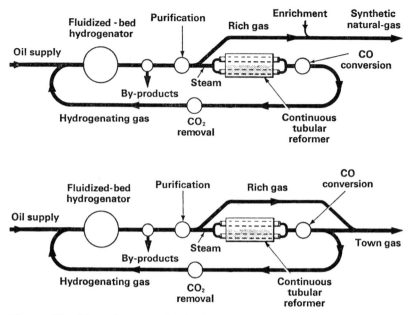

*Figure 47*   *Flow diagrams for hydrogenation of crude oil or heavy fuel oil to produce synthetic natural gas (top) and town gas (bottom) (From Proceedings of Inst. Gas Eng. and Inst. of Fuel conference, Hastings, 1962)*

of the bed. This is promoted by the higher particle density in the downcomer compared with that in the riser tube.

The hydrogenating gas used can be produced either by steam-reforming part of the purified hydrogenator product gas, as shown in Figure 47, or, by some other means such as the steam-reforming of naphtha.

Typical results obtained from a one-million ft³ per day (28 000 m³ per day) plant operated at 50 bars with crude oil feedstock are given in Table 29, which shows that approximately 73% of the potential heat of the feedstock is recovered as rich gas and 22% as an aromatic condensate with a high polycyclic content.

With efficient heat exchange, a thermal yield of rich gas plus condensate of approximately 90% can be anticipated. If the heat losses involved in the manufacture of the recycle gas are deducted, this becomes approximately 86% for rich-gas manufacture. The gas-plus-condensate yield would fall to 82% for high-flame-speed town gas

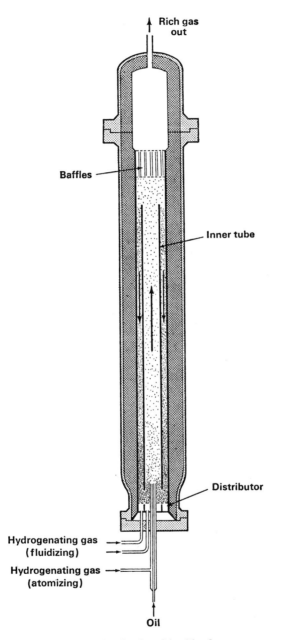

*Figure 48    The fluidized-bed hydrogenator*

153

manufacture when allowance is made for the heat losses involved in the manufacture of the lean-gas element.

The first commercial application of this process, an 8 000 000 ft³ per day (226 000 m³ per day) unit, was installed in Osaka, Japan in 1969.

In place of crude oil or fuel oil, light-distillate feedstock can be used (43), but the CRG process and the recycle hydrogenator appear to be more appropriate and more economical for the latter feedstock.

The properties of the substitutes for natural gas that can be made by the propane-enrichment of the product gas described in Table 29 are slightly closer to those of natural gas than those shown on lines 7 to 9 of Table 5 relating to gas made by the gas-recycle hydrogenator.


## The UK Gas Council's Gas-Recycle Hydrogenator (37)

The UK Gas Council's gas-recycle hydrogenator has already been referred to as an ancillary to the ICI continuous reformer in the production of high-flame-speed town gas. The following is a more detailed description of this process.

Light distillate vapour is thermally cracked and the products hydrogenated by reaction with a lean gas containing hydrogen. The operating temperature range is 700 to 750°C and the pressure 10 to 100 bars. In these conditions a clean gas is produced containing practically no unsaturated hydrocarbons. (Under low pressure conditions, as in the carburetted-water-gas process, little hydrogenation occurs, the process is thermally neutral, and a large proportion of unsaturated hydrocarbons are produced together with some tar.) The distillate is cracked and the fragments react with the hydrogen to produce methane and ethane as follows:

$$(- CH_2-) + H_2 \rightarrow CH_4$$
$$2(- CH_2-) + H_2 \rightarrow C_2H_6$$

The methane/ethane ratio in the product gas varies according to the structure of the hydrocarbons involved, and can be predicted by assuming random breaking of the C — C bonds (38). Benzene nuclei present survive the reaction, but are mainly stripped of side chains and can be condensed from the product gas. These reactions are exothermic and, provided there is some heat exchange between the product gas and the reactants, no external heat source is required and the process may be operated continuously.

154

*Table 29    The hydrogenation of crude oil at 50 bars pressure*

| Crude oil | | | |
|---|---|---|---|
| Specific gravity | | | 0·86 |
| Conradson carbon content | % wt | | 3·5 |
| Calorific value | Btu/lb | | 19 300 |
| | MJ/kg | | 44·9 |
| Rate of supply | lb/1000 ft³ | | 39·0 |
| | kg/1000 m³ | | 624·8 |
| Preheat temperature | °C | | 350 |
| Hydrogenating gas | | | |
| Composition | | | |
| CO₂ | % vol | | 0·3 |
| H₂ | | | 94·0 |
| CO | | | 3·1 |
| CH₄ | | | 1·7 |
| N₂ | | | 0·9 |
| Total | | | 100·0 |
| Rate of supply | ft³/h | | 32 870 |
| | m³/h | | 931 |
| Preheat temperature | °C | | 600 |
| Temperature of fluidized bed | °C | | 750 |
| Gas produced | | | |
| Composition | | | |
| CO₂ | % vol | | 0·2 |
| CₙHₘ | | | 0·3 |
| H₂ | | | 36·3 |
| CO | | | 2·9 |
| CH₄ | | | 45·9 |
| C₂H₆ | | | 13·5 |
| N₂ | | | 0·9 |
| Total | | | 100·0 |
| Calorific value | Btu/ft³stp(sat) | | 821 |
| | MJ/m³(st) | | 31·11 |
| Rate of production | ft³/h | | 35 180 |
| | m³/h | | 996 |

| Carbon balance | |
|---|---|
| In oil supplied | 100·0 |
| In gas produced | 71·7 |
| Benzene | 11·6 |
| Toluene | 1·9 |
| Naphthalene | 3·5 |
| Higher aromatics | 9·2 |
| Carbon deposited | 2·1 |

| Potential heat balance | |
|---|---|
| In oil supplied | 100·0 |
| In gas due to oil | 72·9 |
| Benzene | 10·0 |
| Toluene | 1·7 |
| Naphthalene | 2·8 |
| Higher aromatics | 7·2 |
| Sulphur | 0·3 |
| Carbon deposited | 1·3 |
| Heat of reaction, by difference | 3·8 |

155

A diagram of the recycle hydrogenator is shown in Figure 49. The hydrogen-rich gas used may be subject to prior shift conversion and carbon dioxide removal or not, according to the characteristics required of the enriched gas produced. At the hydrogenator inlet, steam is added to produce a content of 8 % by volume, and sulphur equivalent to 20 ppm w/w of total reactants also is added, preferably as hydrogen sulphide. The hydrogenation temperature is controlled by means of the degree of preheat of the reactants, which is in the range 450 to 550°C for a product gas temperature of 750°C at 25 bars. Operation at the lower pressure limit of the process demands a slightly lower temperature but this should not be allowed to fall below 700°C. The residence time for the reactants is 10 to 15 seconds, and output

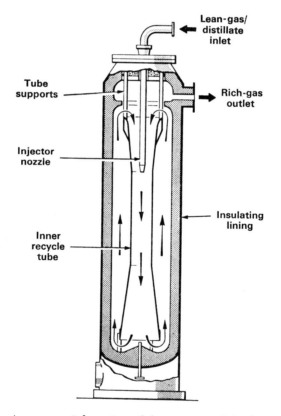

*Figure 49    A commercial version of the gas-recycle hydrogenator*

therefore varies in direct proportion to pressure. The process is flexible and no difficulty is anticipated in scaling-up to 50 million ft³ (1·5 million m³) per day capacity for a single unit.

The lean gas containing hydrogen can be derived from such processes as Lurgi, Shell, Texaco and the steam hydrocarbon reformers.

Typical potential heat balances are given in Table 30. The designations '170' and '115' applied to the light distillate feedstocks refer to the temperature in degrees centigrade at which 95% of the material distils. The heat of reaction shown appears as sensible heat in the make-gas and is relatively small. With efficient heat exchange the potential heat of synthetic natural gas made by this process would be 90% expressed on the basis of the total heating and process feedstock, the heating feedstock being required mainly for the reformer producing the hydrogen-rich gas.

*Table 30    Typical potential heat balances in distillate hydrogenation by the UK Gas Council's recycle hydrogenator*

| Distillate used | LDF 170 | LDF 115 |
|---|---|---|
| Potential heat in products as percentage of potential heat in hydrogenator distillate | | |
| Hydrocarbon gas | 88·9 | 95·0 |
| Benzene | 7·1 | 2·5 |
| Toluene | 0·6 | 0·2 |
| Other monocyclics | 0·3 | 0·2 |
| Naphthalene | 0·2 | 0·1 |
| Higher aromatics | 0·2 | nil |
| Heat of reaction (by difference) | 2·7 | 2·0 |
| Total | 100·0 | 100·0 |

The quality of the supplementary or substitute natural gases that can be produced by propane enrichment is shown in Table 5. The quality of the raw gases produced, with varying degrees of carbon dioxide removal from the hydrogenator gas, can be judged by eliminating the added propane.

# Chapter 12    Miscellaneous Processes

## Catalytic Carbon Monoxide Conversion

The chemical reaction involved in what is generally termed the carbon monoxide shift conversion is expressed as follows:

$$CO + H_2O \rightleftharpoons CO_2 + H_2$$

It is mildly exothermic from left to right, and is effected catalytically. The conversion of 1 % of carbon monoxide results in a rise of approximately 10 degC in the temperature of converted gas. The conventional catalyst is iron oxide promoted with chromic oxide, but other catalysts have recently been introduced.

The equilibrium coefficient of the reaction, $K$, is expressed as follows, where $p$ is the partial pressure of the gases:

$$K = \frac{p(CO)p(H_2O)}{p(CO_2)p(H_2)}$$

From this it will be seen that the presence of water vapour, in excess of that demanded by the reaction, reduces the equilibrium carbon monoxide content. There is no change of volume, and the effect of pressure change on the reaction equilibrium is slight. Increase in pressure does, however, speed up the reaction.

$K$ increases with reaction temperature, rising for example from 0·28 at 550°C to 0·38 at 600°C. The importance of minimizing the conversion temperature is therefore apparent. However the reaction rate also increases, but more steeply, with increasing reaction temperature. For this reason conventional iron-chrome catalysts are normally not used at temperatures below approximately 330°C, and, where gases containing high concentrations of carbon monoxide have to be rigorously converted, multi-stage treatment is employed, the temperature being adjusted between stages. This allows the bulk of the carbon monoxide to be converted at optimum space velocity, even when a high conversion efficiency, and hence a low conversion temperature, is demanded of the final stage. The reaction heat removed between stages can be used for such process purposes as steam-raising and lye-heating or water-heating.

158

# 1 Chromium-Promoted Iron Oxide Catalyst

Iron-chrome catalysts containing roughly 10% of chromic oxide and 80% of ferric oxide are the most commonly used for carbon monoxide shift conversion. A great deal is known concerning their behaviour. Salient points (46) are as set out below and overleaf:

## (a) Initial Reduction of Catalyst

The catalyst has to be reduced initially. The two reactions involved with synthesis gas are as follows:

$$3 Fe_2O_3 + CO \rightarrow 2Fe_3O_4 + CO_2$$
$$3 Fe_2O_3 + H_2 \rightarrow 2Fe_3O_4 + H_2O$$

The reaction with carbon monoxide results in a rise of approximately 120 degC for each 1% by volume carbon monoxide reacted, whereas that with hydrogen produces a much smaller rise. In order to avoid excessive temperature during start-up, reducing gas mixtures containing a high carbon monoxide content must not be used without dilution, say with steam or recycled gas.

## (b) Main Operational Reactions

The principal reactions involved under operating conditions are as follows:

$$CO + H_2O \rightleftharpoons CO_2 + H_2$$
$$Fe_3O_4 + 3H_2S + H_2 \rightleftharpoons 3FeS + 4H_2O$$
$$O_2 + 2H_2 \rightarrow 2H_2O$$
$$O_2 + 2CO \rightarrow 2CO_2$$

Heat evolved in the reactions with oxygen result in a temperature rise of 120 degC per 1% by volume of oxygen reacting when hydrogen is consumed, and approximately 140 degC with carbon monoxide ie respectively 12 and 14 times the heat evolved in the conversion of 1% of carbon monoxide. The content of oxygen, which in any case is rarely present, must therefore be carefully controlled.

The heat evolved by the sulphiding of the catalyst, or absorbed by its being desulphided, is slight. High concentrations of hydrogen sulphide in the reactant gases reduce the activity of the catalyst, but the effect is slight for concentrations below 0·08% v/v of hydrogen sulphide in the gas. The sulphiding reaction is easily reversible. Therefore, depending upon the previous history of the catalyst, and the steam and hydrogen sulphide content of the reactant gas, hydrogen sulphide may be absorbed or given up by the catalyst.

A further interesting point concerning the sulphiding reaction is that the equilibrium constant changes so rapidly in the temperature range of shift conversion that it is possible for the catalyst at the lower temperature of the inlet end of the converters to be sulphided, whilst that at the higher temperature of the outlet end is sulphur-free.

*(c)   Oxidation Reactions*
The reduced catalyst is pyrophoric and must be oxidized under carefully controlled conditions prior to its removal from the converter vessel, or prior to the uncontrolled admission of air to the vessel. The oxidizing reactions are as follows:

$$2Fe_3O_4 + H_2O \rightleftharpoons 3Fe_2O_3 + H_2$$
$$6FeS + 9H_2O \rightleftharpoons 3Fe_2O_3 + 6H_2S + 3H_2$$
$$4Fe_3O_4 + O_2 \rightarrow 6\ Fe_2O_3$$
$$6\ FeS + 13\tfrac{1}{2}O_2 \rightarrow 2\ Fe_2(SO_4)_3 + Fe_2O_3$$
$$2\ FeS + 3\tfrac{1}{2}O_2 \rightarrow Fe_2O_3 + 2SO_2$$

The reactions with oxygen are extremely rapid and result in a temperature rise of roughly 100 degC per 1% by volume oxygen reacted in the gas mixture. The reactions with steam are slow, and slightly exothermic when magnetic iron oxide ($Fe_3O_4$) is involved and slightly endothermic when ferrous sulphide is involved.

Oxidation of the catalyst is carried out slowly with steam until the final phase when a small amount of air, or oxygen-containing gas, may be admitted in order to ensure that it is complete.

The life of the catalyst is limited with regard to oxidation, in one case ten cycles only being guaranteed. In consequence, on plant shutdown, when possible the catalyst is left in the reduced state in contact with treated or inert gas.

*(d)   Operating Conditions*
Iron-chrome catalysts are normally used in the temperature range 330 to 500°C and in the pressure range 1 to 35 bars. No methane is formed under these conditions, although small quantities may appear at higher pressures.

## 2   The Girdler G-66B Low-Temperature Carbon Monoxide Shift Catalyst
As stated, owing to the low rate at which the reaction would proceed, conventional iron-chrome catalysts are not used at temperatures below approximately 330°C. The advantage of operating at lower temperatures is apparent from Figure 50 and catalysts are now

available that permit this to be done at economic space velocities. The Girdler G-66B low-temperature catalyst, made under licence from EI du Pont de Nemours, is such a catalyst. It can be used alone or following a stage in which a conventional catalyst is used.

This catalyst operates in the temperature range 190 to 370°C, and in the pressure range 1 to 30 bars. No carbon deposition or methane formation has been encountered under these conditions. Figure 50 gives a comparison of the operating temperature range with that of conventional catalysts, and of the relevant equilibrium carbon monoxide concentrations under given conditions.

In common with iron-chrome catalysts, the G-66B material is produced in the oxidized state and must be reduced under controlled conditions. If steam-cooled, however, the reduced catalyst will not oxidize when exposed to air and this simplifies start-up procedure after a complete shut down.

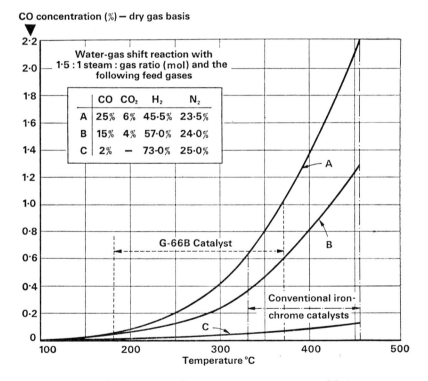

CO concentration (%) — dry gas basis

Water-gas shift reaction with 1·5 : 1 steam : gas ratio (mol) and the following feed gases

|   | CO | CO₂ | H₂ | N₂ |
|---|-----|------|------|------|
| A | 25% | 6% | 45·5% | 23·5% |
| B | 15% | 4% | 57·0% | 24·0% |
| C | 2% | — | 73·0% | 25·0% |

G-66B Catalyst

Conventional iron-chrome catalysts

Temperature °C

*Figure 50    Carbon monoxide concentrations in equilibrium at temperatures in the range 100 to 460°C (Courtesy of Anglo-Continental Fullers Earth Company Limited)*

161

In common with conventional catalysts, G-66B suffers a loss of activity if exposed to unsaturated hydrocarbons, but the resulting deposited gums can usually be removed by oxidation with steam and air at 425°C. Sulphur contents of the order of 10 ppm and chlorine of the same order permanently damage the catalyst. If the G-66B catalyst is used in series with an iron-chrome catalyst, means must be employed for absorbing the hydrogen sulphide traces normally evolved by iron-chrome catalysts during the first few days in operation, even when sulphur-free gas is being treated. A suitable method is the introduction of a layer of zinc oxide on top of the G-66B material.

### 3   Cobalt-Molybdenum Catalyst for Shift Conversion

Cobalt-molybdenum catalyst, normally used for hydrogenation, can be used in the sulphided state as a shift conversion catalyst. If unsaturated hydrocarbons are present in the gas to be treated, the operating pressure and temperature must be sufficiently high to ensure their hydrogenation. These conditions are satisfied by the partially quenched gas from the Lurgi gasifier operating on coal, and cobalt/molybdenum is used without a guard catalyst in this application. A two-stage process is employed with temperature reduction between stages; the treated gas temperature is 400°C.

In an instance quoted (47) the carbon monoxide content was reduced from 24·6% to 7·5%. After approximately a year in use the catalyst became partially choked, mainly with oxides of iron and arsenic derived from the coal. This was removed by sieving and the catalyst was put back into use.

### 4   Miscellaneous Reactions and Effects Occurring during Operation with Shift Catalysts

In the foregoing sections, consideration has been given to the behaviour of hydrogen, hydrogen sulphide, steam, the oxides of carbon and the small quantity of oxygen that may be present during operation or catalyst oxidation. In practice, however, commercial gases may contain other gases and trace substances which influence operation. The principal of these, and their effects, are dealt with below.

*(a)   The Girdler G-66B Catalyst*
This catalyst is deactivated even by 10 ppm of sulphur in any form.

*(b)   Iron-Chromium Catalysts*
These catalysts reduce carbon disulphide and carbonyl sulphide as follows:

162

$$CS_2 + 2H_2O \rightarrow CO_2 + 2H_2S$$
$$COS + H_2 \rightarrow CO + H_2S$$
$$COS + H_2O \rightarrow CO_2 + H_2S$$

Thiophen is unchanged and ethyl mercaptan is said to deactivate this catalyst immediately and permanently (46).

*(c)   Cobalt-Molybdenum Catalysts*
All the organic sulphur compounds likely to be present including thiophen are hydrogenated to hydrogen sulphide by this catalyst, provided it is not fouled by the hydrocarbons referred to below.

*(d)   Effect of Hydrocarbon Gases*
Paraffins and benzene do not impede the operation of shift conversion catalysts. Acetylene, diolefins if accompanied by oxygen, and nitric oxide if accompanied by diolefins and oxygen, poison iron-chrome catalysts.

Cobalt-molybdenum catalysts, although less affected at high operating temperatures and pressures, are similarly affected at low temperatures and pressures. It is probable that the G-66B low-temperature catalyst would be the most susceptible to these effects.

The UK Gas Council's London Research Station (48) showed that the worst hydrocarbon fouling agent occurring in practice is acetylene. It was shown also that cobalt-molybdenum oxides, nickel-molybdenum oxides and nickel subsulphide can all be used successfully as guard catalysts. They would all become fouled, but suffer less on regeneration than the physically weaker shift catalyst.

## Catalytic Removal of Organic Sulphur from Fuel Gases

Many of the heavy metals and their oxides and sulphides are effective in the temperature range 200 to 450°C for promoting the following types of reaction involving organic sulphur compounds:

reduction in the presence of hydrogen,
$eg$ $COS + H_2 \rightarrow CO + H_2S$
hydrolysis in the presence of water vapour,
$eg$ $COS + H_2O \rightarrow CO_2 + H_2S$
oxidation in the presence of oxygen,
$eg$ $COS + O_2 \rightarrow CO + SO_2$

163

Metals that have been used for this purpose include platinum, zinc, copper, iron, cobalt, nickel, chromium and molybdenum. Typical initial forms are zinc oxide plus metallic copper, zinc oxide alone, iron oxide, nickel subsulphide, molybdenum disulphide, and the thiomolybdates of copper, nickel and cobalt.

Cyclic organic sulphur compounds such as thiophen are more resistant to catalysis than the other compounds normally present in fuel gases – namely mercaptans, alkyl sulphides and carbon oxysulphide and disulphide. The only catalysts used to deal with thiophen successfully on a commercial scale are those based on molybdenum.

Difficulties may arise in practice when these catalysts are used, owing to the fact that diolefins such as butadiene and pentadiene, together with other trace substances, may be polymerized on the catalyst surface. This probably accounts for the relative ineffectiveness of highly active hydrogenation catalysts based on molybdenum in dealing with the thiophen in coal gas at low pressure, compared with their effectiveness in dealing with thiophen either in the absence of these substances, or in their presence at hydrogen partial pressures sufficiently high for the olefins and other trace substances to be hydrogenated.

When the reactions proceed under reducing conditions and in the absence of steam, certain of the oxides, such as those of iron and zinc, are used at the reaction temperature as absorbents, by chemical reaction, of the hydrogen sulphide produced, in order to yield a sulphur-free exit gas.

# Chapter 13    Gas Manufacture Costs

The data given in Tables 31, 32 and 33 are subject to the following qualifications.

*Scope*

Costs are intended to be comprehensive for gas manufacture on a new site, up to the inlet of the main storage holder, *ie* site, site preparation, office, laboratory, workshop and other buildings, roads, drains and other service and amenities costs are included.

The capital cost of a tubular reforming or partial-oxidation plant, for example, installed on site already prepared within an existing works provided with an adequate reserve of services capacity, could be as much as 40% less than the estimated cost used in the tables.

*Scale of operation*

1·5 to 2 million cubic metres per day.

*Notional fuel prices used in cost calculations*

|  | £/tonne |
|---|---|
| Coking coal | 7·5 |
| Coal for gasification processes | 4·0 |
| Coke | 12·0 |
| Heavy fuel oil | 8·0 |
| Light distillate | 12·0 |
| Liquefied petroleum gas | 12·5 |
| Natural gas and refinery gas | 10·0 |

It is unlikely that these notional prices will be appropriate for a particular time or place. The costs in Table 32 have therefore been set out in such a manner that correction to the applicable fuel prices can readily be made.

*Capital charges*

An arbitrary capital service charge of 12% per annum has been applied. This can be varied as may be considered appropriate.

With regard to the cost comparison between the continuous reformer (Table 32, Column 6) and the Shell and Texaco processes (Column 8) it should be borne in mind that, in the examples given, carbon dioxide and methane contents of the continuous reformer gas shown

165

*Table 31*    *Specific notional capital costs for 'green field site' gasworks*
*Total capital charges assumed at 12% per annum (1971)*

| Process | Feedstock | | Product gas cal val MJ/m³ | Capital cost £/100MJ daily capacity | Capital charges p/100MJ of gas made | |
|---|---|---|---|---|---|---|
| | Primary | Enriching | | | Load factor 45% | 85% |
| 1 Producer gas | Coke | | 4·75 | 8·0 | 0·59 | 0·31 |
| 2 Blue-water-gas | Coke | | 10·44 | 32·0 | 2·34 | 1·24 |
| 3 Koppers-Totzek | Coal | | 10·81 | 40·0 | 2·93 | 1·55 |
| 4 Continuous tubular reformer | Natural gas | | 12·14 | 16·0 | 1·17 | 0·62 |
| 5 Continuous tubular reformer | LPG | | 12·14 | 17·0 | 1·24 | 0·66 |
| 6 Continuous tubular reformer | LDF | | 12·14 | 18·0 | 1·32 | 0·69 |
| 7 Lurgi | Coal | | 11·77 | 65·0 | 4·76 | 2·51 |
| 8 Shell and Texaco (92% H₂) | HFO | | 11·58 | 35·0 | 2·56 | 1·36 |
| 9 Continuous vertical retorts | Coal | | 18·98 | 63·0 | 4·61 | 2·44 |
| 10 Intermittent vertical retorts | Coal | | 18·98 | 60·0 | 4·39 | 2·32 |
| 11 Coke ovens (Gas works) | Coal | | 18·98 | 52·0 | 3·81 | 2·01 |
| 12 CWG (LDF reforming) | Coke | LDF | 18·98 | 15·0 | 1·10 | 0·58 |
| 13 Lurgi | Coal | LPG | 18·98 | 40·0 | 2·93 | 1·55 |
| 14 Onia-Gegi and Segas | HFO | | 18·98 | 27·0 | 1·98 | 1·04 |
| 15 Uniflow cyclic (Onia) | Natural gas | Natural gas | 18·98 | 9·0 | 0·66 | 0·35 |
| 16 Uniflow cyclic (General) | LDF | | 18·98 | 14·0 | 1·02 | 0·54 |
| 17 Shell and Texaco | HFO | Refinery gas | 18·98 | 14·0 | 1·02 | 0·54 |
| 18 Continuous tubular reformer | Natural gas | Natural gas | 18·98 | 7·0 | 0·51 | 0·27 |
| 19 Continuous tubular reformer | LPG | LPG | 18·98 | 11·0 | 0·81 | 0·43 |
| 20 Continuous tubular reformer (with GC recycle hydrogenator) | LDF | LDF | 18·98 | 16·0 | 1·17 | 0·62 |
| 21 Continuous tubular reformer (with GC CRG process) | LDF | LDF | 18·98 | 14·0 | 1·02 | 0·54 |
| 22 Topsøe single-stage and ICI 500 processes | LDF | LDF | 18·98 | 13·5 | 0·92 | 0·48 |
| 23 Gas Council's CRG process | LDF | | 24·68 | 7·0 | 0·51 | 0·27 |
| 24 Gas Council's CRG process | LDF | LPG | 37·96 | 8·5 | 0·62 | 0·33 |

Conversion factors :
1p/100MJ =   2·4 US cents/100MJ
        = 25·32 US cents/10⁶ Btu
        =  0·1 US cent/1000 kcal

166

*Table 33    Selected gas-making costs from Table 32 adjusted where necessary for the cost of detoxification, organic sulphur reduction and compression*

|  | Feedstock | | Cost of gas manufactured at 85% load factor p/100 MJ | | | |
|---|---|---|---|---|---|---|
| Process | Primary | Enriching | Cost from Table 32 | Cost of de-toxification and sulphur reduction | Cost of compression to 24 bars | Total cost |
| 9 Continuous vertical retorts | Coal | | 4·24 | 0·4 | 0·6 | 5·24 |
| 12 CWG (LDF reforming) | Coke | LDF | 5·98 | 0·4 | 0·6 | 6·98 |
| 13 Lurgi | Coal | LPG | 5·19 | | | 5·19 |
| 14 Onia-Gegi and Segas | HFO | | 4·88 | 0·4 | 0·6 | 5·88 |
| 15 Uniflow cyclic (Onia) | Natural gas | Natural gas | 2·97 | | 0·6 | 3·57 |
| 16 Uniflow cyclic (General) | LDF | | 4·29 | | 0·6 | 4·89 |
| 17 Shell and Texaco | HFO | | 4·01 | | | 4·01 |
| 18 Continuous tubular reformer | Natural gas | Natural gas | 2·87 | | | 2·87 |
| 19 Continuous tubular reformer | LPG | LPG | 3·74 | | | 3·74 |
| 20 Continuous tubular reformer (with GC recycle hydro-genator) | LDF | LDF | 4·14 | | | 4·14 |
| 21 Continuous tubular reformer (with GC CRG process) | LDF | LDF | 3·97 | | | 3·97 |
| 22 Topsøe single-stage and ICI 500 processes | LDF | LDF | 3·86 | | | 3·86 |
| 23 Gas Council's CRG process | LDF | | 3·41 | | | 3·41 |
| 24 Gas Council's CRG process | LDF | LPG | 3·53 | | | 3·53 |

are higher than those of the latter processes. Costs for the production of hydrogen of similar quality from both sources, would be closer.

No credit is given in the costs shown in Table 32 for detoxification and organic sulphur content reduction, in those cases where they are effected, *eg* the Lurgi, Shell and continuous reforming processes. The cost of reproducing these effects would fall within the range 0·2 to 0·4p per 100 MJ in the case of conventional coal-gas/carburetted-water-gas mixtures. Neither is any credit given for the pressure with which certain of these gases are endowed. The value of this, if required say for town gas transmission on this scale, is approximately 0·6p per 100 MJ for 20 bars.

In Table 33 selected total costs of gas manufacture given in Table 32 are set out and then adjusted to render them comparable with regard to detoxification and pressure.

169

# PART TWO    NATURAL GAS

## Introduction

The limitation of space relative to the vast scope of the various aspects of natural gas has prevented any treatment in depth. An attempt has been made, however, to deal in a brief, broad and generalized manner with all fundamental aspects of the subject.

Many of the techniques described concerning the transmission, storage and uses of natural gas in the gaseous phase are applicable also to manufactured town-gas, which is referred to in a number of contexts. Liquefied petroleum gases, which are closely associated with natural gas and can be used for most purposes for which natural gas is used, are also dealt with.

# Chapter 14 The Origins and Characteristics of Natural Gas

Natural gas associated with sedimentary rocks, as distinct from the air, varies in composition from mixtures of almost pure hydrocarbons to mixtures totally devoid of hydrocarbons. Some exceptional gases are shown in Columns 1 to 3 of Table 34.

The principal constituents other than hydrocarbons are nitrogen, carbon dioxide and to a smaller extent hydrogen sulphide. The inert gases helium and argon are commonly present in small quantities; the former in rare cases exceeds 1 % by volume and is recovered. The term *sour gas* is used to denote the presence of hydrogen sulphide which, in parts of Western Canada to quote an extreme example, ranges from 35 % to 85 % by volume.

Substantial quantities of the natural gas so far discovered are found in association with, or are thought to be derived from, either coal or oil. The bulk however, is not so associated and falls into two groups. The minor group is considered to be derived from the microbial (that is, biochemical) degradation of organic matter in shallow sedimentary rocks of no great age, and, like marsh gas, consists mainly of carbon dioxide and methane (see Column 4 of Table 34). The second group derives from deeper rocks of great age and is likely to have resulted from the chemical degradation of organic residues (49).

The term *associated gas* is applied to that produced by the stabilization of crude oil; in other words, it is the gas in excess of that which can be carried in the crude oil at atmospheric pressure. Although associated gases consist mainly of methane and ethane they nevertheless contain appreciable quantities of $C_3$ and higher hydrocarbons and are a major source of liquefied petroleum gases (see Column 5 of Table 34).

Non-associated natural gases may be either dry or may require treatment for the removal of condensate before distribution at pressure. In both cases the highly predominant hydrocarbons present will be methane and ethane, mainly in the ratios of 5 to 50 parts of methane to one of ethane. Analyses of the gas produced from several of the world's major fields are given in Columns 6 to 10 in Table 34.

Gases from strata of great age but with high methane/ethane ratios, such as those of the North Sea and Groningen (Columns 6 and 7 of Table 34), are likely to have resulted from the decomposition of underlying coal (50). A diagrammatic representation of a North Sea natural-gas field is shown in Figure 51.

# Table 34 Characteristics of selected natural gases

| | Gases containing high concentrations of non-hydrocarbons | | Gas of geologically recent period | | Associated gas | Examples of major non-associated gases as marketed | | | | |
|---|---|---|---|---|---|---|---|---|---|---|
| Source | 1 Song Canyon, Utah | 2 San Andres, New Mexico | 3 Lacq, France | 4 Salt Lake, Utah | 5 Aga Jari, Persia | 6 Leman Bank, North Sea | 7 Groningen, Holland | 8 Monroe, Louisiana | 9 Amarillo, Texas | 10 Ashland, Kentucky |
| **Composition** | | | | | | | | | | |
| Methane % vol | 2·6 | — | 69·1 | 96·0 | 66·0 | 94·7 | 81·2 | 94·7 | 72·9 | 75·0 |
| Ethane | 0·8 | — | 2·8 | — | 14·0 | 3·0 | 2·9 | 2·8 | 19·0 | 24·0 |
| Propanes | 0·3 | — | 0·8 | — | 10·5 | 0·5 | 0·4 | — | — | — |
| Butanes | 0·1 | — | 1·5 | — | 5·0 | 0·2 | 0·1 | — | — | — |
| $C_5$ and higher | 0·1 | — | 0·6 | — | 2·0 | 0·2 | 0·1 | — | — | — |
| Hydrogen sulphide | — | — | 15·4 | — | — | — | — | — | — | — |
| Carbon dioxide | 0·4 | 92·1 | 9·7 | 3·7 | 1·5 | 0·1 | 0·9 | 0·2 | 0·4 | — |
| Nitrogen | 94·0 | 7·1 | — | 0·3 | 1·0 | 1·3 | 14·4 | 2·3 | 7·7 | 1·0 |
| Helium | 1·3 | 0·6 | — | — | — | <0·1 | <0·1 | — | — | — |
| Argon | 0·2 | 0·1 | — | — | — | — | — | — | — | — |
| Specific gravity (air=1·0) | 0·97 | 1·47 | 0·75 | 0·59 | 0·87 | 0·59 | 0·64 | 0·58 | 0·68 | 0·67 |
| Calorific value (gross) Btu/ft³ | 55 | nil | 910 | 952 | 1403 | 1037 | 843 | 988 | 1054 | 1161 |
| MJ/m³ | 2·0 | nil | 33·9 | 35·4 | 52·3 | 38·6 | 31·4 | 36·8 | 39·2 | 43·2 |

The gases shown in Columns 1 to 5 are untreated.
The gases shown in Columns 6 to 7 have been subjected to a minor adjustment of hydrocarbon dewpoint.
The gases shown in Columns 8 to 10 have been treated for the removal of LPG and higher hydrocarbons.

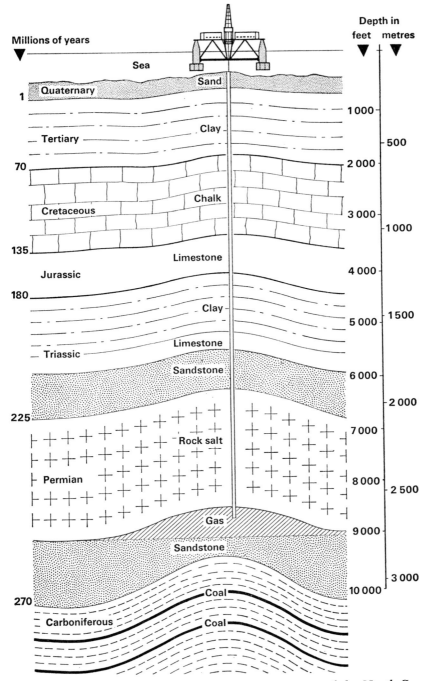

*Figure 51   Typical rock strata in gas-bearing areas of the North Sea*

173

# Chapter 15    The Purification of Natural Gas

The characteristics of the natural-gas deposits throughout the world (shown in Table 34) indicate vast differences. The physical states in which the gases are found also differ greatly. Formation pressures may be 250 bars or more in some cases, and as low as 10 bars in others, with associated temperatures up to 120°C (248°F) in the deep, high-pressure formations, and near ground-level temperature in the relatively rare high-level formations. The bulk of the proven reserves have formation pressures of 80 bars or more.

It is not surprising, therefore, to find that the treatment required to prepare natural gases for use varies greatly. For example, in a number of instances the gas, after passing through condensate knock-out pots, is fed direct to industrial consumers; in other cases it is subjected to several of the treatments described below.

## Removal of Dust

Commonly the well-head gas has a negligible solids content. When dust is carried, gravel packs are sometimes used at the well-base to hold it back or alternatively it is removed by a dust catcher at the well-head.

## Removal of Elemental Sulphur

In those instances where elemental sulphur is carried in sour gas, it separates with the condensate. The only serious drawback arises from its accumulation as a hard deposit on the wall of the bore-hole riser pipe. Where the deposit cannot be scraped off, solvent is injected into the bore hole. At the well head the sulphur and solvent are scrubbed out and separated, the solvent being returned to the bore hole.

## Adjustment of Water and Hydrocarbon Dewpoints

Commonly the moisture and condensible hydrocarbon content of natural gas has to be reduced, as close to the source as is economically acceptable, in order to prevent difficulties in transmission arising from

174

retrograde condensation or hydrate formation or both, as described below. The extent of these reductions and the means of effecting them are detailed in the section entitled *Preparation of Gases for Transmission*.

## 1 Retrograde Condensation

A feature of the handling of gases at high pressure, say above approximately 25 bars, is the substantial differences that appear in the 'real gas' compared with ideal-gas behaviour. One manifestation of this is termed *retrograde condensation*. This phenomenon results from the rise in hydrocarbon dewpoint that accompanies a fall in pressure, which is the reverse of perfect-gas behaviour. This is demonstrated in Figure 52, which shows that condensation commences as the pressure falls isothermally from point A on the line XX to point B. It reaches a maximum at point C. Re-evaporation then commences and is complete at point D.

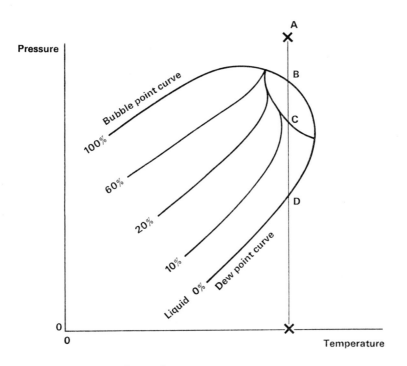

*Figure 52  Retrograde condensation*

175

The extent of condensation of the heavier hydrocarbon content of natural gas and, to a lesser degree, that of the water-vapour content, is increased if the gas is allowed to expand adiabatically from the structure pressure to the desired level required for gas treatment and transmission, and thereby to fall in temperature. In such cases slugs of hydrocarbons and water may appear in the gas stream from the well-head onwards even when relatively dry gases are being handled.

## 2 Hydrate Formation

A further potentially embarrassing feature in the handling of natural gas prior to dehydration is the formation of the hydrates of the lower hydrocarbons. These can produce white deposits, resembling either ice or impacted snow, which impede gas flow.

Hydrates are the product of physico-chemical reaction between $C_1$ to $C_4$ hydrocarbons and water. The conditions of temperature, pressure and gas composition in which hydrates can be formed are predictable (51), but in some cases they may not appear under these conditions without a secondary cause similar to those required to promote crystallization phenomena in general, such as seeding or pressure disturbance.

Although hydrates can theoretically be formed from water in the vapour phase, this does not occur in practice, and the water dewpoints of high-pressure natural gas for transmission are specified to avoid condensation and thus prevent their formation.

Figure 53 shows the conditions in which hydrates were produced over water from Algerian natural gas (52). Sixty-six per cent of the hydrate produced in these experiments was derived from methane, the remainder consisting of the hydrates of ethane, propane and butanes.

Like ice, hydrates are readily soluble in methanol, glycol and similar substances. If these substances are applied to the gas stream prior to the condensation of water vapour, they suppress hydrate formation by lowering the temperature at which hydrates can form, that is they shift to the left the right-hand boundary of the hydrate-formation area shown in Figure 53.

## Preparation of Gases for Transmission

### 1 Raw Dry Gases

Natural gases of low $C_3$ and higher hydrocarbons content are termed *dry*. As an example, with a dry gas at a structure pressure of 250 bars, the first operation could be the removal, in a three-phase separator, of water and hydrocarbon liquid at the well head. This could be followed

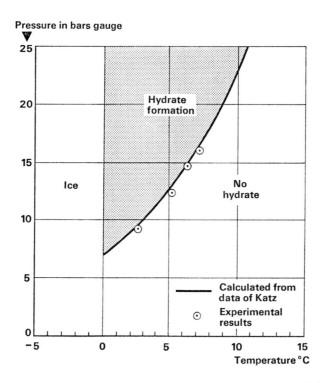

*Figure 53*    *Conditions for hydrate formation (Courtesy of the Institution of Gas Engineers)*

by heating before expansion to a working pressure of say 80 bars, in order to prevent hydrate formation as the result of a drop in temperature.

A further separation of condensates would then occur and be followed by treatment designed to reduce the water vapour and condensible hydrocarbon contents to such a level that the gas would remain dry and free from hydrates under the most critical conditions of temperature and pressure to which it will be subjected on transmission and reticulation, and prior purification if this is necessary. This normally involves drying within the limits 40 to 120 mgH$_2$O/m$^3$, according to local requirements, and the reduction of the hydrocarbon dewpoint to a similar, possibly slightly higher, level.

More often than not, however, the preheat of the crude gas before expansion, for the purpose of avoiding hydrate formation, is rendered unnecessary, either because the dehydration treatment would be carried out at the well-head pressure, or because only a small pressure drop is involved, or because methanol (or less commonly glycol) may have been injected upstream of the well-head choke. This injection of methanol or glycol is particularly necessary if the gas has to be transmitted some distance before treatment, as is the case with some offshore deposits. The methanol or glycol used in this way is removed later with condensate and may be recovered.

Means used for the final adjustment of water-vapour dewpoint are primarily absorption by diethylene glycol (DEG) or triethylene glycol (TEG):

$$DEG = HOCH_2 \cdot CH_2 \cdot O \cdot CH_2 \cdot CH_2OH$$
$$TEG = HOCH_2 \cdot CH_2 \cdot O \cdot CH_2 \cdot CH_2 \cdot O \cdot CH_2 \cdot CH_2OH$$

Less commonly solid adsorbents such as silica gel and activated alumina are used, or else molecular sieves. All these materials would be used in regenerative systems analogous to those shown in Figures 54 and 55. The solid adsorbents or molecular sieves are almost invariably used for the more thorough drying necessary before natural-gas liquefaction.

A recent advance in the preparation of gases for transmission used in Holland, Austria and the USSR, applicable to high-pressure dry gases, involves the Joule-Thomson effect. This is the moderate cooling that results from expanding a gas without doing external work. The technique is to cool the high-pressure well-head gas to such a level that, on expansion to the pressure required for transmission for use or further treatment, its temperature is low enough to reduce the dewpoint to a level that will obviate subsequent condensation. Glycol, $C_2H_4(OH)_2$, or diethylene glycol, which can subsequently be recovered, is added upstream and downstream of the choke in order to prevent hydrate formation. Efficient separators are required in such systems for the removal of the condensed water and hydrocarbon droplets. As well-head pressures are reduced by depletion, the unexpanded gas can be cooled to a progressively lower temperature by heat exchange, with the treated gas if necessary, in order to offset the progressive loss of temperature drop on expansion.

## 2 Raw Wet Gases

Many natural gases, and particularly *associated gases* (those arising from crude-oil production), have contents of $C_3$ and higher hydrocarbons at such a level as to render impractical or uneconomic their

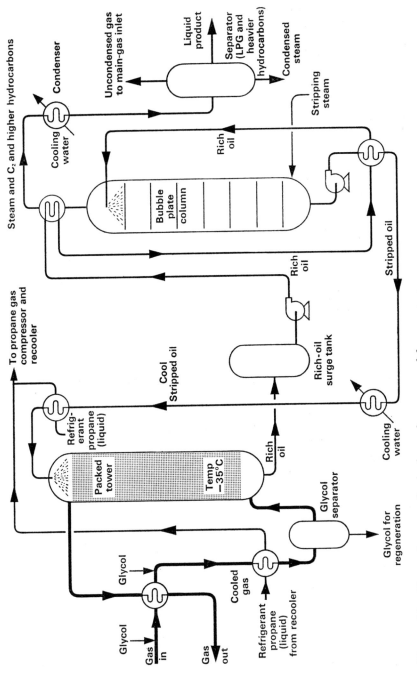

*Figure 54   Type of process for hydrocarbon removal from wet gas*

179

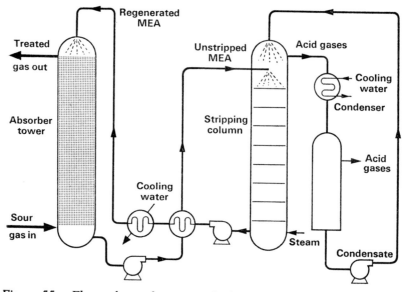

*Figure 55   Flow scheme for removal of acid gases by monoethanolamine solution*

removal by the use of the Joule-Thompson effect, molecular sieves, silica gel or alumina.

The removal of $C_3$ and higher hydrocarbons, which is necessary as a preliminary to long-distance gas transmission, can be a profitable process, as in some cases in North America. (This removal process is additional to the drying process referred to above.) The main technique used in this removal operation is scrubbing with a refrigerated oil, normally in the light middle-distillate range. The procedures for the design of these processes are available in standard texts (53, 54).

A simplified diagram of such a process is given in Figure 54. This operates as follows.

The raw gas is cooled by heat exchange with the outgoing gas and is then reduced to $-35°C$ by means of refrigerated propane. Glycol is added during these stages to prevent the formation of hydrate. The cold gas is then scrubbed with a light wash-oil, which has been cooled by heat exchange and refrigeration to the gas temperature. The scrubbed gas, with some of its ethane and most of the hydrocarbons above $C_2$ removed, passes out from the top of the scrubber tower

180

through the inlet-gas heat exchanger to be warmed up. The cold rich wash-oil leaving the scrubber is pumped through heat-exchange stages, first with the hot product-gas stream from the bubble-plate column and then with the hot stripped oil. It next enters the top of this column and is stripped with steam fed into the base. It is then re-cooled and re-cycled.

The vapours leaving the stripping column are cooled, the products are separated, and the uncondensed gases are returned to the raw-gas stream. Stripping efficiency can be increased with economy in steam by the installation of a vacuum pump between the liquid-products condenser and separator.

A possible future development in this field is the use of active carbon as the adsorbent in a regenerative system, a process that has been used for debenzolizing coal gas. Progress is dependent on the development of suitable heat-recovery systems.

## Removal of Acid Gases (55, 56)

Most natural gases produced require no further treatment other than those already described; the remainder contain acid gases at levels demanding treatment. Prior to this treatment, various proprietary corrosion inhibitors, mainly complex amines, are added to acid-gas gathering lines.

The removal of carbon dioxide to a limit of approximately 3 % by volume is normal for reasons of corrosion prevention and/or reduction in the cost of transmission. Hydrogen sulphide, the other acid gas that may be present, must normally be reduced to a statutory level. Statutory levels range from 1 to 15 ppm vol/vol (1 to 20 mg/m³).

Low hydrogen-sulphide concentrations, for example 500 mg/m³, in gas at pressure up to 30 bars, may be removed in static dry-box purifiers containing oxide of iron (iron sponge). Molecular sieves and a modified version of the Giammarco Vetrocoke process referred to later are also used for dealing with such low concentrations, if necessary at pressures up to 70 bars. All of these treatments are exceptional. Normally the hydrogen sulphide and excess carbon dioxide are removed by the use of one of the processes described below.

All the commonly used processes for acid-gas removal comprise an absorption stage in a liquid reactant or solvent medium. The medium is then regenerated by the stripping of the acid gases from it. All these treatments are invariably costly. The appropriate choice is dependent

upon the following major variables:
the level and related partial pressure of the acid-gas contents
the carbon-dioxide/hydrogen-sulphide ratio
the carbonyl sulphide and mercaptan content
the content of hydrocarbons above $C_2$.

*MEA and DEA Processes*

The most widely used process employs a monoethanolamine solution (MEA) which reacts with the acid gases and is therefore only slightly pressure-sensitive. This is likely to be the cheapest process, at least for acid-gas contents up to $3\%$ by volume. At higher levels pumping and regeneration heat become more costly than those of simple absorption processes. MEA is degraded by carbonyl sulphide, and so, where carbonyl sulphide is present in conditions otherwise favourable, diethanolamine (DEA) is used in place of MEA, with a higher circulation rate. Alternatively, one of the carbonate processes described later may be used.

Figure 55 is a diagram showing the flow system of a typical MEA acid-gas absorption process. The raw gas passes up through a packed tower counterflow to the monoethanolamine solution. The acid gases are absorbed as a result of the following reactions, in which R represents the ethanol radical $- C_2H_4OH$:

$$2RNH_2 + H_2S \rightleftharpoons (RNH_3)_2S$$
$$(RNH_3)_2S + H_2S \rightleftharpoons 2RNH_3HS$$
$$2RNH_2 + CO_2 + H_2O \rightleftharpoons (RNH_3)_2CO_3$$
$$(RNH_3)_2CO_3 + CO_2 + H_2O \rightleftharpoons 2RNH_3HCO_3$$
$$2RNH_2 + CO_2 \rightleftharpoons RNHCOONH_3R$$

The gas leaves the top of this packed column after a controlled degree of stripping, and the used cold absorbent is then pumped, through a heat-exchange system with the hot regenerated MEA solution, to the top of the stripping column.

In the stripping column the sulphides, disulphides, carbonates, bicarbonates and substituted carbamic acid products described above are decomposed by a counter-current flow of steam. The stripped lye is then recirculated, first through the heat-exchange stage with the incoming MEA, and then through a water-cooling stage to the absorber column.

The acid gases leaving the top of the column are cooled. The resulting condensate, augmented with additional water if needed to

182

maintain the appropriate dilution of the MEA, is fed back into the top of the stripper tower, where it serves to scrub out amine vapour carried in the acid-gas stream.

### The Sulfinol Process

The Sulfinol process operates partly by chemical reaction and partly by absorption, and is likely to be more economical than MEA in the range of acid-gas concentrations from 3% to 10% when carbon dioxide is the main contaminant, which is commonly the case. It is highly specific for the removal of hydrogen sulphide. It has the disadvantage of absorbing the heavier hydrocarbons, but the countervailing advantage of removing organic sulphur in the form of mercaptans in addition to carbonyl sulphide and carbon disulphide.

### The Rectisol Process

The Rectisol process employs methanol at $-45°C$. It is not generally regarded as competitive in this application although one project is reported (57).

### Carbonate Processes

The remaining processes mainly use potassium carbonate, or an organic carbonate with added catalysts or activators. They are used when carbon dioxide contents exceed 10% by volume, and operate mainly by physical absorption. They are therefore pressure sensitive. Examples of these are the Catacarb and Giammarco Vetrocoke processes employing potassium carbonate solution plus an activator, which is arsenic in the latter case, and also the Fluor Solvent process, using propylene carbonate. The carbonate processes are used mainly where the removal of carbon dioxide only is involved. In the case of the Giammarco Vetrocoke process, as designed for carbon dioxide removal, the presence of hydrogen sulphide is not permissible since it reacts irreversibly with the arsenical activator.

The Selexol and Purisol processes produce similar results to the carbonate processes. These processes are competitive for treating dry gases of high carbon-dioxide partial pressure.

### General

The hydrogen sulphide in the acid gases leaving the reactant or solvent stripping columns of the processes described above is dealt with mainly in one of three ways. Small quantities are burnt in the atmosphere; larger quantities are either burnt to sulphur dioxide and

183

converted to sulphuric acid, or most commonly converted to sulphur by the Claus process. Carbon dioxide is normally discharged to atmosphere.

A final adjustment of water dewpoint will be necessary after any of the wet purification processes just described. A process employing a solid absorbent (for example, silica gel) is appropriate at this stage.

## Removal of Organic Sulphur

The vitiation of the atmosphere, even in rooms provided with flueless gas appliances, would be regarded as negligible with natural gas having organic-sulphur contents up to 200 mg/m$^3$ (9 grains/100ft$^3$). Sulphur contents at this level are also negligible from the viewpoint of gas-appliance corrosion.

Most natural gases have organic sulphur contents below or near this level. Some sour gases have higher organic sulphur contents, but these are mainly dealt with either by the choice of an acid-gas removal process that will at the same time deal with the excess of organic sulphur (this is applicable to 'dry' gases) or by means of the refrigerated-oil washing process in the case of 'wet' gases, since this process is effective for the removal of organic sulphur as well as higher hydrocarbons.

In the small number of instances where the organic sulphur content of treated gas exceeds the level referred to above, to the extent of roughly 100%, its presence is tolerated.

## Odorizing or Stenching

In common with the town gases produced by modern hydrocarbon-reforming processes, many purified natural gases lack a distinctive odour such as that exhibited by coal gas. Experience shows that such a characteristic odour is essential in order to reduce the risk of the accumulation of toxic or explosive gas mixtures occurring unnoticed until disastrous consequences ensue. It is therefore the practice when such an odour is either lacking, or present at an inadequate level, to *stench* town gas, LPG or natural gas. This is a statutory requirement in some countries.

With leakages of manufactured gases even of low carbon-monoxide content, a lethal gas concentration is reached sooner than an explosive concentration. A higher level of odour could therefore be justified for

184

gases containing carbon monoxide than for natural gas and LNG. With these latter only the relatively minor hazard, the explosion risk, has to be countered. In the UK this is accomplished by odorizing natural gas and LPG to a level that is distinctive and noticeable without conscious effort by the consumer when the gas present reaches one fifth of the minimum required to produce an explosive mixture.

Odour is a subjective quality. The distinctive and noticeable level referred to in the foregoing paragraph, which is also described as the *alert level*, had been classified on an arbitrary olfactory scale as 2 degrees (58). The threshold limit on this scale is 0·5 degrees. There is little doubt that 2 degrees of odoriferousness would be adequate for individuals of normal olfactory sense in normal health, yet it would be imperceptible to some elderly persons. Regardless therefore of the manner in which odorization levels are determined, expressed or rationalized, they are in practice based upon experience with the gases in use. This demands a level adequate to give warning of the hazard for as wide a range of human perception as is practical, without provoking complaints regarding gas leakages of negligible proportions. The odorants used comprise a number of the organic sulphur compounds responsible for the odour of coal gas and naturally occurring gases, and other organic sulphur compounds with similar olfactory properties. These are marketed alone or as mixtures, and in some cases diluted and under proprietary names.

The principal volatile sulphur compounds used are set out below:

| | |
|---|---|
| Tetrahydrothiophen (THT) | $C_4H_8S$ |
| Dimethyl sulphide | $(CH_3)_2S$ |
| Methyl ethyl sulphide | $CH_3·S·C_2H_5$ |
| Ethyl mercaptan | $C_2H_5·SH$ |
| Propyl mercaptan | $C_3H_7·SH$ |
| Tertiary butyl mercaptan | $(CH_3)_3 C·SH$ |

In Europe, THT at the rate of approximately 30 ppm by weight was mainly used until recently for town gas and natural gas, dimethyl sulphide and ethyl mercaptan being used for LPG, possibly owing to their being more volatile and therefore better able to volatilize uniformly from LPG tanks and bottles than THT.

The current trend in the gas industry is away from THT towards dimethyl sulphide and mercaptan mixtures on the basis of the improved cost/effectiveness ratio of the latter.

Several factors other than cost can affect the choice of a stenching agent. For example, if the stenched gas has to be reformed the ease of

185

removal would be important. Another factor is the extent to which the unstenched gas contributes to its odour. For example, the UK Leman Bank gas has a natural odour slightly above the threshold of recognition (58). This was raised to the desired level by the addition of 1·5 ppm by weight of tertiary butyl mercaptan. Following this, in order that the UK natural gas from the various sources should smell the same, gases from other sources are to be odorized with a mixture of dimethyl sulphide and ethyl mercaptan — the natural odorants of the Leman Bank gas — and tertiary butyl mercaptan.

Considerable progress has been made recently (58) in the measurement of gas odour and various other aspects of stenching.

# Chapter 16    The Liquefaction of Natural Gas

Cryogenics, literally the production of frost, is a term applied to the techniques by which heat is abstracted from matter in order to reduce its temperature to below ambient. Such techniques are essential for reducing so-called permanent gases to liquids, since by definition pressure alone at ambient temperature cannot achieve this. Cryogenics has been used to a limited extent for the greater part of this century, so far mainly for the production of liquid oxygen, but also for liquefying nitrogen, hydrogen and rare gases such as helium.

Starting approximately 30 years ago, natural gas was liquefied on a commercial scale in the USA, and during the past decade there has been such an acceleration in this process that natural-gas liquefaction and transportation have become one of the largest-scale examples of cryogenic techniques. It is probable that in the future few large-scale gas utilities will be without facilities for storing and/or producing liquefied natural gas (LNG). It is also likely that it will become to a limited extent generally available like other hydrocarbon products, instead of, as at present, by pre-arrangement between particular distributors or utilities and producers.

The principal natural-gas liquefaction techniques used are described below, but prior to liquefaction the gas must be treated in order to reduce its content of any substances that would solidify during the process. This involves reducing the water-vapour content to $<10$ ppm, and carbon dioxide to $<100$ ppm. Hydrogen sulphide must be reduced to a level intermediate to those described above. Hydrocarbons above the level of $C_5$ must also be dealt with, in some instances being reduced to $<50$ ppm.

These demands normally involve superimposing a final trim on purification processes already carried out in order to render the gas suitable for transmission. In such cases the use of molecular sieves or other solid absorbents such as silica gel or activated alumina are appropriate. The final adjustment of higher hydrocarbon content may be made during liquefaction.

An approximate indication of the temperatures and the order of the heat transfer involved in the liquefaction or evaporation of natural gases can be obtained from Table 35, which gives a selection of physical properties of the separate constituents. The behaviour of multi-component mixtures at pressure and under cryogenic conditions is complicated. Much experimental work is currently proceeding aimed at its elucidation and the development of techniques for the prediction of the properties of such mixtures (59, 60).

A point not indicated in the diagrams shown in this section is that, in order to conserve cold, the low-temperature parts of natural-gas liquefaction equipment are, as far as is practical, enclosed in one or more well insulated 'cold boxes'.

*Table 35  Selected properties of natural-gas constituents*

|  | Boiling point at 1·0 bar absolute | Heat of vaporization at boiling point | | Critical temperature | Critical Pressure | | Ideal-gas-state enthalpy at 273·15K (Datum zero K) | |
|---|---|---|---|---|---|---|---|---|
|  | °C | Btu/lb | MJ/kg | °C | lbf/in² absolute | bars absolute | Btu/lb | kJ/kg |
| Methane | −162 | 219 | 509 | −82 | 673 | 46·4 | 245·6 | 571·2 |
| Ethane | −89 | 210 | 488 | 32 | 708 | 48·8 | 152·6 | 354·8 |
| Propane | −42 | 183 | 426 | 97 | 617 | 42·6 | 126·3 | 293·8 |
| *iso*-Butane | −12 | 157 | 365 | 134 | 544 | 37·5 | 115·0 | 267·4 |
| *n*-Butane | −1 | 166 | 386 | 152 | 553 | 38·1 | 126·1 | 293·3 |
| Pentane | 36 | 154 | 358 | 197 | 487 | 33·6 | 122·8 | 285·7 |
| Carbon dioxide | −78 | 247 | 574 | 31 | 1069 | 73·9 | 82·5 | 191·9 |
| Argon | −186 | 71 | 165 | −122 | 492 | 33·9 | 62·5 | 145·4 |
| Nitrogen | −196 | 86 | 200 | −147 | 705 | 48·6 | 121·9 | 283·5 |
| Helium | −268 | 10 | 23 | −267 | 34 | 2·3 | 610·0 | 1418·9 |
| Water | 100 | 970 | 2256 | 374 | 3206 | 221·1 | 216·3 | 503·1 |

Critical temperature— the temperature above which a gas cannot be liquefied.
Critical pressure    —the minimum pressure required to liquefy a gas at its critical temperature.

# Liquefaction

## 1  Expansion-Cycle Processes

As stated in the previous chapter, if natural gas at high pressure and ambient temperature is expanded at a nozzle without performing external work, its temperature falls slightly. If the cooled gas so produced is used to cool a further quantity of high-pressure gas before it passes out of the system, this latter gas will be cooled still further. A repetition of this process, in conditions of adequate heat exchange between the incoming and outgoing gas, results in the conversion of one or two per cent of the high-pressure gas into LNG at the expense of a loss of pressure of the remainder of the gas.

This process is extremely wasteful of energy and although used to lower the $C_5$ and higher hydrocarbon contents of certain high-pressure dry gases, as already explained in Chapter 15, in practice it is usually modified when used to produce LNG. In this modification, termed the *Claude Cycle*, the gas is expanded in conditions in which it performs external work. The heat extracted from the gas in these conditions is increased to the extent of the heat equivalent of the external work done.

Several plants of this type are in operation, exploiting the difference between the high pressure of the natural gas as received, and the lower pressure requirement of the distribution system, in order to produce a small supply of LNG for peak-shaving. In the greatly simplified example shown in Figure 56, the power output of the expansion turbine is used to re-compress the low-pressure flash gas released by the LNG entering the low-pressure LNG storage tank, together with the boil-off required to maintain the low temperature of the LNG

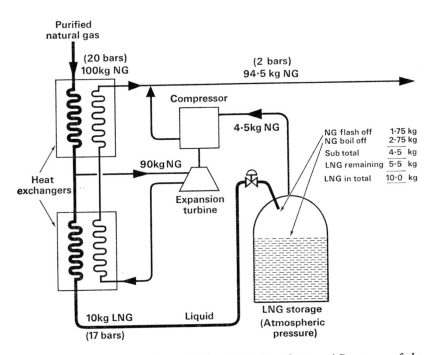

*Figure 56  The expander cycle for LNG liquefaction (Courtesy of the UK Gas Council)*

stock. The LNG stock, for peak shaving, is normally large relative to the rate of LNG production.

The proportion of the natural gas liquefied depends on the extent of the pressure let-down and the efficiency of the expansion turbine. In practice a pressure drop from 50 to 10 bars should liquefy 10% of the natural gas expanded (61).

In the example shown in Figure 56, 10% of the natural-gas supply is liquefied under pressure. This is reduced to 8% after flashing into the low-pressure LNG storage tank. Boil-off for temperature control during off-peak periods then reduces the net available for peak-shaving to 5·5% of the total feed gas.

Figure 56 shows the whole of the feed gas purified to the level required for liquefaction. This could be economical if little needed to be done. Alternatively, the main gas stream could be appropriately dried as necessary for the expansion stage, and the stream for liquefaction could be split off and purified separately.

## 2   Mechanical Refrigeration Cycles

Where it is desired to liquefy more of a natural gas supply than is possible by exploiting, in an expander cycle, any excess gas-pressure available, mechanical refrigeration is employed.

If we consider the thermodynamics of a hot-gas engine we find that the theoretical maximum possible efficiency with which the heat energy of a given hot gas can be converted into mechanical energy is proportional to the fall in its temperature. When this process is reversed, therefore, it follows as a corollary that the efficiency with which work can be used in order to extract heat from a gas is in inverse ratio to the reduction in temperature required. From this it can be inferred that the least thermally efficient process for the extraction of heat would be to cool by mechanical means a heat carrier to such a temperature that it could extract in one stage all the heat necessary for the liquefaction of natural gas. The most thermally efficient means would be to extract heat in infinite stages with infinitely small temperature differences between the mechanically cooled heat carriers and the gas to be cooled.

In considering the means of heat transfer from a coolant and the gas to be cooled, the extraction from the latter of the latent heat demand of a boiling coolant is a far more efficient process than the transfer of sensible heat.

The mechanical refrigeration cycles described below are designed to give effect, to the maximum economical extent in practice consistent with the cycle chosen, of the two principles set out above.

*(a)   The Classical Cascade or Multiple-Refrigerant Cycle*
A greatly simplified version of a cascade cycle is given in Figure 57. This shows three refrigeration circuits. In the first the temperature of the natural gas is reduced to $-38°C$ by the evaporation of liquid propane, then to $-100°C$ by the evaporation of liquid ethylene, at which stage it liquefies under pressure. In the final stage the LNG is subcooled to $-160°C$ by boiling methane so that it will remain liquid in the low-pressure LNG storage tank.

The gaseous refrigerant in each case is drawn off by a compressor, recompressed and water-cooled. Following this the resulting liquefied propane is recycled to the first stage. The ethylene, after recompression and cooling, is liquefied in the propane evaporator and recycled in the second stage. The vaporized methane is compressed, water-cooled, cooled in the propane evaporator and liquefied in the ethylene evaporator, before passing on for recycling to the third stage, the methane evaporator.

The term *cascade cycle* derives from the transfer or overflow of heat from the colder stages to the warmer, as described. In practice there are more stages than shown in Figure 57. There are, for example, two or more loops comprising evaporator and compressor for each refrigerant before it is cooled and recycled through the system.

The multi-stage versions of this process are more efficient in terms of power than other systems, but capital and maintenance costs are high owing to the multiplicity of compressors, vaporizers and connections. It is also claimed that difficulties are experienced in balancing the various compression stages.

*(b)   The Auto-Refrigerated Cycle (ARC) and other Mixed-Refrigerant Cycles (MRC)*
The first large-scale mixed-refrigerant cycle was developed by l'Air Liquide of France. It retains the principle of the classical cascade but reduces capital and maintenance costs and simplifies operation. This is achieved at the expense of an increase in power demand.

Figure 58 is a greatly simplified diagram of a cycle that comprises four stages of heat exchange. The mixed refrigerant is derived from condensate from the natural-gas stream, and consists of liquid $C_1$, $C_2$, $C_3$ and $C_4$ hydrocarbons together with a small amount of nitrogen if this is condensed. Condensate leaving the natural-gas line at the separator $E$ in Figure 58 is refluxed for use in refrigerant make-up or modification. This reflux equipment, which is not shown, can be augmented with efficient columns so that ethane gas, and $C_3$ and higher liquefied gases, can be individually separated from wet natural

191

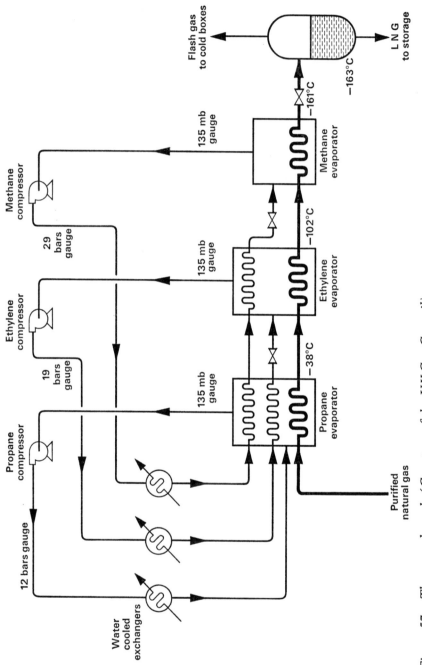

*Figure 57   The cascade cycle (Courtesy of the UK Gas Council)*

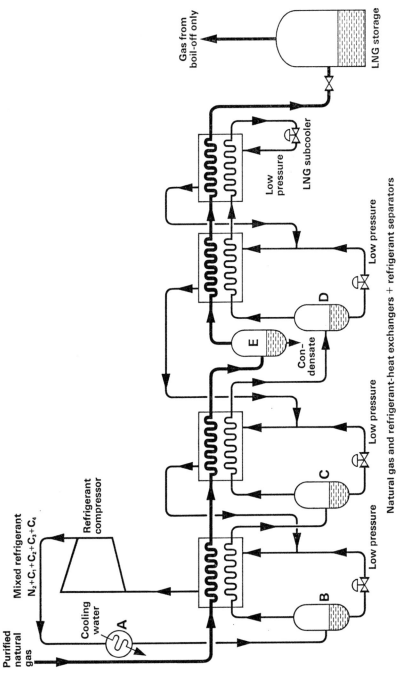

*Figure 58  The auto-refrigerated cascade (ARC) cycle (Courtesy of the UK Gas Council)*

gases in order to produce a dry gas composed almost entirely of methane (61, 62).

The theoretical minimum power requirement per million cubic metres of natural gas liquefied per day varies from approximately 10 000 to 12 000 hp (7 457 to 8 950 kW) according to its initial pressure and LPG content. The requirement for the classical cascade in practice is 21 000 to 25 000 hp (15 660 to 18 640 kW), whereas that for the ARC or MRC process will be approximately 20 % higher.

The cycle is operated as follows. A single compressor draws off, from the first cooling stage, the mixed refrigerant vapours produced at a similar low pressure in all stages, which pass counterflow to the natural gas through the system. These vapours are compressed, and all the surplus heat arising from the process is transferred to water in the cooler A.

The relatively high-boiling-point refrigerant required for the first cooling stage condenses on the outlet of the compressor and is separated at point B. This refrigerant is then vaporized at low pressure in the first stage, where it cools both the natural gas and the uncondensed high-pressure refrigerant from which, as stated, the highest-boiling-point material has now been removed. The refrigerant composition is so controlled that in this first stage a refrigerant of appropriate boiling point for the second stage is condensed from the high-pressure mixed-refrigerant stream. This is separated at point C. The process of producing in one stage the appropriate refrigerant for the succeeding stage is repeated as often as is designed for. The liquid methane produced at pressure in the third stage shown is sub-cooled in the fourth stage so that it will remain liquid in the low-pressure LNG storage tank.

A number of ARC natural-gas liquefaction plants are in operation producing LNG mainly for peak-shaving functions. The currently (1971) largest Mixed Refrigerant Cascade plant was constructed in North America by Air Products and Chemicals Incorporated and is termed MRC. Analogous plants have been designed by BOC-Airco (63), Prichard Rhodes, Lummus and others, for the liquefaction of both wet and dry gases.

*(c)   The Liquid Nitrogen Refrigerant Process*
An interesting peak-shaving liquefaction system in which liquid nitrogen is used as coolant has been built by BOC-Airco (64). It is particularly appropriate for use where the nitrogen content of the feed gas is at such a level, 2 to 4 %, that gas-quality problems would arise owing to boil-off if it were not separated – that is, where it is advan-

tageous to separate most of the nitrogen. A number of advantages are claimed over the cascade cycles. It has yet to be established exactly where the economic balance lies.

*(d)   Cold Gas Refrigeration Systems—Sulzer (65) and Stirling cycle CGR (66)*

Small-scale natural gas liquefaction is expensive and is economically justified only in special circumstances. One justification is the re-liquefaction of LNG storage-tanks boil-off on land or sea. The need to re-liquefy boil-off gas from LNG storage can arise either from a desire to prevent a change in the quality of the stock resulting from the preferential boil-off of lighter constituents, or from a desire to conserve the peak-shaving LNG stock.

At reception terminals or large satellite LNG storage centres, where no other liquefaction facilities are available, a small purpose-built plant for the re-liquefaction of boil-off gas can be economical. Such a plant has operated throughout 1970 in the UK (65) using helium gas in a closed-circuit expander cycle for the re-liquefaction of 2 to 3 tonnes of natural gas per day. The operation of this plant (built by Sulzer) is as follows (See Figure 59).

Helium gas enters a reciprocating compressor with an oil-free labyrinth piston. After compression to 12 bars it is water-cooled to ambient temperature. It is then further cooled to 96K in a counterflow heat exchange with the returning stream of cold expanded helium. This stream of cold helium at approximately 12 bars is then used to re-liquefy the boil-off gas in a condenser from which the LNG flows by gravity into the main LNG storage tank.

Leaving the condenser at 116 K the helium stream passes through two expansion turbines in series operating against oil brakes for the removal of work output, thus increasing the drop in temperature of the helium. The helium stream leaves these turbines at 92 K and 6 bars pressure and enters the counterflow heat exchanges already described, where it cools the helium leaving the compressor and after-cooler. Stand-by units, not shown, are provided for all the major items of equipment.

A refrigeration system for ethylene and methane re-liquefaction, already in use aboard ships, can be modified for use on land for re-liquefaction of boil-off gas, for small-scale natural-gas liquefaction, or for augmenting the refrigerating capacity of a larger system (66). This is based on the Stirling cycle and is claimed to be economical only over the low-capacity range of 4 000 to 40 000 m³ of natural gas

195

per day. Refrigeration is effected by the compression, cooling and expansion of either gaseous helium or hydrogen.

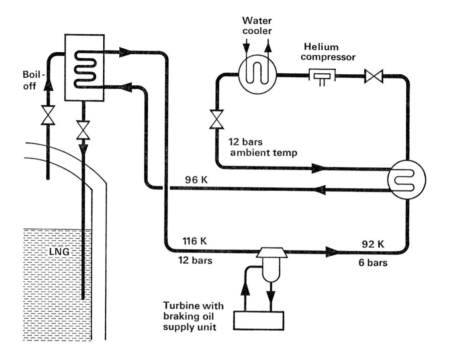

*Figure 59    Refrigeration cycle for re-liquefaction of boil-off (Courtesy of Sulzer Brothers Limited)*

## Separation of By-Products (67)

### 1    Hydrocarbon Separation

Liquefaction plants can be designed to separate part of the ethane and the bulk of the hydrocarbons above $C_2$, to produce a 'light' LNG that is mainly methane; alternatively, a 'heavy' LNG can be produced from a 'wet' gas. This can contain as little as two-thirds methane, the remainder being hydrocarbons in the $C_2$ to $C_5$ range.

On the evaporation of heavy LNG it would be necessary to remove the bulk of the $C_3$ and higher hydrocarbons content if the product gas is to be transmitted under pressure, which is the normal requirement. At La Spezia in Italy, where this is done, the separated hydrocarbons

196

above $C_2$ are used to make synthetic natural gas by the UK Gas Council's CRG Process.

The economics of the separation of ethane should be examined where there is a local need for ethylene manufacture. This leads to an interesting possibility referred to in the following sub-section 4.

## 2   Nitrogen Disposal (68)

The nitrogen content of natural gases containing less than approximately 2% by volume can be liquefied together with the other constituents. It will tend to boil off preferentially from the LNG storage tank without appreciable ill effect. Higher concentrations will demand an extension of the liquefaction stages and separation facilities so that the nitrogen can be removed either as a liquid, or, as is more likely, as gaseous nitrogen, possibly together with some natural gas.

Liquefaction is used at Alfortville (68) by means of an expander cycle to liquefy Dutch Groningen gas containing 14·3% by volume of nitrogen. Advantage is taken of this process to separate the 0·045% by volume of helium present, at marginal cost. The final products are gaseous low-pressure natural gas, nitrogen and helium. It is self-supporting for cold.

Two methods under consideration at Stuttgart for producing LNG from the Groningen gas (69) involve the removal of about 60% of the nitrogen content as nitrogen gas and 36% in a natural gas of a slightly higher nitrogen content than the feed gas. This latter gas can be enriched to make it interchangeable with the feed gas.

## 3   Helium Recovery

Helium is economically recovered by cryogenic means from natural gas. Where no surplus of gas pressure is available, and natural-gas liquefaction or the separation of the constituents other than helium is not effected, the minimum concentration of helium required to render separation economical is 0·4 to 1·0% by volume. Such a separation is effected in Saskatchewan from two gases consisting mainly of nitrogen and containing 1% and 2% helium respectively. In the USA nitrogen recovery is effected in association with helium recovery from similar and other types of gas.

When natural gas has to be liquefied in any case, the separation of helium at the marginal capital and process cost involved in adapting the process to this purpose becomes economical at concentrations as low as 0·2 to 0·4%. At the Alfortville installation already referred to in this section, the recovery of 0·045% by volume is effected at a marginal cost in the process of nitrogen separation. Economical recovery

197

at this low concentration may also be economical if the energy demand can be supplied entirely by the excess pressure of the gas over its required pressure.

## 4   The Recovery of Cold

In a broad sense the cold produced by the evaporation of LNG can be regarded as a by-product. Its utilization for the liquefaction of ethylene produced from separated ethane has been examined in relation to heavy LNG deliveries to Barcelona (70). In this case the net cold that would be available, although adequate, is low owing to the demands for the separation and sub-cooling of the bulk of the consituent hydrocarbons other than the methane.

The evaporation of dry 'light' LNG has a much greater potential for cold production, and the economics of using this for the purpose proposed above, or for air liquefaction or food processing has been examined (71).

No projects to utilize the cold in any of these ways are as yet in operation, but Tokyo Gas (72) and Gaz de France are incorporating air separation plants sited adjacent to their reception and regasification terminals at Negishi and Fos. A small volume of the nitrogen production will be used to adjust the calorific value of the gas.

An ingenious proposal involving the use of cold-carrying media (cryophores) for the storage of cold has been described (73). LNG is vaporized during the daily peak and the 'cold' is transferred to an appropriate carrier such as propane or 2-methyl butane. During the night this cold is used as part of that required to liquefy an equivalent amount of natural gas. The process appears to be a more elaborate and costly alternative to storage in the gas phase — the normal means of meeting diurnal variations in gas demand.

## Evaporation of LNG

## 1   Base-Load Evaporators (74)

*(a)   Open-Surface Types*
Open-surface evaporators comprise either vertical pipes or panels of an appropriate material and design to withstand the temperature and pressure of the LNG fed from a header into their base. These evapor-

ator elements hang from a steel structure and are warmed on the outside with a down-flowing stream of cold water.

In the case of the Marston Excelsior panel type, when sea water is used as a heat source, the aluminium panels are sprayed with a sacrificial coating of aluminum plus 1 % zinc, 2 mm in thickness. The panels are made up of hollow extruded sections arranged side by side and tack-welded to increase rigidity.

A simple flow valve on the LNG supply is controlled by an impulse from a pre-set gas-flow recorder, and a flow valve on the water supply is controlled by an impulse derived from the temperature of the gasified LNG. At the UK Canvey Island installation the sea water used suffers a fall of 4 degC (7 degF) in temperature. Ice forms at the base of the panels to an extent roughly equal to their weight, and some protection from wind is provided. Design pressures vary from 75 to 7 bars on the gas side, and outputs from 57 to 16 tonnes of LNG per hour.

*(b)   Indirect Evaporators*
An indirect evaporator produced by Marston Excelsior also uses sea water as a heat source. It is passed through a bundle of aluminium tubes in the base of a cylindrical vessel, which is 50 % filled with propane (See Figure 60).

In the upper half of this vessel the propane vaporized by the sea water condenses on the small-bore finned aluminium tubes in which the LNG is evaporated. The condensed propane recycles to the lower half of the vessel, which is maintained at a pressure of 4·5 bars absolute.

Since propane boils just below 0°C at this pressure, the natural gas is heated only to $-2·5°C$; its temperature is therefore raised to slightly above 0°C by means of a small trimming exchanger in series with the evaporator. This comprises a seamless aluminium tube designed to withstand the pressure of the natural gas that passes through it, and in addition a nest of aluminium tubes placed within it through which sea water is allowed to pass.

The control system and pressure ranges are similar to those of the direct evaporator described in the previous section. A twin-vessel installation at Canvey in the UK has a working pressure of 69 bars absolute and a total capacity of 50 tonnes of LNG per hour. In the absence of an economical supply of sea water or river water as a heat source, a closed water-circulation system maintained by external heating at say 20 to 25°C can be used.

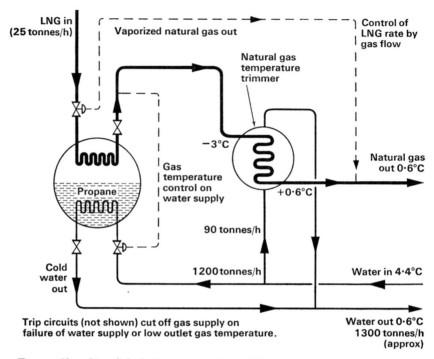

Labels in figure:

LNG in
(25 tonnes/h)

Vaporized natural gas out

Control of
LNG rate by
gas flow

Natural gas
temperature
trimmer

−3°C

Propane

Gas
temperature
control on
water supply

+0·6°C

90 tonnes/h

Natural gas
out 0·6°C

Cold
water
out

1200 tonnes/h

Water in 4·4°C

Trip circuits (not shown) cut off gas supply on
failure of water supply or low outlet gas temperature.

Water out 0·6°C
1300 tonnes/h
(approx)

*Figure 60   Simplified diagram of the Marston Excelsior indirectly
heated LNG vaporizer (Courtesy of the International
Institute of Refrigeration)*

## 2   High-Performance Evaporators for Peak Shaving

The absence of a natural heat source, especially if combined only with
a peak-load demand for use of the vaporizer, enchances the importance of plant efficiency, of capital cost, and of the relativity of capital
cost and process costs.

The development of a series of compact high-performance evaporators for peak-shaving use, with natural-gas outputs ranging from
10 000 to 130 000 m³/h (7 to 90 tonnes/h) has been described (75).

A steam-heated version of these evaporators is shown in Figure 61.
The special feature of this design is the use of bundles of externally
finned copper tubes, provided with inserts of corrugated finned copper
coils, within which the LNG is vaporized. The high basic cost per unit
of the tubing used is more than offset by the resulting manifold reduction
in resistance to heat transfer, relative to alternative materials in simpler

200

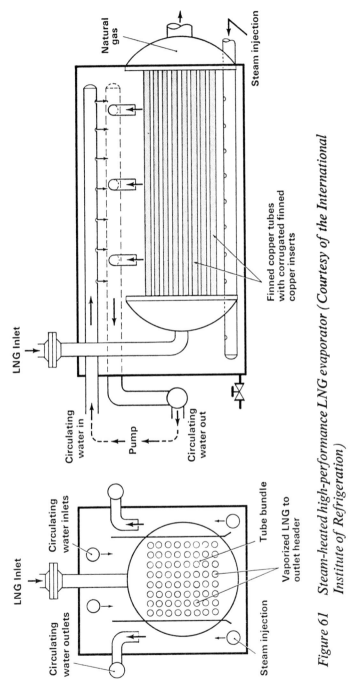

*Figure 61 Steam-heated high-performance LNG evaporator (Courtesy of the International Institute of Refrigeration)*

201

designs. The tube bundles are arranged above the steam-heated water in the base of a rectangular vessel and the heat transfer from the steam-heated water is enchanced by its being recirculated to create turbulence.

Alternative designs are also proposed, with submerged burners in place of the steam manifold for heating the water. Turbulence is created by means of the circulation of the products of combustion in place of recirculation of the water. These alternative designs are claimed to be marginally lower in overall cost than the steam-heated version.

# Chapter 17  Natural-Gas Transmission and Distribution

During the first century of the existence of the gas industry, say to 1920, gas distribution was a simple matter. Even in the UK, where the industry was most highly developed during this period, few gas supply systems were integrated, and most supplied less than 1 million ft³ (28 000 m³) of gas per day. Even a large undertaking, making 18 million ft³ (0·5 million m³) per day would supply gas at pressures up to 15 in (400 mm) water gauge only, through several cast-iron mains jointed with lead and yarn radiating from the manufacturing centre. These mains would then be connected into a network of smaller cast-iron mains throughout the supply area, culminating in the wrought-iron pipe leading to the individual consumer's meter.

A manual record would be made of the hourly gas stock, make and output. The distribution pressure would be varied, with few exceptions, by the manual loading of governors on the outlet of the gas storage holders, according to a scale based on experience.

During the past half century these techniques have been transformed, in the first instance resulting from the integration of gas undertakings making gas, but latterly and to a much greater extent, as the result of the need to transmit massive quantities of natural gas from the point of discovery to the consumer, commonly at a great distance. A single modern 36-inch (900 mm) high-tensile-steel pipe continuously operated at 69 bars absolute, for example, would deliver more gas, thermally, than the total town-gas consumption of any European country prior to the large-scale discovery of natural gas in Europe.

The high pressure at which natural gas (and the gas delivered from modern gas-making plant based on hydrocarbon oil or gaseous feedstocks) is available, demands changes in pipe materials, and jointing and laying techniques if it is to be economically exploited. Furthermore, a great part of the pipe system will operate at such pressures that changes will involve substantial variations in its gas content. This enables the transmission and reticulation system to effect a share in the gas-storage function, which could be the determining factor in their design.

Further effects of operation at higher pressures and loadings are the resulting complications in pressure governing the need for the more rapid transmission of control information, and the need for the automatic distant control and operation of various items of equipment involved in transmission and reticulation.

In the following section the principles involved in the flow of gases, the determination of transmission and reticulation pressures, the choice of materials for pipes, the sizing and routing of pipes and the control of pipeline networks are dealt with briefly but fundamentally. A more detailed authoritative account of UK practice is available (76).

## Transmission as Gas

### 1 Flow Formulae

The basic flow formulae employed for gases in turbulent flow are as follows:

*For gases at pressures above 1·20 bar*

$$Q = 182\cdot0 \sqrt{\frac{D^5(P_1^2 - P_2^2)}{SfL}} \times \sqrt{\frac{520\,Y}{T}}$$

*For pressures below 1·20 bar*

$$Q = 187\cdot7 \sqrt{\frac{D^5\,\Delta H}{SfL}} \times \sqrt{\frac{520}{T}}$$

where $Q$ = Flow rate, $ft^3/h$ measured at 60°F, 30 inches Hg, dry (UK Gas Industry Standard)

$D$ = Internal pipe diameter, inches

$P_1$ = Upstream gas pressure, $lbf/in^2$ absolute

$P_2$ = Downstream gas pressure, $lbf/in^2$ absolute

$\Delta H$ = Pressure drop, inches water gauge

$S$ = Specific gravity of gas

$f$ = Pipe-line friction factor (coefficient of friction)

$L$ = Length of pipe, feet

$Y$ = Super-expansibility factor of the gas

$T$ = Absolute temperature of the gas, °F (T = t + 460).

A hand-operated computer developed by Polyflo (77) for all fluids is particularly useful for determining natural-gas flow data. The calculator is designed on the following simplification of the basic formulae, in which the incorporated base friction factor for air is related to average experience with commercial pipes. Air-flow temperature is taken to be 60°F.

*For gases at pressures above 1·20 bar abs.*

$$Q_{air} = 182\cdot0 \sqrt{\frac{D^5(P_1^2 - P_2^2)\,Y}{C_r f_{ba} L}}$$

$$= 2242\,D^{2\cdot623} \left\{ \frac{(P_1^2 - P_2^2)}{C_r Z L} \right\}^{0\cdot541}$$

*For pressures below 1·20 bar abs.*

$$Q_{air} = 187\cdot7 \sqrt{\frac{D^5 \Delta H}{C_r f_{ba} L}}$$

$$= 2318\,D^{2\cdot623} \left( \frac{\Delta H}{C_r L} \right)^{0\cdot541}$$

204

where $Q_{air}$ = Air flow rate, ft³/h measured at 60°F, 30 inches Hg, dry (UK Gas Industry Standard)

$$f_{ba} = 0.0213 \left(\frac{D}{Q_{air}}\right)^{0.152} = \text{Base friction factor for air at } 60°F$$

$$C_r = 0.00354 \; ST \left(\frac{\eta_t}{S}\right)^{0.152} = \text{Factor for viscosity, density and temperature for air at } 60°F \; (ie \; t = 60°F)$$

$$Z = \text{Compressibility factor of the gas} = \frac{1}{Y}$$

$\eta_t$ = Viscosity at the appropriate temperature, centipoises.

In the above formulae a $C_r$ factor must be used for air if its flow temperature deviates from 60°F, and for all other fluids at any temperature. This factor corrects for the deviation of the temperature, viscosity and specific gravity of the fluid involved from that of air at 60°F, and produces answers that are sufficiently accurate for most purposes for pressures up to 7 bars.

Where greater accuracy is required a further multiplying factor $C_f$ can be added below the line to correct for the difference between the friction factors for air and the fluid involved $(f_b)$:

$$C_f = \frac{f_b}{f_{ba}} \quad \text{where } f_b \text{ for gases} = 0.0392\left(\frac{D\eta_t}{QS}\right)^{0.152}$$

$C_r$ and $C_f$ factors for paraffinic hydrocarbon gases, appropriate for natural gases, are given in Figure 62. When mean gas pressures exceed 7 bars the $C_r$ factors given in Figure 62 should be corrected for the deviation of natural gas from ideal-gas behaviour by multiplying it by the compressibility factor obtained from Figure 63. The compressibility factor is the reciprocal of the super-expansibility factor $Y$, and applied in this way it replaces $Y$ shown above the line in the formulae. The mean gas pressure needed for the determination of the compressibility factor for a particular problem can be obtained from Figure 64.

For still greater accuracy it would be necessary to substitute the known friction factor for the particular pipe to be used, in place of the average value used in the determination of $f_{ba}$.

The hand-operated computer is designed to facilitate the application of the correction factors referred to above. The simplified

205

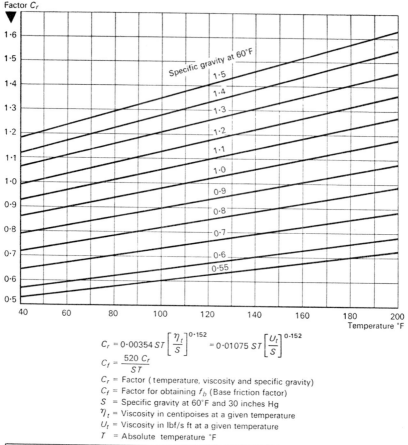

$$C_r = 0.00354\,ST\left[\frac{\eta_t}{S}\right]^{0.152} = 0.01075\,ST\left[\frac{U_t}{S}\right]^{0.152}$$

$$C_f = \frac{520\,C_r}{ST}$$

$C_r$ = Factor (temperature, viscosity and specific gravity)
$C_f$ = Factor for obtaining $f_b$ (Base friction factor)
$S$ = Specific gravity at 60°F and 30 inches Hg
$\eta_t$ = Viscosity in centipoises at a given temperature
$U_t$ = Viscosity in lbf/s ft at a given temperature
$T$ = Absolute temperature °F

| | $C_f$ Factors | | | | | | | | | | |
|---|---|---|---|---|---|---|---|---|---|---|---|
| Temp | Specific gravity at 60°F and 30 inches Hg | | | | | | | | | | |
| °F | 0·55 | 0·6 | 0·7 | 0·8 | 0·9 | 1·00 | 1·1 | 1·2 | 1·3 | 1·4 | 1·5 |
| 40 | 1·00 | 0·99 | 0·97 | 0·94 | 0·92 | 0·90 | 0·88 | 0·86 | 0·85 | 0·83 | 0·82 |
| 60 | 1·00 | 0·99 | 0·97 | 0·94 | 0·92 | 0·90 | 0·88 | 0·87 | 0·86 | 0·84 | 0·83 |
| 80 | 1·01 | 1·00 | 0·98 | 0·95 | 0·93 | 0·91 | 0·89 | 0·88 | 0·87 | 0·85 | 0·83 |
| 100 | 1·01 | 1·00 | 0·98 | 0·95 | 0·93 | 0·91 | 0·89 | 0·88 | 0·87 | 0·85 | 0·84 |
| 120 | 1·02 | 1·01 | 0·99 | 0·96 | 0·94 | 0·92 | 0·90 | 0·89 | 0·88 | 0·86 | 0·84 |
| 140 | 1·02 | 1·01 | 0·99 | 0·96 | 0·94 | 0·92 | 0·90 | 0·89 | 0·88 | 0·86 | 0·85 |
| 160 | 1·03 | 1·02 | 1·00 | 0·97 | 0·95 | 0·93 | 0·91 | 0·90 | 0·89 | 0·87 | 0·85 |
| 180 | 1·03 | 1·02 | 1·00 | 0·98 | 0·95 | 0·93 | 0·91 | 0·90 | 0·89 | 0·87 | 0·86 |
| 200 | 1·04 | 1·03 | 1·01 | 0·98 | 0·96 | 0·94 | 0·92 | 0·91 | 0·90 | 0·88 | 0·86 |

(*Viscosity data taken from CNGA bulletin No. TS-353*)

*Figure 62* $C_r$ *and* $C_f$ *factors for paraffinic gases (Courtesy of Polyflow Incorporated, USA)*

206

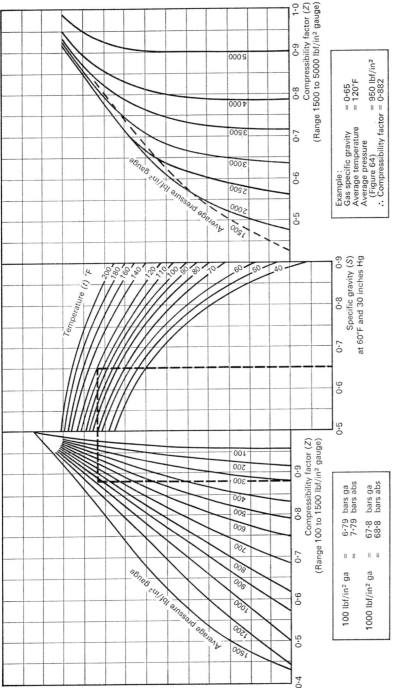

*Figure 63 Chart for determining the compressibility factor of natural gas ( Based on Deviation of natural gas from ideal-gas laws by G. G. Brown, Petroleum Engineer, Vol. X, Feb/April 1940)*

207

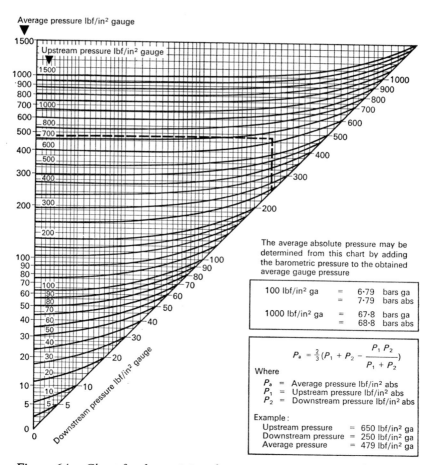

*Figure 64*    *Chart for determining the average pressure in gas lines*

formulae can be used in the metric form since the $C_r$, $C_f$ and $Z$ factors are dimensionless. The converted formulae are as follows:

*For gases at pressures above 1·20 bar*

$$Q_m = 0.1241 \; D_{mm}^{2.623} \left( \frac{P_1^2 - P_2^2}{C_r Z L_m} \right)^{0.541}$$

*For pressures below 1·20 bar*

$$Q_m = 0.001\,237 \; D_{mm}^{2.623} \left( \frac{\Delta H_{mm}}{C_r L_m} \right)^{0.541}$$

208

where $Q_m$ = Flow rate, $m^3/h$ air at 15°C and 1 013·25 mbar pressure, dry (IGU standard)

$D_{mm}$ = Internal pipe diameter, mm

$P_1$ = Upstream gas pressure, bars absolute

$P_2$ = Downstream gas pressure, bars absolute

$L_m$ = Length of pipe, metres

$\Delta H_{mm}$ = Pressure drop, mm water gauge.

An alternative time-saving treatment of the basic formulae would be to use the characteristics of a standard natural gas instead of air, and correct for the deviation in the characteristics of the natural gas involved from that of the standard. However, such comparative data are not available.

## 2  Transmission and Reticulation Pressures

From the basic formula governing flow it is apparent that the higher the starting pressure in a given system carrying a given flow rate of gas, $Q$, the smaller will be the pressure drop, eg

$$Q \propto \sqrt{(P_1^2 - P_2^2)}$$

therefore $Q \propto \sqrt{\{(P_1 - P_2)(P_1 + P_2)\}}$

therefore $P_1 - P_2$ varies inversely as $P_1 + P_2$.

From this it also follows that the energy required to replace this pressure drop will be smaller the higher the initial pressure $P_1$.

It is not surprising therefore that current studies, which are generally computerized, lead to the use of stout, high-tensile-strength steel pipes operated at starting pressures up to almost 100 bars for long-distance transmission. After falling by roughly one-third this pressure would be restored, and if necessary this process would be repeated in successive stages. The result of a study in which the only other variable was pipe-wall thickness is given in Figure 65 as an example of the advantage of increasing operating pressure.

Another inference from the pressure-flow relationship is that the spacing of the re-compression stations on a long-distance transmission line is likely to be close. In practice this is commonly approximately 70 miles. Table 36 gives the results of one US study (78) comparing the economics of 11 and 14 stations on a 1 000-mile line of 30 inch (762 mm) ID pipe.

Generally speaking, codes of practice based on the consideration of public safety restrict the operating pressure of mains traversing or approaching built-up areas, especially dense conurbations where the limit can be as low as 6 bars gauge, possibly with a higher level where the carrier pipe is contained in a steel sleeve.

For bulk gas deliveries to industry, long-distance transmission practice, subject to the restrictions referred to above, is likely to be followed, resulting in the delivery of gas at substantially higher pressure than is demanded in use. This would be governed down in two or more stages, where necessary with slight indirect preheat prior to decompression, in order to remove the risk of formation of ice or hydrate deposits in the governors. There will be exceptions to this, since occasional demands arise for the supply of gas to industry at pressures up to 10 bars gauge.

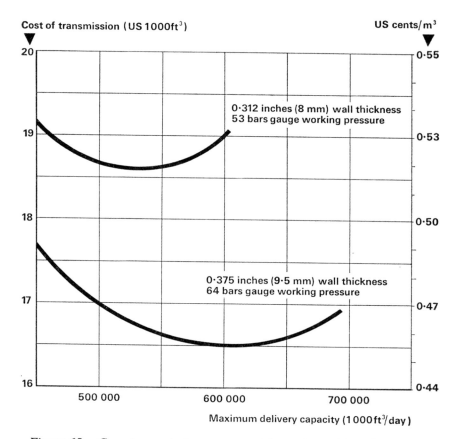

Cost of transmission (US 1000ft³)  US cents/m³

0·312 inches (8 mm) wall thickness
53 bars gauge working pressure

0·375 inches (9·5 mm) wall thickness
64 bars gauge working pressure

500 000 600 000 700 000

Maximum delivery capacity (1 000 ft³/day)

*Figure 65 Gas transmission costs with various 30-inch pipeline systems (Courtesy of the Institution of Gas Engineers)*

**Table 36**   *Example of the economics of station spacing on a 1 000-mile line (Courtesy of the Institution of Gas Engineers)*

| | | | |
|---|---|---|---|
| Daily delivery capacity | 1 000 ft³ | 608 000 | 608 000 |
| Station spacing | miles | 71·4 | 90·9 |
| Stations required | | 14 | 11 |
| Horsepower per station | | 12 500 | 20 000 |
| Total system horsepower | | 175 000 | 220 000 |
| Plant investment | $ million | 195·751 | 196·872 |
| Operation and maintenance | $ million/annum | 4·065 | 4·048 |
| Fuel-gas and loss | $ million/annum | 3·842 | 4·709 |
| Fixed charges at 13·0% | $ million/annum | 25·448 | 25·593 |
| Total cost of transportation | $ million/annum | 33·355 | 34·350 |
| Annual deliveries at 95% load factor | 1 000 ft³/annum | 210 824 | 210 824 |
| Total cost of transportation | cents/1 000 ft³ | 15·8 | 16·3 |

The most economical pressure for the feeder mains to domestic, commercial and small industrial consumers is likely to be above, and therefore limited by, the permitted level of say 6 to 20 bars.

The gas pressure requirement within households or commercial establishments is only of the order of 20 mb. Only a part of the difference between this pressure and the reticulation pressure will be needed to overcome pipe friction. The surplus pressure is disposed of by a series of governors at appropriate points, the last of which is at the inlet of each consumer's meter. These controlled major changes of pressure permit correlated changes in the specification and materials used for the pipes.

## 3   Gas Compressors

*(a)   Large-Scale High-Pressure Transmission*
It is reported from the USA (78) that the size of the reciprocating compressor units used for large-scale high-pressure gas transmission has increased from 1 000 to 5 000 hp (746 to 3 730 kW) during the past 20 years and that fuel consumption has been reduced by 30%. The development of large centrifugal machines with electric motor or gas-turbine prime movers has been even more dramatic; these are now available in units exceeding 15 000 hp (11 200 kW).

From a cost comparison given in 1967, it can be seen (Table 37) that great savings in all costs, other than fuel or power, arise from the

211

substitution of reciprocating units by these large rotary compressors. The extent to which this advantage is outweighed by the fuel or power cost per unit of gas delivered, resulting from the relatively high cost of power compared with raw fuels and the relatively low efficiency of the gas turbine compared with the other systems, will depend upon local circumstances.

The large gas-turbine centrifugal units are likely to prove the more economical in most cases, but the alternatives will no doubt be used in particular circumstances. Further capital savings are made possible by outdoor installation where practical, and operating labour cost savings by automation and telecontrol supervision.

*Table 37    Gas compression costs, excluding fuel and power*

| Station power | 15 000 hp (11·2 MW) | 15 000 hp (11·2 MW) | 15 000 hp (11·2 MW) |
|---|---|---|---|
| Station equipment | Single-unit electric-motor-driven centrifugal compressor | Single-unit gas-turbine-driven centrifugal compressor | Six 2 500 hp (1·87 MW) reciprocating compressors |
| | million US$ | million US$ | million US$ |
| Investment | 2·1 | 3·0 | 4·2 |
| Annual charges | million US$ | million US$ | million US$ |
| Fixed charges at 13% | 0·27 | 0·39 | 0·54 |
| Operation and maintenance expense (excluding power and fuel) | 0·16 | 0·19 | 0·23 |
| Total | 0·43 | 0·58 | 0·77 |

*(b)    Reticulation and Line-Packing*

The power demanded of single compressor units required for reticulation and line packing is of a lower order than that required for large-scale high-pressure transmission.

The need for reticulation compressor units in natural-gas supply systems should arise only from the need to withdraw gas from low-pressure storage. Where local circumstances permit, the simplest way of effecting this is to use gas from a high-pressure source in an ejector; otherwise simple rotary boosters are used.

For line-packing and certain peak-load reticulation demands, prime movers with a power of the order of 1 000 hp (746 kW) may be required. Variable delivery volumes, pressures and pressure/volume ratios are commonly required from a given compressor. In such cases reciprocating compressors are used, normally but not invariably with reciprocating engine drive.

## 4  Materials used for Gas Transmission and Reticulation Pipes
Formerly gas-distribution pressures ranged up to two bars gauge only and cast-iron pipes were used in all stages until close to the point of use, where a change would be made to seamed wrought-iron pipe. Modern techniques involve pressures up to 100 bars for natural gas and 30 bars for manufactured gas. This results in the use of high-tensile-steel pipes for all main transmission lines, and in the reticulation system at least for pressures exceeding those appropriate for cast iron.

At the consumer end, wrought-iron pipes were replaced by protected seamless steel pipes, but these are now being replaced in turn, at an increasing rate, by incorrodable plastic pipes, which are more economical in many cases. Plastic pipes are also replacing cast-iron reticulation pipes up to diameters of 6 inches (150 mm). The use of cast-iron pipes is therefore continuously diminishing and is currently restricted to medium-pressure and low-pressure uses within the reticulation system and mainly in the pipe-diameter range of 18 to 4 inches (450 to 100 mm). The larger pipes are likely to be spun cast, and the smaller are likely to be of 'ductile' cast iron.

*(a)  High-Pressure Steel Pipes*
There are many specifications, recommendations and regulations concerning the installation of high-pressure steel pipelines. Those of the UK Gas Council, reprinted in 1967 and revised in 1970 (79), are comprehensive in scope and include relevant UK and USA standards for operation up to 70 bars absolute. The following is a summarized extract of some of the main features of these recommendations.

*(i)  Gas Characteristics*
The water and hydrocarbon dewpoint of the gas carried at working pressure should at all times be below the temperature of the pipeline. Care should be taken to eliminate dust and minimize the compressor-oil-fog content of the gas.

*(ii)  Pipe Materials and Specifications*
Seamless, longitudinally welded or spirally welded steel pipes of appropriate API and BS specifications are recommended.

The yield strengths of the commonly used pipes are as follows:

| Seamless or electric welded | Specified minimum yield strength | |
|---|---|---|
| | lbf/in² | kN/m² |
| API 5L Grade B | 35 000 | 241 |
| API 5XL Grade X42 | 42 000 | 290 |
| API 5XL Grade X46 | 46 000 | 317 |
| API 5XL Grade X56 | 56 000 | 386 |
| API 5XL Grade X60 | 60 000 | 414 |

*(iii) Wall thickness of pipes*
The minimum recommended pipe wall thickness, which is defined as the normal wall thickness less the maximum tolerance for the under-thickness of the wall, is obtained from the following formula:

$$t = \frac{PD}{2fS}$$

where $t$ = design thickness of pipe wall, inches (mm)
$P$ = maximum working pressure, lbf/in² absolute (MN/m²)
$S$ = minimum yield strength of pipe wall, lbf/in² absolute (MN/m²)
$D$ = outside diameter of pipe, inches (mm)
$f$ = a design factor of 0·72 maximum.

A scale of overriding least nominal wall thickness is provided (Table 38), from which it will be seen that these thicknesses produce effective design factors substantially below 0·72 in most cases.

Two further overriding provisions are as follows: For highly stressed pipelines above 24 inches diameter the minimum design factor, $f$, should not exceed 0·65 for an interim period until further study is made of the possible occurrence of unstable shear fractures in such pipes. This factor is below that produced by the least nominal wall thickness shown in Table 38.

It is also proposed that seamless pipes with bitumen or coaltar coatings should not be used at levels in excess of 56% of their minimum yield strength. This provision also is of a temporary nature until evidence of the cracking of these coatings has been investigated.

# Table 38 Effective design factors (f) based on minimum wall thicknesses for a selection of grades of steel (Courtesy of the Institution of Gas Engineers)

| Outside diameter of pipe inches (mm) | Least nominal wall thickness† inches (mm) | Grade of steel | Maximum working pressure lbf/in²ga (bars ga) | | | |
|---|---|---|---|---|---|---|
| | | | 100 (6·8) | 350 (23·8) | 500 (34) | 1 000 (68) |
| | | | f | f | f | f |
| 6⅝ (159) | 0·188 (4·8) | B | 0·06 | 0·20 | 0·29 | 0·58 |
| | | X42 | 0·05 | 0·17 | 0·24 | 0·48 |
| | | X52 | 0·04 | 0·14 | 0·19 | 0·39 |
| | | X60 | 0·03 | 0·12 | 0·17 | 0·34 |
| 12¾ (324) | 0·250 (6·4) | B | 0·08 | 0·29 | 0·42 | * |
| | | X42 | 0·07 | 0·24 | 0·35 | 0·69 |
| | | X52 | 0·06 | 0·20 | 0·28 | 0·56 |
| | | X60 | 0·05 | 0·17 | 0·24 | 0·49 |
| 18 (450) | 0·250 (6·4) | B | 0·12 | 0·41 | 0·59 | * |
| | | X42 | 0·10 | 0·34 | 0·49 | * |
| | | X52 | 0·08 | 0·28 | 0·40 | * |
| | | X60 | 0·07 | 0·24 | 0·34 | 0·69 |
| 24 (610) | 0·312 (7·9) | B | 0·12 | 0·40 | 0·58 | * |
| | | X42 | 0·10 | 0·34 | 0·48 | * |
| | | X52 | 0·08 | 0·27 | 0·39 | * |
| | | X60 | 0·07 | 0·24 | 0·34 | 0·67 |
| 30 (762) | 0·375 (9·5) | B | 0·12 | 0·42 | 0·60 | * |
| | | X42 | 0·10 | 0·35 | 0·50 | * |
| | | X52 | 0·08 | 0·28 | 0·40 | * |
| | | X60 | 0·07 | 0·25 | 0·35 | 0·70 |
| 36 (914) | 0·375 (9·5) | B | 0·14 | 0·51 | 0·72 | * |
| | | X42 | 0·12 | 0·44 | 0·60 | * |
| | | X52 | 0·10 | 0·34 | 0·49 | * |
| | | X60 | 0·08 | 0·29 | 0·42 | * |

Notes

*Indicates f exceeds 0·72

†The minimum wall thickness used in calculating f has been based on the maximum tolerances for under-thickness of the pipe wall according to the specifications generally used in these sizes ranges, ie

— 12½ % for pipe not exceeding 18 inches diameter.
— 5% for pipe exceeding 18 inches diameter.

## (iv) Designed Gas Velocity

With gas of normal negligible dust content there is no need to limit the designed gas velocity. Where dust is present it is rarely necessary to set limits below 70 ft/s (21·3 m/s), although in the worst cases it may be necessary to limit it to 40 ft/s (12·2 m/s).

## (v) Allowance for Pipe Expansion and Contraction

Provided the final tie-in welds are made within the temperature limits of 32°C to 4°C, no provision need be made for the expansion or contraction of underground pipes in normal circum-

215

stances. Where gas temperature conditions or routing demands it, allowance should be made by the provision of free loops or expansion bellows.

### (vi) Protection from Corrosion

It is unsafe as well as uneconomical to use unprotected steel pipes. The main protection takes the form of a pitch or bituminous enamel coating (79), reinforced with glass fibre, or a plastic tape cladding or sheath. Recently in the USA extruded polypropylene cladding has been used. This protection is backed up where necessary by cathodic protection (80) which operates as follows. The corrosion of steel in the soil results from a flow of current between the less reactive areas, which become cathodes in a system in which the soil moisture is the electrolyte; the more reactive areas become anodes and are corroded. To counteract this the negative terminal of a direct-current source is attached to the pipe and a positive terminal is buried in the soil some distance away. A negative electric current is applied to the pipe, maintaining a negative pipe/soil voltage of slightly less than one volt relative to a given reference. In cases of exceptionally high risk a sacrificial anode of zinc or magnesium can be installed.

These two forms of protection are closely inter-related. A coating lacking in adhesion and impermeability can render cathodic protection inadequate or uneconomic. Satisfactory coatings permit the current requirement to be contained within the limits 0·001 to 0·020 mA/ft² (0·01 to 0·2 mA/m²) of pipe surface.

Internal protection is achieved by the application of a priming paint (79).

### (b) Cast-Iron Pipes (81)

As already stated the role of cast-iron pipes in transmission and reticulation is declining as the result of competition from steel and plastic piping.

The grey pit-cast pipes formerly used are now replaced by spun grey cast of a higher tensile strength for sizes above 12 inches (300 mm) diameter, and by ductile iron below this diameter. The latter is a form of cast iron in which the graphite is dispersed as nodules instead of the normal convoluted flake form in which it is present in grey cast-iron. This renders it more ductile without reducing its resistance to corrosion (82) and gives it a tensile strength approaching that of mild steel. Both spun cast and ductile iron are used for pressures up to 7 bar gauge.

216

The joints used are normally still of the socket and spigot design (Figure 66), but the caulked yarn and lead joints of the past have been replaced by relatively flexible mechanical joints. In these joints a synthetic rubber ring, protected by a lead sheath, is forced into a tapered socket by the tightening action of bolts on a pressure ring.

In the example shown in Figure 66 (centre) it would be possible for the spigot to withdraw from the joint in some circumstances unless restrained. Where these are used, therefore, concrete blocks are in-

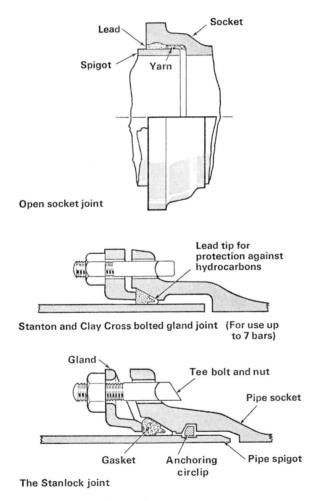

*Figure 66    Three typical pipe joints*

217

stalled to limit movement at sharp bends. A self-locking version of this joint is now available (bottom), so far for pipes up to 12 inches (300 mm) diameter. The locking feature is a circlip in the form of a floating split-ring. This circlip is forced into the recess in the joint socket by the entry of the spigot into the joint, but when the spigot is fully entered the circlip contracts and overlaps into the spigot recess. This locks the joint and renders external restraint unnecessary.

(i)  *Dust in Mains (83, 84)*
Dry natural gas is commonly distributed through systems composed mainly of cast-iron pipes previously used to distribute saturated manufactured gas containing oxygen. These pipes may contain substantial deposits, mainly of iron oxide, which, as they dry, become detached as dust particles and carried forward in the gas stream to district governors and ultimately to consumers' appliances. This dust has to be blown out or mechanically dislodged from the pipes, and while this is in progress dust filters are used at key points throughout the system. Final traces of dust may be dealt with by a process of oil fogging similar to that used for joint-sealing dealt with below.

(ii)  *Leakage from Cast-Iron Mains*
Leakage from the types of cast-iron pipe joint used in the past, increases substantially, even at low pressure, on the change-over from saturated manufactured gas to dry natural gas, LPG or LPG/air. This increased leakage results from the higher Wobbe Number of the latter gases, and also from the drying out of moisture from the yarn behind lead joints and the shrinkage caused by loss of absorbed hydrocarbons from synthetic rubber joints.

These shrunken joints can be plimmed up again by fogging the gas with glycol or similar solutions in the case of the yarn/lead joints, or a hydrocarbon oil of low volatility and appropriate hydrocarbon type and viscosity in the case of the rubber jointing rings. In order to minimize the points of application the hydrocarbon oil is sprayed into the gas stream at high pressure (up to 160 bars) in order to produce a persistent fog.

Another technique is to fill the pipe with a bituminous sealant and then pump it out. This treatment is lasting and effective not only in reducing leakage but also in laying traces of dust.

More effective treatments are used for larger mains. In these the mains are taken out of use in sections and treated after cleaning, the joints being sealed internally by various means. In one method the sealing material used is a two-part polysulphide rubber comprising a base polymer and an activator (85). This latter method although costly reduces leakage to a level that permits higher operating pressures.

In some instances a solution to both dust and leakage problems can be found by using the old pipe as a sleeve to carry a plastic pipe of slightly smaller diameter.

### (c) Plastic Pipes

Pipes made of unmodified polyvinyl chloride (PVC) have been used for many years in the USA and Europe. This material is virtually un-susceptible to stress cracking but a few isolated incidents have nevertheless occurred in the field in Holland. Although the incidents were traced to the presence of abnormal concentrations of naphtha-lene in the gas (virtually absent from natural gas and most manufac-tured gas) they provoked some investigations. One of these (86) indicated that both the unmodified PVC and the improved modified versions subsequently introduced should withstand the effect of the sorption of aromatic hydrocarbons from the most aggressive of the aromatic-containing gases likely to be encountered. This resistance should be maintained for a period greatly in excess of 50 years in conditions of extreme surcharge loads, and with gas pressures up to at least 5 bars absolute.

Various pipes are now available made of PVC modified to increase the impact strength at 0°C by up to ten times that of the unmodified form.

More or less concurrently with the development of the modified PVC dealt with above, piping made of high-density and medium-density polyethylene (PE) came into use. This latter material, although more costly per unit of long-term strength (87), has the following ad-vantages over the modified PVC. Sizes up to an internal diameter of 3 inches (75 mm) can be coiled, which reduces the cost of handling and laying. PE can be fusion-welded and can therefore be tested immedi-ately, whereas PVC cannot be fusion welded and is usually solvent-welded. Although the solvent-welded joints are satisfactory they take up to an hour to set, which delays testing. The stress resistance of PE at low temperature is higher than that of PVC, and its fracture behaviour is better.

Following the research by Brighton and Benton referred to above on the effect of the sorption of aromatic hydrocarbons (86), research has been carried out on the effect on both PVC and PE piping of the

219

sorption of other chemical species likely to be added to manufactured or natural gas (88). The conclusions drawn were in general reassuring.

Costs are available indicating savings of roughly 30% for plastic-pipe systems in practice relative to the use of cast-iron mains and steel services (87). There is little doubt, therefore, that the use of plastic pipes will rapidly increase, at least in the pipe sizes currently employed –up to 6 inches (150 mm) internal diameter–and with normal reticulation pressures up to 3 bars absolute. There are good prospects for plastics applications in larger-diameter pipes also. Plastic pipes should be protected from direct sunlight.

One or two instances of the use of reinforced epoxy resin pipes have been reported. Special circumstances no doubt justified the use of this stronger but much more expensive material.

## 5  The Sizing of Pipes—Notional Costs

The factors determining gas transmission and reticulation pipe sizing for a given load are as follows:

Initial gas pressure available
Terminal gas pressure required
Pressure restrictions
The use of compression stages
The variation of pipe costs with size and strength
Pipe-laying costs.

The simplest problems are those where the initial pressure available is equal to or greater than the permitted gas pressure, the distance the gas has to travel is short enough and the terminal pressure low enough for compression stages to be obviously unnecessary. Many natural-gas reticulation projects fall into this category, and the pipe diameter required can be readily and sufficiently accurately determined by use of the Polyflo calculator already described.

A complication arises if the pressure is inadequate, which is the case with some manufactured gas and with natural gas stored at low pressure. It is then necessary to equate the cost of compressing to various pressures up to the permissible level with the cost of the laid pipes in the corresponding sizes. The number of cases to be tested are greatly restricted by the coarse scale governing commercial pipe sizes and capacities. For example, the difference in the capacity of a 10-inch (250 mm) ID pipe compared with an 8-inch (200 mm) pipe under the same conditions is approximately 75%.

In the foregoing case the pipe size indicated can be increased in order to create line-storage capacity to a desired level; this is dealt with later together with the storage aspect itself.

220

A further complication is that involved in long-distance transmission where decisions have to be made regarding the appropriate operating pressure, the optimum spacing of recompression stations for each pressure, and pipe size to be employed (78). Computers may be used in the solution of these problems and advantage should be taken of the most refined flow formulae available for the pipes to be employed. Currently this information is obtainable from the Institute of Gas Technology, Chicago.

Finally, a special case is presented by the discovery offshore of high-pressure natural gas. The cost of installing pipes underwater can be several times greater than the corresponding costs on land and can lead to operation with lower gas quality and higher gas pressure than would be economical on land. Whether or not this is done, a notional estimate of the ratio of cost involved in open ground *versus* undersea routing is roughly 1 :3.

The largest capacity pipes in use in the world will be those employed in the USSR where vast gas resources have been discovered 3 000 to 6 000 km distant from potential consumers. There pipes of 1 200 mm diameter are in use, those of 1 400 mm are being constructed (1971), and pipes 2 500 mm in diameter are in process of development.

*Notional Pipe-Laying Costs*
The cost of laying transmission and reticulation pipes varies greatly with local conditions, and the overall unit-basis gas-distribution cost will be subject, in addition, to other variables relating to the distances, loads and system load-factors involved and the pressures used. Notional costs have therefore little value other than that of roughly indicating the scale of cost involved.

Figure 67 gives an indication of the cost of laying high-pressure transmission lines across open country and Figure 68 shows the comparative cost of transmitting various loads over a distance of 1 000 miles. For each size of pipe shown in Figure 68 the overall cost of transmission increases with loading at the point where the cost of the further multiplication of recompression stages outweighs the effect of the resulting increase in loading.

Table 39 gives an indication of the cost of laying cast-iron pipes. The savings arising from the use of plastic pipes is small relative to cast iron if the greater part of the cost results from the breaking and reinstatement of the ground. Substantial savings are possible where these costs can be avoided either by 'thrust' laying of plastic or other pipes beneath the hard surface, or, in cases of relaying, by using the old cast-iron pipe as a sleeve for the laying of a plastic pipe capable of

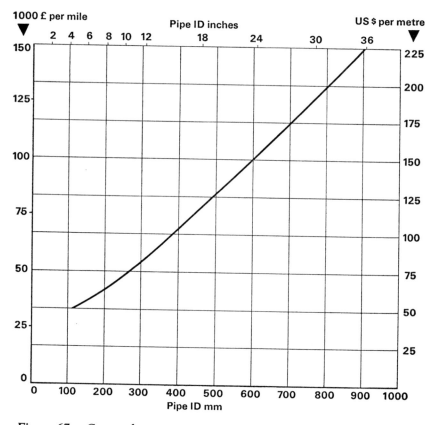

*Figure 67   Comprehensive notional costs of laying pipes for natural-gas transmission and reticulation (1971)*

*Table 39   Comprehensive notional costs of laying ductile-cast-iron pipes (1970)*

| Type of Surface | 4-inch (102 mm) ID | | 6-inch (152 mm) ID | | 8-inch (203 mm) ID | |
|---|---|---|---|---|---|---|
| | US $ per metre | £ per mile | US $ per metre | £ per mile | US $ per metre | £ per mile |
| Tarmac on concrete | 26 | 17 000 | 33 | 21 500 | 37 | 24 000 |
| Tarmac on hardcore | 22·5 | 15 000 | 30 | 19 500 | 34 | 22 000 |
| Soft Verge | 12 | 8 000 | 17·5 | 11 500 | 21·5 | 14 000 |
| Arithmetic mean | 21 | £13 500 | 27 | £17 500 | 31 | £20 000 |

222

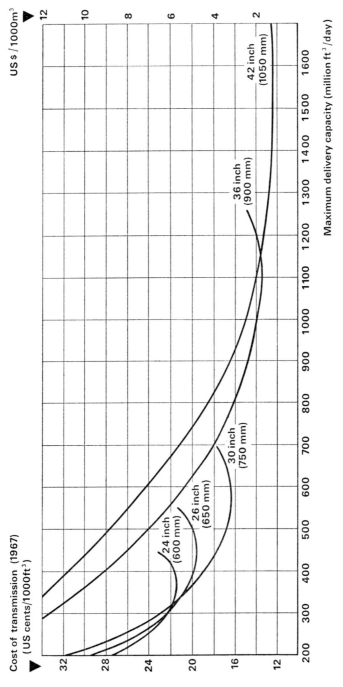

*Figure 68   Gas transmission costs over 1 000 miles with various pipe sizes
(Courtesy of the Institution of Gas Engineers)*

withstanding a higher reticulation pressure and, hence, loading than the existing cast-iron pipe.

Plastic pipe shows to the greatest advantage in systems in which reticulation mains and services are of the same material and integrated by means of simple jointing techniques. One comparison (87) with other systems on an estate divided for test purposes produced the following results:

|  | Cost per property |
|---|---|
| Small-bore plastic mains and services | £33 approx |
| Small-bore steel-pipe mains and services | £36 approx |
| Cast-iron main and steel services | £43 approx |

## 6  The Routing of Pipelines

*(a)  Legal Considerations (79)*

Although gas undertakings have some statutory authority to place pipes and related equipment in roads, such powers are normally limited. In the UK, where the procedures are of a most elaborate nature, a major transmission project will require further permissions from some or all of the following authorities or interested parties:

The appropriate highway authorities, for roads
Owners of private land to be traversed
Local planning authority for pipes or apparatus above ground
Forestry Commission for certain tree felling
The appropriate river board, conservancy board, or
    internal drainage board for crossing inland waterways
British Rail where railway property is concerned
Where railway bridges are involved, notice must be served also
    on the highway authority and any independent bridge authority.

Where pipes are to be laid across country it is advisable to contact the bodies listed below, even if they are only indirectly affected, together with any other known interested parties:

Country Landowners' Association
Forestry Commission
Ministry of Agriculture, Fisheries and Food
Department of the Environment
Local archaeological societies
National Coal Board
National Farmers' Union
Nature conservancy.

## (b)  Routing

The route finally chosen will be the most economical compromise between the shortest permissible route and that along which the costs of laying, reinstatement and compensation are lowest. This involves the avoidance of built-up areas except at the terminals, and a major degree of avoidance of natural obstacles and of unsuitable ground such as marshes or areas of possible subsidence.

## 7   The Control of Pipeline Networks

### (a)   Dynamic Simulation of High-Pressure Systems

The integration of gas-supply systems into large networks with a multiplicity of pipe junctions, terminals and compressors has resulted in the development of the analysis of high-pressure networks (89, 90) and of computer programmes that permit such networks to be dynamically simulated (91). The need for this in high-pressure to medium-pressure networks arises from the greater effect of the pressure variations in these networks than in low-pressure systems, in which the gas put in at one point comes out almost immediately at another, and for which steady-state analysis is adequate.

A comparison has been made (91) of the following three computer programmes available for this purpose. Fairly good agreement was obtained.

The GE Simulator developed by the General Electric Company, Schenectady, USA

Pipetram developed by Electronic Associates Inc, USA

The ERS developed by the Engineering Research Station of the UK Gas Council.

Among other functions, dynamic analysis makes possible the determination of the effects of supply variation or failure, of the time available for remedial action and of the relative merits of alternative remedies. In addition it gives a more accurate measure of the ability of the system to meet current or future estimated daily swings in output. The critical points in the system can be determined and proposed improvements tested.

For these and other reasons, dynamic simulation is becoming increasingly essential both for the efficient design and development of complex modern high-pressure and medium-pressure systems, and for their effective control and automation.

225

*(b)   Day-to-Day Control*

Ideally a system for the day-to-day control of gas transmission and reticulation would demand a continuous record of the following data:

*(i)*   The gas flow into the particular supply area as a whole, and into and out of storage stations, together with such sub-area reticulation system flows as are necessary to indicate the required degree of detail in deployment.

*(ii)*   High-pressure and low-pressure gas stocks, including line-pack gas available. (It is improbable that this latter could be made available either technically or economically at short intervals of time. The control would therefore fall back on the potential of the line pack under certain predetermined conditions as indicated by the dynamic simulation system referred to above.)

*(iii)*   Gas pressures on mains, governor inlets, and compressor and jet booster inlets and outlets, at selected key points.

These data would be transmitted from the points of measurement to the central control room by one or other of the various telemetry systems available, using either micro-wave radio or land line. Selected items would be continuously transmitted and others intermittently.

At the control-room the information would be automatically processed where necessary and that required for control would be printed out or displayed for the operator at least hourly. Automatic visual or sound signals can be built into the system to indicate a condition of alarm.

The immediate problem of the control staff is to check that the deployment of the gas stocks and flows are satisfactory, or to adjust them where they are not. For this purpose various distant control systems are available.

The less urgent but more important problem is to check actual against predicted performance under the following mains heads:

Hourly and cumulative gas made and received

Hourly and cumulative gas sent out

Gas stocks (including estimated minimum stocks for the current 24 hours).

These data are then used, together with any revision of weather forecast available, to produce a frequently revised forecast for the remainder of the 24-hour period of the profiles of gas input, output and stock levels.

For the control of such extensive areas as those of the UK area boards, which are among the most complex in the world, it would be necessary to set up highly automated sub-area centres but with some degree of manual supervision and control.

Although no areas are as yet equipped for such a degree of centralized control as is set out above, the equipment needed for determination, transmission and proeessing of the data is now available. Equipment is becoming increasingly available also for the distant control or the automatic operation of the various items of equipment such as the holder valves, governors and compressors involved.

To the extent that it becomes economical, control systems are tending to become centralized and automated roughly on the lines indicated above (92).

## The Transmission of Natural Gas in Pressure Vessels

From the early part of this century combustible gases have been transported in both low-pressure bags and high-pressure cylinders, for use, for example, as automotive fuel. Proposals to transport natural gas in the gaseous phase for this and other uses recur periodically. More recently (93) an attempt has been made to demonstrate that for sea-going hauls of up to 600 nautical miles the use of pressure vessels would be more economical than liquefaction. It is probable, however, that gaseous-phase transportation of natural gas in pressure vessels will remain an esoteric technique.

## Transmission as Liquid

### LNG Transmission by Pipeline
In the USSR, where some of the largest natural-gas discoveries in the world are 3 000 to 6 000 km (1 850 to 3 700 miles) distant from the furthest potential users, consideration has been given (94, 95) to the transmission of natural gas in the liquid phase. Optimal temperature and pressure conditions have been computed at $-100°C$ to $-120°C$ ($-148°F$ to $-184°F$) and 30-40 bars. In these conditions it is felt that it should be practical to use steels with from zero to 1·5 per cent nickel in place of the alloy having 3 per cent nickel that would currently be used.

Studies have also been made in Canada (96), so far with inconclusive results.

It emerges that the capacity of a given size of pipe for natural gas in the liquid phase is three to four times as great as for natural gas in the gaseous phase. The optimum spacing of re-cooling and re-pressurizing stations is roughly three times that of gas re-compression stations.

The cost of liquefaction, and the higher cost of the heavily insulated pipeline, appear under current conditions to outweigh the advantages of LNG transmission where it is required as a gas *en route* or at the terminal or terminals.

The situations most favourable to LNG transmission would be those requiring the natural gas to be in the liquid phase at the terminal —for transport by sea for example.

The future development of cheaper steels (94), possibly without nickel, and of cheaper insulations systems, could change the cost balance indicated above.


### Evaporative Two-Phase Non-Isothermal Pipelines
A study is also in progress (96) of a high-pressure pipeline supplied with LNG that is progressively evaporated along the pipeline and is delivered as a cold gas. This technique is unlikely to be of interest away from relatively inaccessible arctic areas, where great advantage would stem from the concentration of all the processing and transmission plant at the well-head. One aspect of this system is that the carrying capacity of a given gas pipeline increases several times by cooling the gas to $-70°C$ ($-94°F$), mainly owing to the decrease in the compressibility factor of the gas.


### Two-Phase Flow in Isothermal Pipelines
Two-phase flow occurs in natural-gas pipelines as a result of either or both of the following causes; retrograde condensation, or the use of the gas pipeline for the simultaneous transfer of condensate separated at the well-head. This latter technique is useful for offshore gas discoveries. In both cases the resulting impediment to the gas flow can be great if equilibrium conditions are allowed to be established between the pipeline and the terminal separation points. It is normal therefore to periodically scavenge the accumulated liquid from the pipe at intervals by means of a loosely fitting cylindrical or spherical 'pig' inserted upstream and removed downstream.

Provision is made for the insertion and removal of the pigs in the pipeline design, and the interval between 'pigging' will vary, from say, once per shift to once in several days, according to the quantity of liquid involved.

## LNG Transportation by Sea

Although offshore natural gas is transported to shore by pipeline, and consideration has been given to longer-distance submarine pipes, as, for example, from North Africa to Southern Europe, long-distance natural-gas transportation across the ocean by LNG carrier is now accepted as the more economical means.

Many LNG tanker designs have been considered (97). All are significantly different from dry-bulk carriers. A common requirement is that the LNG compartments should have primary and secondary barriers within the hull, both capable of holding the LNG cargo.

Primary barriers may be of Invar, stainless steel or aluminium alloy. Secondary barriers may be of the same materials or they may be non-metallic. Either may take the form of self-supporting structural barriers, relatively independent of the hull, or LNG-tight $\frac{1}{2}$-mm to 1-mm membrane barriers relying upon the ship's structure for support.

At this stage it is difficult to decide which type of barrier is on balance advantageous, and as a result both types are being developed. Designs incorporating two structural barriers, two membrane barriers and one of each type are available for tankers to meet the rapidly growing international trade in LNG.

The materials used for insulation between primary and secondary barriers and hull include balsa wood, perlite, and polyurethane and PVC foam.

A system has been developed in which a thin stainless-steel primary barrier is supported on a rigid balsa-wood and plywood insulation assembly. The latter is designed to hold LNG if the primary barrier fails, and therefore serves in addition as a secondary barrier (98). This combines the advantages of the insulation system of the LNG carrier *Methane Progress* with the Technigaz membrane used in the *Pythagore*.

Subsequent developments include designs aimed at increasing the safety of the primary tank in order to dispense with the secondary membrane. One such design, claimed to be more economical than membrane tanks for capacities up to 20 000 tonnes, involves the use of five spherical LNG tanks supported at their equators by a continuous cylindrical skirt (99). Another development involves the use of storage aboard at pressure in order to permit a higher LNG temperature (100). This is termed the *Medium-Condition Liquefied-Gas Process*.

Safety and reliability are paramount considerations in the design of LNG tankers, and capital service and insurance together are the main cost element.

The boil-off from the cargo tanks normally forms part of the carrier's fuel but can be re-liquefied (see page 196).

229

**Costs**

A rough estimate has been given (101) of the investment cost involved in the currently known potential LNG projects. Somewhat higher alternative estimates have been advanced for the tankers involved. These estimates indicate the following rough costs:

$200 millions for providing $500 \times 10^6$ m³/day (gas phase) liquefaction capacity

$50 millions for providing $500 \times 10^6$ m³/day (gas phase) storage and re-gasification

$60 millions for providing 120 000 m³ (liquid phase) tanker.

The projects reviewed covered transportation from Africa and the Caribbean to the US Atlantic Seaboard, from Alaska to Southern California, and from Russia, the Persian Gulf and other areas to Japan.

The overall average unit-basis capital costs for these projects are given in Table 40 below on a notional load-factor and interest rate, together with an estimate of process and other costs.

These rough estimates, which are likely to prove much lower than the cost of future projects, show that the international LNG trade is highly capital intensive. The overall costs indicate that LNG will be imported mainly as a peak-shaving and premium fuel and will yield a low net price at well head. In common with synthetic natural gas its use as a low-premium bulk fuel, as defined in Chapter 19, is likely to be conditional upon pollution-control considerations.

*Table 40    Notional unit-basis costs relating to LNG projects executed and approved before 1971*

| | Average capital costs | | Unit basis cost (Assumed system load factor 90% Assumed capital service 15%) | | | | | |
| | per 1000 ft³/day US $ | per 1000 m³/day US $ | per 1000 ft³ gas delivered US c | | | per 1000 m³ gas delivered US $ | | |
| | | | Capital | Other costs | Total | Capital | Other costs | Total |
| Liquefaction | 400 | 14 140 | 18·3 | 6·5 | 24·8 | 6·46 | 2·30 | 8·76 |
| Ships | 440 | 15 560 | 20·1 | 27·0 | 47·1 | 7·10 | 9·55 | 16·65 |
| Terminals and regasification | 100 | 3 530 | 4·6 | 1·5 | 6·1 | 1·62 | 0·53 | 2·15 |
| Total | 940 | 33 230 | 43·0 | 35·0 | 78·0 | 15·18 | 12·38 | 27·56 |

## LNG Transportation in Vehicles by Road and Rail

Using as a base the LNG storage installation associated either with a liquefaction plant or a reception terminal for overseas supplies, satellite LNG storage centres beyond a short radius will be supplied by road or rail tankers. These means for conveying cryogenic liquids such as oxygen have been in use for many years, and great progress has been made in increasing their size and lowering their operating costs.

Although tank trucks and skid-mounted transportable vessels can be used in special cases, rail tank cars and similar cars adapted as highway trailers should provide the great bulk of land-based LNG transporters.

The design, operation and size limitations on these rail tankers and road trailers will be governed by various regulating authorities. Rail tankers of capacities up to 50 tonnes of LNG have been designed, and road trailers with an approximate capacity of 17 and 20 tonnes are in use in the USA.

A recent study (102) gives some projected notional costs for USA conditions (Figure 69). Depending upon the 'turn-around' time for the rail cars the break-even distance for the cost of these two forms of transport is estimated to be from 150 to 300 miles (240 to 480 km). Beyond this distance rail transportation is shown to be cheaper. The cost effect of change of capacity, especially of the relative scale of these vehicles, would be great. The rail-tank-car design in question comprises a Type 304 stainless-steel vessel within a carbon-steel shell. The space between the two shells is filled with perlite and is evacuated. The LNG is carried at low pressure. Highway trailers of similar basic designs and with a capacity of 17 tonnes are available.

A different design of trailer in use (103), with a capacity slightly exceeding 20 tonnes of LNG, employs inner and outer jackets, both of 5083 aluminium and also evacuated between. These trailers operate at 4·8 bars absolute in order to allow transfer at pressure into tanks operated at 4·4 bars absolute. Heat leakage is stated to be equivalent to only 0·7% per day of the contents.

A semi-trailer truck with a capacity of 8·8 tonnes has been in intermittent use for several years conveying LNG required for experimental purposes from Le Havre to Switzerland. This truck comprises a 9% nickel-steel inner tank and a carbon-steel outer tank, the space between the tanks being packed with perlite powder and evacuated.

231

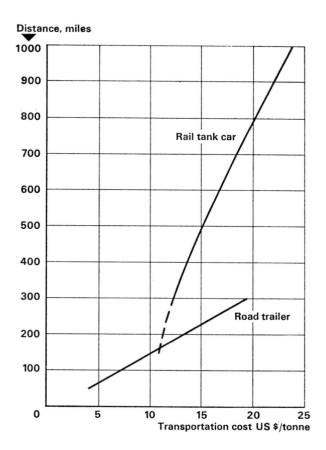

*Figure 69*   *LNG transportation costs (Courtesy of Lox Equipment Company, USA)*

232

# Chapter 18   Natural-Gas Storage

Daily and seasonal variations of gas outputs in town-gas systems based on both manufactured and natural gas, and the roles of gas storage in relation to them, are dealt with in Part Three. There it is shown that the need for gas storage capacity to reconcile production and distribution system load-factors in the short term (that is, over the period of a day or so) is satisfied either by varying the gas pressure in the supply system ('line pack', as described below) or from the low- and high-pressure gas holders as also described in this chapter.

Seasonal variations in gas demand cannot economically be dealt with by these three means but, instead, first by the planned interruption of some supplies, secondly by the use of supplementary gases such as LPG or manufactured gas, and finally by the use of natural gas stored in the liquid phase or the gaseous phase, in a natural reservoir.

## Storage in the Gaseous Phase

### 1   Line Storage or Line Pack
As stated in Chapter 17, bulk natural-gas transmission pressures are high. In a typical case the starting pressure would be 70 bars. After falling by roughly one third this pressure would be restored, if necessary in successive stages.

Although the permitted pressures in the reticulation systems linked with such a high-pressure bulk supply are likely to be substantially lower, especially when traversing dense conurbations, they will still be greatly in excess of the required terminal pressures. The marginal cost of laid high-tensile-steel pipes is such that it is economical to design them, with the aid for example of dynamic simulation systems such as those described earlier in Chapter 17, to make a substantial contribution, through the pressure drop in the system, to the diurnal peak gas demands. The pressure in the system would then be restored during the off-peak period. Such pipes are designed to serve the dual purposes of storage and reticulation.

A study has been made of some of the design aspects of high-tensile-steel pipelines subject to the cyclic pressure variations arising from their use for gas storage. This indicates that special care must be taken in their design to allow for the resulting fatigue (104).

Dependent on the marginal cost of high-tensile-steel pipe-laying (that is, the difference between the cost of laying a pipe large enough to effect the transmission function alone and that of effecting in addition a part of the storage function) it is possible that the major part of the diurnal output load peak gas could be supplied from line pack.

## 2 Low-Pressure Gas Holders
Until the advent of high-pressure gas-transmission systems, low-pressure gas storage was used almost exclusively for the diurnal peak gas demand. In addition the storage capacity would be designed to supply gas deficiencies arising either from the under-estimation of the daily output, or the over-estimation of, or breakdown in, the gas made or supplied.

The familiar low-pressure gas holders are mainly of two types, the water-luted interlocking light-steel-shell type (Figure 70), which rises and falls from a water tank, and the waterless piston type, in which a piston supported by the gas pressure rises and falls within a steel shell (Figure 71).

The water-sealed multi-lift holder would throw a gas pressure of from 100 to 300 mm water gauge according to the number of lifts inflated; the waterless holder would, until empty, maintain a pressure of 300 mm water gauge or more, as designed, regardless of the position of the piston. A third type of low-pressure holder, the Wiggins plastic membrane type, throwing up to 600 mm water gauge of pressure, has been brought into limited use during the past 20 years, mainly in units with a capacity of less than 30 000 m$^3$. These pressures are all low relative to present-day distribution requirements.

With the advent of dry high-pressure manufactured or natural gas, neither type of low-pressure holder is appropriate, but the waterless types have least disadvantages since they maintain higher pressures and do not re-humidify the gas. The water-sealed type can, however, be oil-filmed in order to prevent the addition of water vapour to the gas.

Even before the advent of high-pressure natural gas, the gas supply from low-pressure holders commonly had to be boosted or compressed before being passed on to the district. These holders still serve a purpose over a limited radius. Their construction continues and, where gas at high pressure is available, an alternative to the gas compressor stage is an ejector which is fed during daily peak periods with the base-load high-pressure gas, and which extracts from the low-pressure storage the additional gas required during these periods. The mixed gas passes on to the district at intermediate pressure.

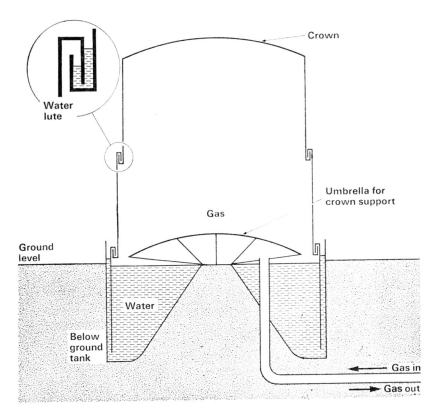

*Figure 70    Water-luted low-pressure gas holder*

### 3    High-Pressure Gas Storage

With increasing reticulation-system pressures arising from the availability of high-pressure gas supplies, and the higher loading of reticulation pipes resulting from increasing gas demands, the unsightly low-pressure gas holder becomes increasingly uneconomical and inappropriate.

The current trend, therefore, is to make up the deficiency of the line pack and existing low-pressure storage by the construction of high-pressure storage-vessel installations. A large number of such installations have been, or are being, constructed in, for example, the UK. Figure 72 shows a typical example, which comprises a number of interconnected convex-ended long cylindrical steel shells 3·7 m in diameter

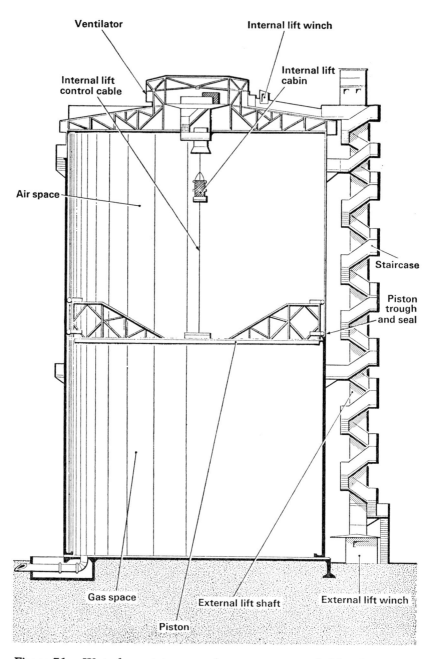

*Figure 71    Waterless piston-type low-pressure gas holder (Courtesy of Clayton Son & Company Limited)*

236

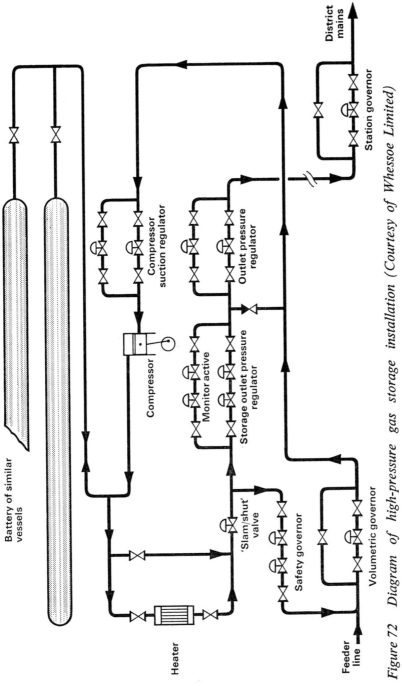

Battery of similar
vessels

Compressor
suction regulator

Compressor

Monitor active

Storage outlet pressure
regulator

Outlet pressure
regulator

Heater

'Slam/shut'
valve

Safety governor

Volumetric governor

Feeder
line

District
mains

Station governor

*Figure 72  Diagram of high-pressure gas storage installation (Courtesy of Whessoe Limited)*

237

by 61 m long. One vessel of this type at 24 bars will contain approximately 600 000 ft³ (21 000 m³) expressed at atmospheric pressure. The UK Gas Council's Engineering Research Station has investigated some of the design aspects of such vessels (104).

The arrangement shown in Figure 72 provides for a controlled flow at a regulated suction pressure to be compressed and passed into the pressure vessels during off-peak periods. During peak periods the gas would be withdrawn through the heater shown to prevent danger of condensation, and, after two stages of pressure regulation, passed on to the station governors. An alternative arrangement of comparable cost involves the replacement of the pressure vessels shown by a length of high-tensile-steel main of similar capacity.

## 4   Below-Ground Gas Storage (Gaseous Phase)

The use by man of underground storage for natural gas is stated to have been first practised in depleted gas sands in Ontario, Canada, in 1915 (105). The practice spread and by 1946 depleted oil- and gas-bearing reservoirs with an estimated capacity of 250 000 million ft³ (7 000 million m³) were in use in the USA.

In addition, from 1946, water-bearing porous formations, termed *aquifers*, were sought for and used, the water being displaced by the gas, and *vice versa*, as gas was pumped into, or taken from, the structure.

The conditions demanded of aquifers for high-pressure gas storage correspond to those of natural-gas deposits; a good depth of a porous formation, permeable both vertically and horizontally, overlaid by a cap or caps of impermeable rock. The means used to search for and exploit such formations are similar to those used in the search for and exploitation of natural gas, although to be of value they need to be substantially closer to the gas consumers than the original natural-gas sources. To be economical their depth should not be greatly in excess of that demanded for the retention of the desired pressure.

A sketch of an aquifer in Iowa, USA (105) is shown in Figure 73. Either fresh or salt water may be present. In the example given it is fresh water and the use of the aquifer for gas storage does not affect the quality of the water.

In addition to the above formations, many artificial underground cavities have been created, mainly in salt deposits by leaching, and to a smaller extent in sandstone, shale and other rocks by mining. These salt cavities are used largely, and the mined cavities exclusively, for materials other than natural gas, mainly for LPG, and are dealt with in the following section.

238

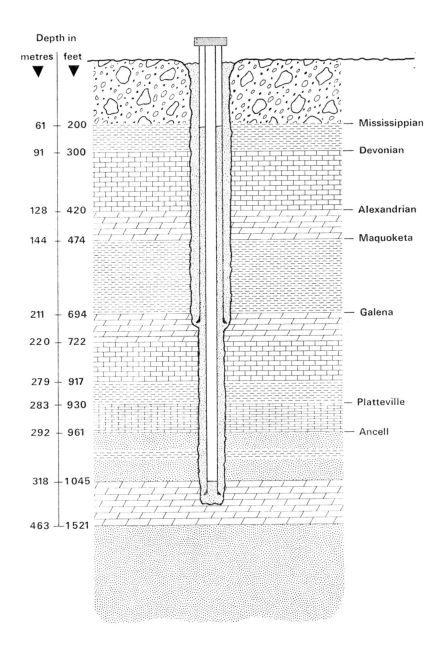

*Figure 73    Cross-section of a typical aquifer in Iowa, USA (Courtesy of the Institution of Gas Engineers)*

239

## Storage of Liquefied Natural Gas

The need to store natural gas as a liquid in bulk arises from two considerations. Firstly, buffer stocks are required at the production and terminal ends when LNG is liquefied for transport, which is mainly by ship. Secondly, the modern trend is for large gas-supply undertakings to store LNG to meet extreme peak gas demands. Normally this would be produced by liquefying off-peak gas.

Currently tanks of from 50 000 to 70 000 tonnes of LNG capacity are available according to type. The forms used so far are above-ground double-walled metal tanks, below-ground frozen-earth storage and pre-stressed-concrete tanks which may be below ground to any desired extent. Mined cavities in rock, which are economical for LPG and naphtha, have not so far been used for LNG; they are attractive in the sense that operation at pressure would be feasible, but various technical and economic problems remain to be solved.

Although small satellite LNG storage vessels operate under pressures of the order of 4 bars gauge, all the bulk-storage systems described above are operated at <0·1 bar gauge. It is unlikely that it will prove economical to design for pressures above this level (106).

All bulk storage tanks have self-supporting (free-span) roofs. Those that are sited above ground are diked, ie bunded, either individually or in groups. This, together with the high standards used in their design and construction, renders them as safe as light-spirit storage tanks from the fire hazard point of view.

Although they are not comprehensive, standards covering many important aspects of design are already set in the USA by the American Petroleum Institute's Standard 620. No doubt this will be extended. Other countries are considering the adoption of these standards, or the establishment of comparable ones.

One comparison of the approximate estimated cost, under UK conditions, of construction of the various storage systems now available (106) indicates that currently the above-ground double-walled tank is the lower in cost, and more predictable in behaviour than the alternatives in the capacity range up to 20 000 tonnes likely to be required for peak shaving (Figure 74). In addition, although it has to be bunded, and is more obtrusive than either form of below-ground storage, it is less subject to geological constraints, as far as siting is concerned, than in-ground storage.

For the construction of larger tanks one or other of the designs involving the use of pre-stressed concrete, possibly metal lined, is likely to prove more economical (107).

240

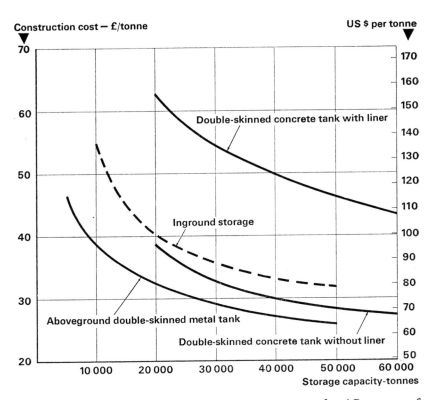

**Construction cost — £/tonne**

**US $ per tonne**

Double-skinned concrete tank with liner

Inground storage

Aboveground double-skinned metal tank

Double-skinned concrete tank without liner

Storage capacity-tonnes

*Figure 74    Approximate costs of LNG storage tanks (Courtesy of The Gas Council)*

In all cases there is a boil-off of natural gas due to heat transfer from ambient media. An appraisal of the economic optimum boil-off rate for a 20 000-ton above-ground steel storage tank to be used for peak shaving resulted in an estimate of 0·04% per day (108). This rate would be much less critical at, for example, a loading terminal provided with useful outlets for the boil-off.

Another important disadvantage of boil-off is the change that it can produce in the composition of the LNG. Where this cannot be tolerated, a small re-liquefaction system, as described in Chapter 16, can be used.

**1    Above-Ground Metallic Tanks**
All above-ground metallic tanks built so far are double walled. The inner wall is of 9% nickel-steel or aluminium alloy; carbon steel is

241

used for the outer wall. A powdered or fine granular insulating material such as perlite is used for the walls and roof. In order to prevent pressure on the inner tank, arising from compression of the wall insulation through compaction resulting from thermal movement of the tank wall, a resilient lining is provided on the outside of the inner metal wall. The space between the two metal shells is maintained at a pressure slightly above atmospheric, by the use of either nitrogen or natural gas.

The general arrangement of the tank described above is shown in Figure 75 together with two versions of a recently introduced design feature for suspended-roof construction. This modification allows all the components subject to the roof design pressure to be transferred to the outer container, thus allowing the components to be constructed in mild steel, thereby reducing the cost of the tank.

## 2 Pre-Stressed Concrete LNG Storage Tanks

The suitability of pre-stressed concrete for the construction of tanks for the storage of LNG and other cryogens has been investigated in the USA and confirmed in practice, for example by LNG tanks at Barcelona in Spain, and Staten Island, USA. The view has been expressed that for the largest capacity tanks that may be built in the future, it should prove more appropriate than metals (107). This view is attributed mainly to the relatively greater resistance that a pre-stressed reinforced tank would offer to buckling, but also to its lower expansion coefficient.

A number of designs have been proposed for above and below ground or partly below ground tanks, with and without metallic inner linings or outer casings.

In the design for a tank on order for Stuttgart (109), where safety considerations are even more than usually important, a pre-stressed reinforced-concrete outer wall surrounds a self-standing pressure-resistant nickel-steel inner tank. Perlite insulation will be used for the roof, and the insulation between the steel tank and the concrete casing will be 'Styrpor' panels (300 mm), and mineral-wool panels (1 000 mm), all maintained under 50 mm water gauge nitrogen pressure. The whole tank will be surrounded by earth back-filling.

In another design (110) the roles of steel and pre-stressed reinforced concrete are reversed (Figure 76). An inner concrete tank, with which the LNG will be in contact, is insulated mainly with perlite and surrounded by a carbon-steel pressure tank. The perlite insulation space will be blanketed with dry natural gas and the pressure equalized between this and the inner tank. The insulation is

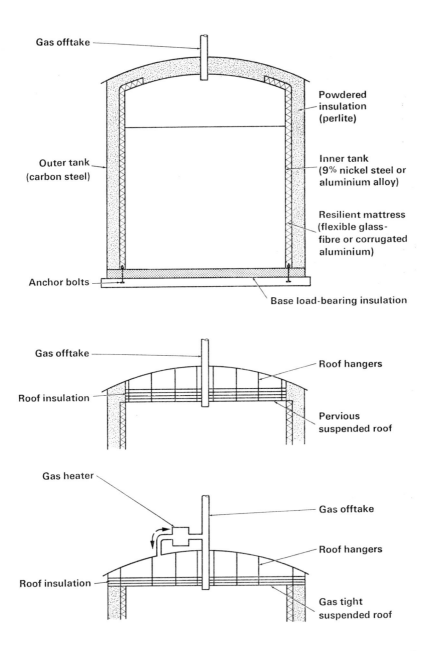

*Figure 75* *General arrangement of conventional double-wall LNG storage tank and alternative roof designs (Courtesy of the International Institute of Refrigeration)*

243

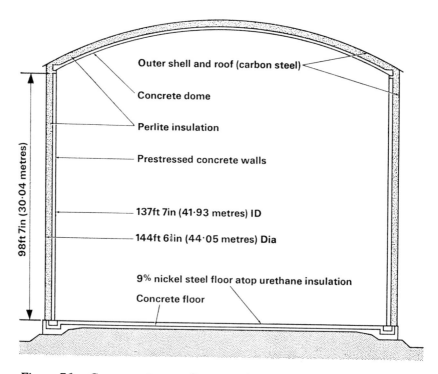

98ft 7in (30·04 metres)

Outer shell and roof (carbon steel)

Concrete dome

Perlite insulation

Prestressed concrete walls

137ft 7in (41·93 metres) ID

144ft 6⅜in (44·05 metres) Dia

9% nickel steel floor atop urethane insulation

Concrete floor

*Figure 76    Cross-section and general dimensions of pre-stressed reinforced concrete and steel LNG storage tank (Courtesy of The Preload Engineering Company, USA)*

designed to limit the heat influx to 300 000 Btu (316 MJ) per hour, equivalent to roughly 0·1 % boil-off per day.

Figure 77 shows a number of optional configurations for concrete tanks, most of which do not require metallic wall linings or casings.

### 3    Frozen In-Ground Storage of LNG

Frozen in-ground storage, in common with a completely in-ground concrete tank, is less obtrusive and more compact than above-ground storage. The fire risk should also be at its minimum. An in-ground unit with a capacity of 16 000 tonnes was installed without difficulty at Arzew in Algeria, and operated successfully. It appeared, therefore, that this type of construction would prove competitive with steel-walled tanks elsewhere, at least for storage units of 20 000 tonnes or more.

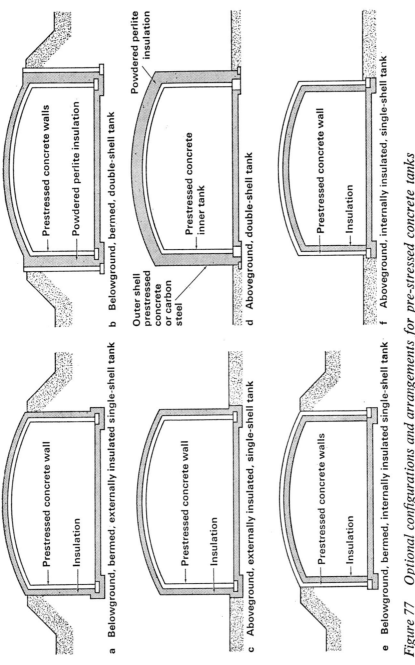

**a** Belowground, bermed, externally insulated single-shell tank

Prestressed concrete wall

Insulation

**b** Belowground, bermed, double-shell tank

Prestressed concrete walls

Powdered perlite insulation

**c** Aboveground, externally insulated, single-shell tank

Prestressed concrete wall

Insulation

**d** Aboveground, double-shell tank

Powdered perlite insulation

Prestressed concrete inner tank

Outer shell prestressed concrete or carbon steel

**e** Belowground, bermed, internally insulated single-shell tank

Prestressed concrete walls

Insulation

**f** Aboveground, internally insulated, single-shell tank

Prestressed concrete wall

Insulation

*Figure 77  Optional configurations and arrangements for pre-stressed concrete tanks
(Courtesy of The Preload Engineering Company, USA)*

245

Four units of the design shown in Figure 78, each of 21 000 tonnes, were subsequently constructed at an LNG reception terminal at Canvey Island in the UK. Construction proved more lengthy and costly than anticipated and the boil-off rate was substantially higher than expected. It emerged that the behaviour of the frozen ground, and the possibility of irregular upward and lateral movement resulting from frost heave, is difficult to predict in new circumstances. Currently for UK conditions, concrete tanks and above-ground metallic tanks are likely to prove less costly overall, especially when the process costs involved in the higher boil-off rate from underground storage are taken into account.

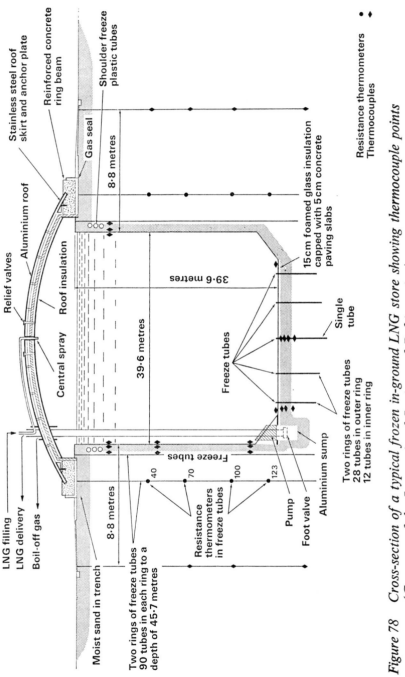

*Figure 78  Cross-section of a typical frozen in-ground LNG store showing thermocouple points (Courtesy of the International Institute of Refrigeration)*

247

*Chapter 19*     Applications of Natural Gas and Other
Gaseous Fuels in Industry

Gaseous fuels are available at the turn of a valve and are easily controlled. Used on a wide variety of burner types, they can produce a range of shapes, sizes and qualities of flames beyond the scope of other fuels. Their waste gases are free from solid particles, and with few exceptions are sufficiently low in sulphur content to produce no corrosion, although their nitrogen-oxides content is comparable to that of waste gases from other fuels.

Natural gas, liquefied petroleum gases and manufactured gas can therefore fulfil most industrial-fuel roles more cleanly, more conveniently and in many cases more efficiently than other fuels.

These advantages are at their minimum in large-scale fuel-intensive industries such as power generation, industrial steam raising, steel and iron making and cement manufacture, where solid and liquid fuels are used with high efficiency. The superiority of gaseous fuels in this area, expressed as a cost advantage on a heat unit basis, varies from nil to 1·3 : 1. These are arbitrarily termed low-premium uses.

In most small-scale industrial-fuel uses, and in some substantial-scale uses in low-fuel-intensive industries, gaseous fuels show to greater advantage. These are arbitrarily termed high-premium uses, showing cost advantages per heat unit of from 1·3 : 1 to 3 : 1, the highest premium values being achieved in plants specifically designed to make the best use of the gaseous fuel.

The upgrading of solid fuel into the gaseous state and delivering it to industry involves a cost increase on a heat-unit basis comparable to the highest premiums arising from the use of the gas. Gas made from such materials under present-day conditions, therefore, would find little use in fuel-intensive industries. The use of hydrocarbon oils as gas-making feedstock involves less cost and improves the prospects of gas in industry, but even gas made in this way would demand a premium value in use of the order of 2 : 1 or 3 : 1 to be economical.

In contrast, natural gas in many areas is available on such a scale that, after meeting the demands of domestic and commercial users where gaseous fuels command the highest premiums, and also those of high-premium industrial users, there is sufficient to overflow at such prices that it can compete for the lowest premium uses. In extreme cases it may still be competitive even where it is less efficient and less

248

convenient than the alternative fuels, as may be the case when it is used for cement making.

The principal industrial uses for fuels of all kinds are set out in Table 41. The potential range of application of the three principal fuel gases over the industrial area is indicated.

The first group of uses shown are almost exclusive to LPG since they are dependent on its transportation and storage in the liquid phase. In times of war, town gas has been used for vehicle propulsion, and natural gas, either under pressure or liquefied, is currently being experimented with for this use. These applications, however, are unlikely to become extensive, though LNG will become a contender with liquid hydrogen and hydrocarbon fuels for hypersonic aircraft if and when they evolve.

The second group consists of the high-premium uses in which manufactured gas, in spite of its cost, can compete with solid and liquid fuels.

The third group comprises applications in which the premium for a gaseous fuel is insufficient to render town gas economical, but sufficient in some areas to render natural gas and butane economical.

The last group comprises industries using massive quantities of fuel, in which gaseous fuels show to the minimum advantage.

The fuel applications shown in Table 41 cover, for practical purposes, the whole of industry. Many industries generate steam and power and these operations have been indicated separately in order to show the effect of scale on their potential for fuel-gas application.

This method of presenting the fuel-gas potential of industry is over-simplified, which is essential in a brief treatment. Practically every major industry involves a whole range of operations demanding either fuel or power on vastly differing scales. The scale of these demands will be a major factor in determining whether or not a gaseous fuel is the most economical. It follows therefore that the separate functions within each industry can be viewed in a similar manner to that in which the whole of industry is viewed in Table 41.

When this is done it may be that, to take the extreme example of an integrated steel works, the simultaneous use of coal, coke, a range of fuel oils, liquefied petroleum gases, manufactured coal gas, producer gas, and blast-furnace gas can be shown to be economical.

At the other extreme lies the 'total-energy' concept whereby a single fuel source is used, firstly to meet the electrical energy demand and secondly to meet the heat demands by means of the pass-out steam and/or hot waste gases arising from the power generation, or by degrading part of the power back into heat. As thus defined, few

249

industries other than electricity undertakings are likely to find the total-energy concept practical or economical, firstly because of the difficulty of balancing the electrical energy demand and the pass-out heat demands, and secondly because of demands in other, more appropriate, energy forms for particular functions. Even if the definition is relaxed to include the use of part of the fuel independently of power production, it would still be highly restrictive if the main fuel source was coal or fuel oil, but less so if it was gas.

A more enlightened approach to on-site power production in industry than the total-energy concept is to determine the low-grade process-heat requirement in the form either of steam or hot waste gas. Where the supply of this is demanded on a scale sufficient to justify the installation of on-site power plant, after allowing for the cost of appropriate standby equipment if any, this can be done. The remainder of the fuel and power requirements can be provided in the most appropriate and economical manner.

Examples of actual or potential applications of fuel gases under the heads of the first three groups of industries shown in Table 41 are set out below but, as explained above, some uses for LPG and other fuel gases, *eg* space heating, can be found in factories in all industries.

## Examples of Actual and Potential Applications of Fuel Gases in Industry

### Group 1

*Civil Engineering and Other Site Uses*
These applications are manifold and, in the absence of piped gas, normally involve the use of LPG. They include the provision of personnel amenities such as space heating, hot water and cooking facilities. Building materials can be de-frosted, surfacing materials melted, and metals cut, brazed, soldered, melted or heated for bending. Apart from these heating functions LPG will also floodlight the site.

*Agricultural Uses*
Carbon dioxide enrichment of glasshouse atmospheres, by the combustion of gas, is a widely accepted technique for accelerating growth and increasing yields. So also is the practice of heating livestock pens.

New applications of gas firing for crop drying are continually being developed, largely because of the capability for effecting drying by direct contact without contaminating the crop. Gas is also used for curing and processing tobacco.

*Table 41*    *Potential industrial applications of fuel gases*

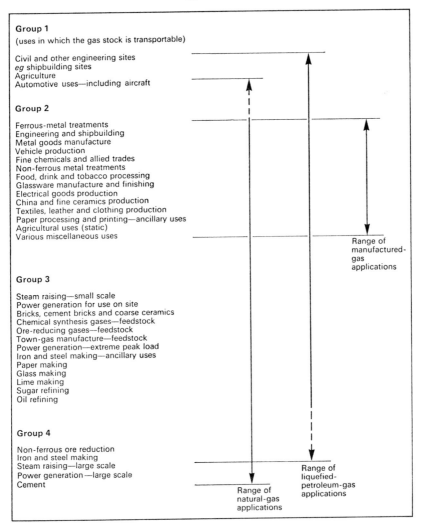

**Group 1**
(uses in which the gas stock is transportable)

Civil and other engineering sites
*eg* shipbuilding sites
Agriculture
Automotive uses—including aircraft

**Group 2**

Ferrous-metal treatments
Engineering and shipbuilding
Metal goods manufacture
Vehicle production
Fine chemicals and allied trades
Non-ferrous metal treatments
Food, drink and tobacco processing
Glassware manufacture and finishing
Electrical goods production
China and fine ceramics production
Textiles, leather and clothing production
Paper processing and printing—ancillary uses
Agricultural uses (static)
Various miscellaneous uses

Range of manufactured-gas applications

**Group 3**

Steam raising—small scale
Power generation for use on site
Bricks, cement bricks and coarse ceramics
Chemical synthesis gases—feedstock
Ore-reducing gases—feedstock
Town-gas manufacture—feedstock
Power generation—extreme peak load
Iron and steel making—ancillary uses
Paper making
Glass making
Lime making
Sugar refining
Oil refining

**Group 4**

Non-ferrous ore reduction
Iron and steel making
Steam raising—large scale
Power generation—large scale
Cement

Range of natural-gas applications

Range of liquefied-petroleum-gas applications

251

*Automotive Uses*
It is assumed that the use of LPG to propel road-vehicle engines in normal circumstances, if taxed comparably with petrol, would be uneconomical. It is also assumed that the limited contribution that its use would make to the reduction of pollution would not be used to justify tax remission generally.

On the basis of the above assumptions the uses of LPG in this field are likely to be limited to those set out below:

As auxiliary fuel in diesel engines for use when under maximum load

As an alternative to petrol in dual-fuel vehicles, for use in conditions where pollution could demand it, *eg* for vehicles operating on factory floors or in congested shopping areas

As a fuel for purpose-built engines of public-transport vehicles, *eg* taxis and omnibuses operating in congested areas.

In aviation LPG is less attractive than currently used fuels in present circumstances, and less attractive than LNG in the concept of hypersonic aviation.

**Group 2**

*Ferrous-Metal and Non-Ferrous-Metal Treatments; Engineering and Shipbuilding; Metal-Goods Manufacture; Vehicle Production*
The heat treatments of metals are among the most important industrial uses of all gaseous fuels. Gases are used to provide heat for the following types of operation in the above-mentioned industrial activities.

Reheat and soaking pits

Reversing regenerative furnaces for general heat treatments

Furnace-heating billets for rolling into wire

Annulus heating of 'lift-off' bright annealing furnaces

Heating non-ferrous rods prior to extruding

High-velocity heating for stress relieving of pipework and vessels

Bale-out furnaces in die-casting

Aluminium slab heating and heating of liquid-holding furnaces

Rapid heating of massive billets by direct impingement of hot products of combustion

Firing zinc galvanizing tanks

Steel straight hardening, carburizing, carbon nitriding

Non-ferrous metal melting

Precious metal refining

Turbine-blade mould firing

Heating of steel plates prior to blasting and protective coating
Gas/air mixture is fed to externally heated catalytic reformers to produce controlled atmospheres for reducing, or neutral atmospheres for metal heat treatments.

*Metal Goods Manufacture; Shipbuilding; Vehicle Production; Electrical Goods Production*
The direct-fired drying of paints, and stove enamel protective surfaces on metal parts or metal strip. In the latter case forced-convection ovens using high-velocity ejector nozzles may be employed.
Metal cutting and welding
Vitreous enamelling either in muffle or continuous furnaces.

*Fine Chemicals and Allied Trades*
The provision of heat for small-scale endothermic reactions
The concentration or drying out of solutions
Heat for solvent and other extraction processes.

*Food and Drink Processing*
The superiority of gaseous fuels in food processing stems not only from ease of control but also from their purity, which permits direct heating. The combustion products cannot contaminate the food. Examples of these processes are as follows:
Baking bread, biscuits and cakes
Confectionery and soft-drink manufacture
Barley drying to 2% moisture for maltsters
Meat and prepared-cereals processing
The spray-drying of food such as potato granules
Milk and soup concentration or drying
Preparation of meat extracts and concentrates.

*Glassware Manufacture and Finishing; Electrical Goods Production*
The main purpose of gaseous fuels in glassware manufacturing and finishing, and those aspects of electrical-goods manufacture involving glassware, lies in the following processes:
Glass melting and tempering furnaces
Annealing
Numerous second-stage finishing processes in the production of bottles, electric light bulbs, fluorescent tubes, vacuum ware, and any operations involving the use of large numbers of sharp-pointed flames

253

Welding together sections of cathode-ray tubes
Glass-wool and slag-wool production.

### China and Fine Ceramics Production

As with food processing it is not only ease of control but the purity of the products of combustion of fuel gases that justifies their use in fine ceramics.

Furthermore the flexibility, and the close control of temperature profile and atmosphere composition that they permit, result in increased output, improved product quality and reduced losses.

These considerations apply over practically the whole range of china, high-grade sanitary ware, and high-grade earthenware.

### Textiles, Leather and Clothing Production

Sulphur-free atmospheres of controlled temperature and humidity have many applications in the treatment of textiles, leather and clothing, such as degreasing, dying and latex treatment. Gaseous fuels are particularly suitable for these applications.

### Paper Processing and Printing

Gaseous fuels may be used for the drying of paper or print by direct heating.

### Agricultural Uses

Where the agricultural functions set out under this head in Group 1 are within the reach of piped fuel gas, this will be competitive with LPG.


## Group 3

### Small-Scale Steam Raising

The economic balance that justifies the use of the lowest-price fuels for steam raising for any purpose on a massive scale rapidly changes with the reduction in scale. This leads to the use of natural gas or, in the absence of natural gas, first to the use of middle distillates and then to LPG and finally even to manufactured gas.

### Bricks and Other Coarse Ceramics; Cement Blocks

In the heavy clay industry the ousting of solid fuels by natural gas and butane is not only enabling manufacturers to meet the provisions of Clean Air legislation but it also gives economic benefits.

The special advantage of these gases in the ceramics industry lies in their purity, and the flexibility and temperature-profile control they permit; these result in increased output, and particularly in improved product quality and reduced losses. They are also very suitable for producing the steam/waste-gas atmosphere needed for the rapid curing of cast breeze and cement blocks.

*Chemical Synthesis Feedstock*
Natural gas at high pressure has a marginal premium value over LDF for the large-scale production of hydrogen or mixtures of carbon oxides and hydrogen needed for hydrocarbon-oil reforming, the synthesis of ammonia, methanol and other chemicals, and the reduction of ores. The value of liquefied petroleum gases is intermediate between that of natural gas and LDF in these applications. LPG is used on a large scale in the USA for the production of ethylene, butadiene and acetyl chemicals.

*Town-Gas Manufacture*
In high-flame-speed town-gas manufacture, natural gas and LPG have the following uses:
As sources of enrichment for lean gases (*eg* continuous reformer gas) made from either LPG or LDF
As natural-gas/air, or LPG/air, they are used to supply entire small communities, or as peak-shaving devices.

*Power Generation Peak Load and Other Uses*
LPG is employed for starting up solid-fuel and oil-fired boilers supplying turbo generators. It is a potential standby fuel for gas turbine generating equipment run on interruptible gas supplies. Its use for peak-load turbines will be economical in some circumstances.

*Iron and Steelmaking — Ancillary Uses*
The high price and developing shortage of coke, and the current fall in the value of coke-oven gas, is producing changes in the steel-works' fuel balances. Although fuel oil is normally the most economical auxiliary fuel for application at *tuyére* level in order to replace coke, natural gas and LPG can be used if available at a lower price thermally.
LPG is an alternative to LDF for the enrichment of blast-furnace gas. A reported novel use of LPG is that of under-firing coke ovens, to release the coal gas so used, in order that the latter can be devoted to town-gas supply during periods of peak output.

255

*Paper Making*
The main heat requirement for paper making is for steam raising, but this may be outside the economic range of some fuel gases. LPG is used as an auxiliary fuel, for example to provide radiant heat or a drying atmosphere exterior to the steam-heated drying drums, thereby producing a worthwhile saving in steam.

*Lime Burning*
The increasing relative cost of solid fuels is leading to the use of alternative fuels for lime burning. Particularly in small-to-moderate-scale operations, the use of hot gases made by the partial combustion of fuel oil, or alternatively the use of natural gas or unreformed LPG, is becoming more economical.

*Sugar Refining*
The principal use for fuel in this industry is for steam-raising. Therefore, when operated on a large scale, fuel gases can compete on terms approaching price equality only on a thermal basis. Small-scale operations of this kind, where they exist out of reach of natural-gas supplies, are possible subjects for conversion to LPG.

## The Effect of Fuel-Gas Characteristics on Utilization

The basic characteristics affecting the combustion of gases and their interchangeability are the Wobbe number, defined as the calorific value of the gas divided by the square root of its density, and the flame speed, usually expressed on an arbitrary scale on which hydrogen is deemed to be 100 (Table 42). The manner in which these characteristics affect gas utilization, and the limits, expressed diagrammatically, within which they can be varied without demanding the adjustment, adaptation or replacement of the appliance burners using the gas, is dealt with in Chapter 1.

Also in Chapter 1 it is stated that in order to maintain a given degree of pre-aeration of the gas fed to an aerated burner, the gas modulus, M — defined as the square root of the pressure divided by

Wobbe Number: $M = \left(\dfrac{\sqrt{P_1}}{W_1}\right)$ — must remain constant. Gas pressure

must be increased in proportion to the square of the change in Wobbe Number. The practical effect of this for the principal types of fuel gas is shown in Table 43.

Characteristics that may affect the utilization of fuel gases in industry, not referred to in Chapter 1, are now dealt with.

## Table 42    Characteristics of fuel gases

| | Modern high-flame-speed gases | | Low-flame-speed gases | | |
|---|---|---|---|---|---|
| | Cyclic reformer gas | Enriched continuous reformer gas | North Sea natural gas | Commercial propane/air | Commercial butane/air |
| Specific gravity (air=1·0) | 0·550 | 0·470 | 0·618 | 1·166 | 1·256 |
| Calorific value   Btu/ft³stp(sat) | 500 | 500 | 1033 | 787 | 815 |
|          MJ/m³(st) | 18·98 | 18·98 | 39·20 | 29·87 | 30·94 |
| Wobbe number    UK† | 674 | 730 | 1315 | 730 | 730 |
|          SI* | 25·69 | 27·71 | 49·92 | 27·71 | 27·71 |
| Weaver flame-speed factor 'S' | 40·4 | 39·9 | 14·1 | 16·0 | 16·0 |
| Organic sulphur    ppm w/w | 100 | 15** | 15** | 25** | 25** |

**Stenching additive

$$\text{†Wobbe Number UK} = \frac{\text{cal val Btu/ft}^3\text{stp(sat)}}{\sqrt{\text{sp gr}}}$$

$$\text{*Wobbe Number SI} = \frac{\text{cal val MJ/m}^3\text{(st)}}{\sqrt{\text{sp gr}}}$$

## Table 43    Gauge gas pressures required to maintain the gas modulus (M) constant, assuming 2 inches water gauge is adequate for gas with a Wobbe Number of 730 (27·71 IGU metric units).

| | UK units 30 in Hg 60°F (sat) $M = \sqrt{\dfrac{2 \text{ in water gauge}}{730}}$ | | SI units 1013 mbar 15°C (dry) $M = \sqrt{\dfrac{5 \text{ mbar gauge}}{27·67}}$ | |
|---|---|---|---|---|
| | Wobbe number | Gas pressure in W G | Wobbe number | Gas pressure mbar gauge |
| High-flame-speed gas | 730 | 2·0 | 27·71 | 5 |
| Commercial propane/air | 730 | 2·0 | 27·71 | 5 |
| Commercial butane/air | 730 | 2·0 | 27·71 | 5 |
| Natural gas (North Sea) | 1315 | 6·5 | 49·92 | 16 |
| Commercial propane gas | 1990 | 14·8 | 75·54 | 37 |
| Commercial butane gas | 2270 | 19·4 | 86·17 | 48 |

Note:
1 mbar (gauge) = 0·75 mm Hg (gauge) = 0·4 inch water gauge

257

**Emissivity**

The emissivity of the clear aerated flames of fuel gases is low compared with that of fuel oil or coal flames. Even the diffusion flames of fuel gases have very low radiating capacity and intrinsic luminosity (Table 44). Natural gas is similar, but LPG substantially better, in this respect, compared with modern manufactured gases. Undebenzolized coal-gas flames have the highest intrinsic luminosity of all fuel-gas flames but are unsatisfactory in other respects, and this gas is therefore debenzolized before distribution.

For most appliances designed to use gas, emissivity is of no great importance, since clear flames can be used to produce radiating surfaces, and further, the clean combustion products from clean flames can be circulated at high velocities against conducting surfaces. By these means the lower level of flame radiation is offset. Alternatively, the lower emissivity of gas flames, compared with fuel-oil or coal flames, can be offset by raising the flame temperature to the level at which the increased radiation from carbon dioxide and water vapour offsets to the desired extent the effect of the lower free-carbon content of the flame. The preheat involved in this technique may not be costly and will result in increased efficiency if effected by means of a self-recuperative burner as described on page 265.

*Table 44    Diffusion flame emissivities and gross/net calorific value differences of various fuels*

| Fuel | Emissivity (Black body=1·0) | Difference between gross and net calorific value    % |
|------|------------------------------|-------------------------------------------------------|
| Town gas }<br>Natural gas } | 0·20 or less | 10 |
| Liquefied petroleum gas | 0·40 | 8 |
| Gas oil | 0·60 | 6 |
| Fuel oil | 0·85 | 6 |
| Bituminous coal | 0·95* | 4 |
| Anthracite | — | 2 |

*Pulverized

When gas is used in plant originally designed to take full advantage of flame radiation (for instance, open-hearth furnaces and to a smaller extent glass tanks) a problem arises that demands burner and plant modification. One solution in these circumstances is to produce a radiating flame by two-stage combustion, the first stage of which is designed to produce carbon. This technique, though successful with natural gas and LPG, is impracticable with high-flame-speed gas.

Many installations using non-gaseous fuel, *eg* steam raising plant, though designed to take into account high flame radiation, are not dependent upon it for efficient operation, and suitably designed gas burners in many cases can maintain rated output and efficiency. Burners designed to thermally crack part of the feed gas are helpful in this context (111).


### Carbon/Hydrogen Ratio

The carbon/hydrogen ratio of fuel gases, whether manufactured or otherwise, is substantially lower than that of alternative fuels. As a result the latent-heat content of the waste gases is substantially higher in the products of combustion from gaseous fuels. Since it is normally uneconomical to recover this heat, resultant stack losses, with a given waste-gas temperature, are greater with gaseous fuels than with alternative fuels.

The measure of this difference is shown in Table 44. Frequently the loss of efficiency from this cause is counteracted by the effects arising from the relative ease of control of gas burners, and the cleanliness of the flame and combustion products.


### Sulphur Content

As can be seen from Table 42, the sulphur content of all the gases shown is so low as to present no obstacle, in the form of corrosion by oxides of sulphur, to the utmost economic degree of heat exchange with waste gases. Coal gas, not shown in the table, would be an exception to this unless treated for the removal of organic sulphur.


### Gas-Burner Design and the Conversion of High-Flame-Speed Gas Appliances to Natural Gas

Currently small diffusion burners on appliances designed for high-flame-speed gas are replaced by aerated burners on change-over to LPG or natural gas; otherwise the slower-burning flames would lift off the burner before more than a fraction of the rated thermal output had been reached. The relative flame-speed factors are given in Table 42.

259

The conversion of low-pressure self-aerated burners, in its simplest form, involves reductions for two purposes in the primary-jet aperture area. The first, to allow for higher Wobbe Number ($W_2$) of natural gas, would involve reducing the orifice area roughly in inverse ratio to the Wobbe Number change, $ie$ $\dfrac{W_1}{W_2} = \dfrac{730}{1315}$. This would maintain the thermal discharge at the pressure $P_1$ used for the high-flame-speed gas. This pressure must now be increased to $P_2$ so that the gas modulus is maintained constant in order to maintain unchanged the pre-aeration: $M = \dfrac{\sqrt{P_1}}{W_1} = \dfrac{\sqrt{P_2}}{W_2}$. This means that the orifice pressure must be increased directly as the square of the Wobbe Number change: $\dfrac{P_2}{P_1} = \left(\dfrac{W_2}{W_1}\right)^2 = \left(\dfrac{1315}{730}\right)^2$. Since the gas discharge is proportional to the square root of this pressure, this would involve an increase in thermal output in the proportion 1315/730. To correct this a second reduction in the primary-jet area, roughly in inverse ratio to the change in Wobbe Number, would be required.

These changes in the area of the primary-jet arise from the higher Wobbe Number of natural gas. If natural-gas/air or LPG/air is used, of a Wobbe Number equal to that of the high-flame-speed gas replaced, no change is necessary. On the other hand if undiluted LPG vapour is used, a greater reduction in primary-jet area is demanded, since LPG Wobbe Numbers exceed those of natural gas (Table 43).

With the delivery to the flame-port area of the same thermal equivalent of natural gas, with the same proportion of its stoichiometric air as for former high-flame-speed gas supply, there remains the great difference in flame speed, which would result in the flames leaving the burner unless action was taken to avoid it. This action normally takes either or both of the forms of an increase in the flame-port area, or the introduction of a flame-stabilization device such as those shown in Figure 79.

Finally, stable natural-gas flames having been produced of corresponding thermal output to that of high-flame-speed gas, the issue arises of whether there is sufficient combustion space above the burners to allow for the slower combustion rate of the LPG or natural gas. If there is not, and an appropriate de-rating cannot be accepted, it may be possible to achieve it by re-siting the burner; otherwise re-design of burner or combustion space becomes necessary.

Although current practice in the UK and elsewhere involves the conversion of the diffusion (neat) flame burners used in domestic, commercial and small industrial appliances to aerated burners, the

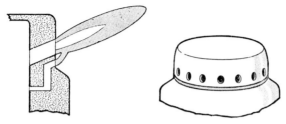

**Auxiliary flame**

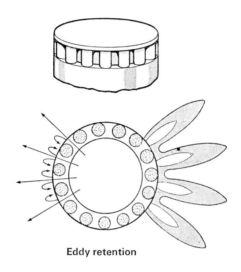

**Eddy retention**

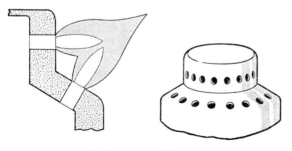

**Impingement of flames**

*Figure 79   Flame stabilization devices for small-scale self-aerated burners (Courtesy of the Institution of Gas Engineers)*

261

search continues for small stable diffusion-flame burners for the combustion of natural gas and LPG.

Three versions of stable non-aerated burners are (1971) under test for domestic and commercial uses in the UK (112). These are shown in Figure 80 and operate as follows:

*(a)  The Pinhole Burner*
This is supplied with gas at a pressure of 200 mm water gauge, which issues from a row of pinhole jets provided with minute retention flames on both sides.

*(b)  The Uniplane Burner*
Gas is discharged through a slit at the base of the wall and the flame is retained by the grid shown.

*(c)  The British Petroleum Company Matrix Burner*
This operates on a different principle from those of the other burners shown. Gas issues at low pressure, and with a low efflux velocity, from a matrix of slits produced by the juxtaposition of a number of hexagonal tube heads. The air supply is naturally induced by means of a slight flue effect and emerges through the hexagonal outlets. This burner, operated under pressure, will no doubt also find industrial uses (113).

**Design and Conversion of Large-Scale Industrial Gas Burners**
The problems associated with flame speed and Wobbe Number, arising in the design of burners for low-flame-speed gases (natural gas and LPG) or in the conversion of burners from the use of one gas type to another, are more readily overcome in the case of many large-scale gas-using appliances than with domestic and commercial appliances. This is mainly owing to the following advantages of the large-scale installations:

Higher gas pressure is available.

The air supply may be forced, or more effectively induced by fan or flue effect.

The cost of flame-stabilization devices can more readily be borne.

Pilot flames, if used, can be larger and therefore less vulnerable.

Although it is desirable to minimize burner noise, standards can be relaxed relative to those demanded in domestic and commercial establishments.

Burner maintenance facilities are more readily available.

On the other hand, however, the scope of the requirements deman-

262

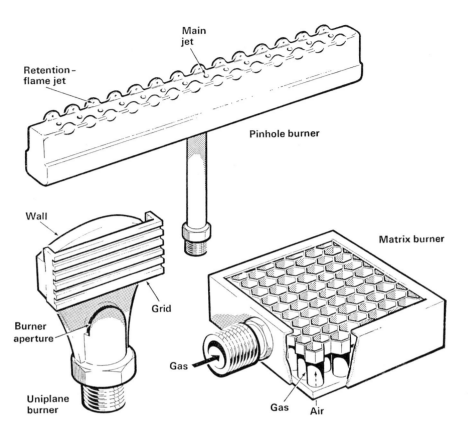

*Figure 80    Non-aerated burners for natural gas (Courtesy of the Institution of Gas Engineers)*

ded of large industrial burners in terms of efficiency of combustion, speed of heating, intensity of heat-release, flame characteristics, automatic operation and safety, transcends that of smaller burners. On balance, therefore, the techniques employed in the design or adaptation of these large burners are even more refined than those employed for small low-pressure types.

Some of the devices used to stabilize the flames of domestic, commercial and small industrial burners are applied to large industrial burners. An example of the use of flame impingement on an industrial burner of a capacity up to 400 000 Btu/h (117 kWh) is shown in Figure 81.

Alternatively, various aerodynamic devices depending upon the greater gas and/or air pressure available on large industrial installations can be used to increase the stability of the flames. The two-stage aeration injector shown in Figure 82 is one of a number of such devices, using starting gas pressures up to 2 bars gauge or more. This can feed a highly aerated gas mixture at a high pressure to various configurations of burners at rates up to 1 500 000 Btu/h (440 kW). Such highly aerated or stoichiometric mixtures of gas and air at pressure are less likely to require flame-stabilizing devices than less well aerated low-pressure mixtures.

The passage of the flame through a refractory-lined tube or tunnel, the playing of it upon a high-temperature surface, or the pre-heat of the air and/or the gas, are all of use in stabilizing the flames of low-

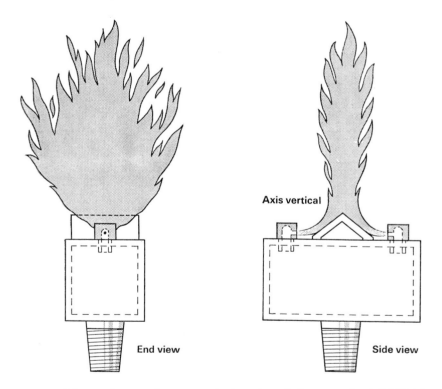

*Figure 81    Multi-gas burner with fan-shaped flame — the SE-NEAT burner (Courtesy of Aeromatic Company Limited)*

264

flame-speed gases, although in most cases they will be contrived for other purposes. This is the case with the self-recuperative burner (114) shown in Figure 83.

The scope of the various flame characteristics that can be produced for use in industry using high-flame-speed gas is great and extends beyond the range of other fuels. With few exceptions, burners exhibiting this range of shapes, sizes and other qualities can readily be adapted to the use of natural gas and liquefied petroleum gases.

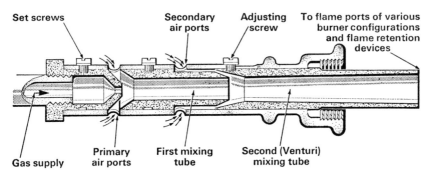

*Figure 82    Two-stage gas injector (Courtesy of Aeromatic Company Limited)*

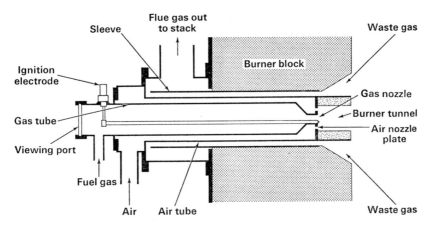

*Figure 83    Self-recuperative burner (Courtesy of the Institution of Gas Engineers)*

265

PART THREE    THE EFFECT OF LOAD VARIATION
              AND FEEDSTOCK OR NATURAL-
              GAS AVAILABILITY ON THE TECH-
              NIQUES OF GAS MANUFACTURE
              AND NATURAL-GAS SUPPLY


Chapter 20    Gas Output Load-Variations and their Effect
              on Gas Production


## Variability of Gas Outputs and the Role of Gas-Storage Plant

The rate of gas output in town-gas systems varies throughout the day; the maximum rate is usually many times the minimum. The primary storage capacity required to meet these variations, and cover the daily output when the rate of gas manufacture is constant, can readily be calculated. In many European systems it is equivalent to approximately 20% of their peak day's output.

The capital cost of high-pressure or low-pressure gas-storage plant is such that it is economical to provide only for this diurnal variation storage plus a reserve of capacity, determined by experience, to meet such contingencies as interruptions in gas make or transmission, and the effect of errors in the prediction of make or deliveries.

Gas output normally changes considerably throughout the year. This seasonal change varies greatly from one area to another and, expressed in terms of the ratio of the maximum to the minimum day's output, many town-gas supply systems in Europe show figures of from 2:1 to 4:1, and in American natural-gas supply systems ratios of 6:1 or more are reached. Since it is uneconomical to install storage plant to meet this seasonal variation, daily gas makes are planned to meet daily outputs, and manufacturing-plant capacity of one sort or another is normally installed to meet the climatic peak day's output, although this may be reduced by planned load shedding.

The foregoing considerations do not apply where natural underground gas-storage capacity is available, such as that provided by depleted natural-gas or oil reservoirs, salt-bed cavities, or aquifers in sand or porous limestone overlaid by impermeable rocks or clay. Where this type of storage capacity is available it becomes economical to store gas in order to equalize the demands on gas-manufacture

266

plant from one season to another. In such cases the economic balance is sought between the expenditure of capital on seasonal and peak-load plant, and on the exploitation of the natural storage resources.

A typical graph showing the output variation throughout the year in a supply system with a variation of 3:1 between the predicted maximum and minimum possible daily outputs is given in Figure 84. In the hypothetical system to which this graph relates, weather is the predominant factor influencing output, and is assumed to vary considerably from average or predicted figures. In this example the winter loads have been reduced by the planned shedding of interruptible supplies.

The modern trend towards the distribution of dry gas at high pressures, affecting both manufactured and natural gas, has revolutionized the form of constructed storage plant. Such low-pressure holders as are installed are of the waterless type but, increasingly, high-pressure systems comprising groups of high-tensile-steel *bullets*, or lengths of high-tensile-steel mains, are used together with line-packing systems as dealt with in Chapter 18.

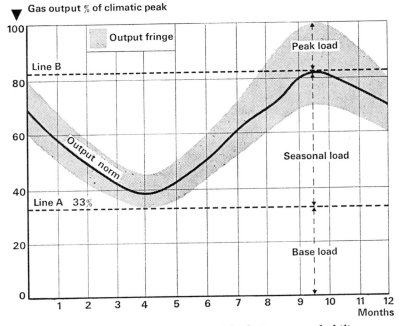

*Figure 84    Daily gas output norm with deviation probability over a period of seven years (based on no increase in normal output for the year)*

267

# Definitions of Output in Terms of Various Load Elements

It is convenient to consider the output shown in Figure 84 as being made up of the following three elements:

That below the line A, which may be termed the base load and which, with a high degree of probability, provides a 100% loading throughout the year for the plant making it.

That represented by the space between the line A and the line B, which has been arbitrarily drawn on the level of maximum normal output. This second part, termed the seasonal load, includes the greater part of the output *fringe*, as the gap between the lines of maximum and minimum output may be termed. It is therefore variable daily as well as seasonally, and provides an average load factor of approximately 50% for the plant making it.

That part of the output fringe above the line B, *ie* above the normal maximum output. This is arbitrarily termed the peak load, is entirely variable and, in a given year, might result in anything from a negligible loading to a 100% loading of the plant standing in readiness to make it.

# Economic and Technical Considerations Involved in the Provision of the Various Parts of the Gas Output

Any attempt to manufacture, by means of a single process, such incompatible elements of gas output as those described above would result in loss of efficiency, waste of capital, or both. A large modern gas undertaking, after achieving the maximum economic degree of integration of its manufacture and supply system in order to cheapen gas production and minimize output variation (possibly with the help of planned load shedding) might employ at least three techniques, each designed mainly for one of the three parts into which the output load has, somewhat arbitrarily, been divided.

The principal considerations governing the choice of these techniques are set out in the following paragraphs, under the headings of the various load elements, and show, as would be expected, a shift in emphasis from process-cost considerations for base-load gas manufacture to capital-cost considerations for the manufacture of the peak-load gas.

268

# 1  Base-Load Plant Requirements

## (a)  Process
Low process costs are of paramount importance. This involves the use of the cheapest process materials available, or increased efficiency or substantially reduced capital costs in the use of higher-grade feedstocks.

## (b)  Capital
The effect of continuous operation at full output is to minimize the capital cost per unit of gas made, and capital can therefore be invested to the maximum extent for labour saving or process efficiency.

## (c)  Operation
Maximum reliability of operation is demanded. A low level of flexibility can be tolerated.

# 2  Seasonal-Load Plant Requirements

## (a)  Process and Capital
A balance has to be maintained between process and capital costs. The emphasis shifts from process-cost considerations to capital-cost considerations as the load factor of the plant making this gas falls.

## (b)  Operation
Flexibility of operation would be required to deal with the output fringe, and the plant would need to be shut down and started up at least annually.

# 3  Peak-Load Plant Requirements

## (a)  Process
Process costs are the least important consideration. It is, however, desirable that the process labour requirement should be small in order to prevent difficulty in manning at short notice.

## (b)  Capital
Capital costs are of paramount importance, since on a unit basis they will be increased ten or even fiftyfold owing to the limited period of operation of the plant in any year. Assuming that the unit-basis capital costs for the various gas-making plants, including ancillaries, range from, say, 0·4p to 2·5p per 100 MJ of gas output on the basis of

269

full loading, then taking as an example peak-load plant operated for two weeks in a year, these costs would be increased to 10p to 65p per 100 MJ.

It is not surprising, therefore, that many expedients are used in peak-load gas manufacturing techniques to minimize the quantity of plant constructed specifically for peak-load purposes. Such expedients include bringing back into use obsolete plant and the overloading of base-load and seasonal-load plant with sacrifice of normal standards of efficiency. Normally the uses of LPG/air or natural gas are the lowest-cost climatic peak-shaving techniques.

## Effect of Load Factor in Synthesis-Gas Manufacture

Synthesis-gas and hydrogen manufacture are not subject to the influence of daily or seasonal load-variations in the same way as town-gas manufacture.

The plants making these gases should normally be maintained at high loading based on long-term planning, since the product of the synthesis can usually be stored economically on a much greater scale in terms of daily plant output than town gas. For the same reason, temporary unplanned interruptions in gas manufacture are less important.

## Chapter 21

The Modern Trend in the Selection of Gas-Making Processes in Areas beyond the Economic Transmission Range of Natural Gas

## Selection of Gas-Making Plant in Areas where Liquid Hydrocarbons are the Most Economic Basic Gas-Making Materials

### 1 Synthesis Gas and Hydrogen Manufacture from Liquid Hydrocarbons

Where light distillates are available, the trend, as with the utilization of natural gas or liquefied petroleum gas for this purpose, is towards the continuous tubular reformer operating at pressures up to 36 bars. Where heavier oils are the more economical, the normal practice is the use, at high pressures, of the 'omnivorous' Shell and Texaco processes.

### 2 Town-Gas Manufacture from Liquid Hydrocarbons

*(a)    Small-Scale Town-Gas Manufacture from Liquid Hydrocarbons*
Small supplies, say up to 150 000 ft³ (4 250 m³)/day, outside the economic gas transmission range of large gasworks, can be provided in the form of liquefield-petroleum-gas/air mixtures. Works that are required to meet an intermediate demand, in similar circumstances, say from 150 000 to five million ft³ (4 250 to 142 000 m³)/day, tend to use low-pressure processes. For example, where liquefied petroleum gases are economically available, a lean gas subsequently cold-enriched can be made by the use of continuous tubular reforming plants such as Vickers-Zimmer or Otto. For light distillates a whole range of cyclic processes capable of producing town gas direct are available. These include Onia-Gegi, MS, Silamit and UGI.

*(b)    Large-Scale Town-Gas Manufacture from Liquid Hydrocarbons*

*(i)    Liquefied Petroleum Gas Feedstocks*
Liquefied petroleum gases can be made into a lean gas, which is subsequently cold-enriched. If the final gas is not required to be under pressure or detoxified, either large-scale cyclic catalytic plants or continuous tubular reforming plants can be used; the difference in

271

the cost of the gas made is likely to be small. However, where the gas is required to be under pressure (this is becoming a requirement more often under present conditions) and detoxified, the continuous tubular reformer should produce substantially cheaper gas.

*(ii) Light Distillate Feedstocks*
The main considerations governing the choice of plant when light distillates are the economic oil fraction available are similar to those applicable to the use of liquefied petroleum gases, with the following provisos. Though it is possible to manufacture a lean gas from light distillates in cyclic plants, the use of light distillate for cold enrichment would not be legal in some countries without the payment of duty, quite apart from the practical difficulties involved. Normally, therefore, in any case where a low-pressure undetoxified gas is required from a cyclic process, a gas of town-gas quality is made direct from light distillate.

If, however, a detoxified gas at pressure is required, a lean gas can be made by the use of the ICI or some comparable version of the continuous tubular reformer. Enrichment may be effected by the use of methane, refinery gas, liquefied petroleum gases or light distillate, in the latter case by employing either the recycle hydrogenator, the catalytic rich-gas process developed by the UK Gas Research Station or the ICI (500) process. Alternatively, a town gas may be made direct in the tubular reformer, for example by the Topsøe process.

*(iii) Crude or Heavy Oil Feedstocks*
With heavy oil, as with the lighter feedstocks, the main consideration is whether or not the gas is required to be at pressure and detoxified. If it is not, the cyclic processes available, *ie* Segas and Onia-Gegi, can be used. Alternatively, for the production from heavy oil of lean gas at pressure for detoxification, the oxygen-using Shell and Texaco processes stand out. If these latter processes are used, however, a difficulty arises with regard to the enrichment of the lean gas, and this is usually resolved by using lighter materials for the purpose.

A second alternative for processing crude or heavy oil is the fluid-ized-bed gasification process of the UK Gas Council, described on page 151.

*(c) Effect of Load Element on the Foregoing Trends*
Generally, the lighter the feedstock the lower the capital cost. This implies that the cheapest plants employing liquefied petroleum gas or light distillate feedstocks are likely to be used for seasonal loads, and

272

that the use of the more expensive plants using heavy oil would be restricted normally to base loads, even in circumstances where heavy oil was substantially cheaper than the lighter materials.

In large-scale gas manufacture, climatic peak shaving is likely to be achieved by the addition of LPG/air, or by the use of LNG, either as a substitute for other forms of enrichment or in the form of methane/air or methane/ballast-gas.

## Selection of Gas-Making Plant in Areas where Coal is the Basic Economic Raw Material

### 1   Synthesis-Gas Manufacture from Solid Fuels

Although some synthesis gas is still made from producer gas, and blue and semi-water gas, a strong trend is developing towards the use of processes using oxygen, such as the low-pressure Winkler process and its successors, and the high-pressure Lurgi process. Full-scale, low-pressure installations, using oxygen and fuel dust, have also been installed, such as those of Koppers Totzek and Rummel.

### 2   Town-Gas Manufacture

Where coal is the economic material the choice lies between the carbonization of a coking coal in coke ovens or vertical retorts, yielding a low-pressure high-flame-speed gas, or the processing of any of a wider range of coals as described on pages 20 to 51 to produce either high-flame-speed or low-flame-speed gas as desired, at a wide range of pressures.

The capital costs of all these processes are intolerable for seasonal and peak-load gas production. Thus, where coal is the basic economic gas-making material, either a high production system-load-factor must be achieved (eg by planned load-shedding), or hydrocarbon oils or gases must be used for the seasonal load, in low-capital-cost processes, to produce an acceptable system-load-factor for the coal-using plant. As with systems based on natural gas and liquid hydrocarbons, the use of LPG/air is likely to be the most economical technique for climatic peak shaving, subject to the limitations imposed by its effect on the mixed gas characteristics, and subject also to competition from LNG.

273

# Chapter 22 The Modern Trend in Gas-Supply Techniques based on Abundant Natural Gas

## Considerations Governing the System-Load-Factors of Natural-Gas Production and Supply Facilities

The cost effect of operating long-distance natural-gas transmission systems, such as those of the USA and USSR, at less than full loading, plus the increase in production costs that this would impose (since production and transmission loads must match), means that such systems are normally designed to operate at approximately full load.

Where gas fields are sited relatively less distant from areas with high densities of premium-gas consumers, as in the case of North Sea and other European deposits, the most economical production and transmission loading may be closer to that of the reticulation system. For North Sea gas, for example, the current production and transmission system-load-factors are approximately 60%. This roughly matches the anticipated future normal reticulation system-load-factor. This, in turn, will result from the restriction of gas supplies, by pricing, mainly to domestic, commerical and premium-industrial-gas users, but ameliorated by bulk fuel sales which, as far as is economical, will be interruptible.

Premium uses are arbitrarily defined as those for which gas, by virtue of its form-value and purity, commands a premium of 30% over the cost of the cheapest bulk fuel. For most bulk-fuel uses, natural gas can command premiums over alternative fuels of only 10 to 20% if supplied as required, but may command no premium on an interruptible supply basis. The spill-over of natural gas into bulk-fuel uses in the circumstances detailed in the second paragraph above would be limited to that required to achieve the desired gas-field depletion rates. The difference between the value of this bulk-fuel gas on a continuous-supply basis and that on an interruptible basis, compared with the relative supply costs on these bases, would be the economic factor determining the load form such supplies would take, but political forces may also have influence.

The determination of the economic depletion rate of a gas field would involve estimating the current capacity and any probable increase over the depletion period. The level of capital service rates, the prices that could be charged in the main sectors of supply, and the potential demands and load factors in these sectors over this period,

274

would also have to be estimated. Finally, the differential cost of replacing natural gas by gas manufactured from the future economic process material when the field was depleted, for those premium sectors that could bear this cost, would be determined.

In the circumstances it is not surprising that depletion periods for particular gas discoveries of twenty-five to thirty-five years are commonly decided upon on an arbitrary basis, subject to any overriding physical consideration within the gas-bearing structure that might limit the extraction rate.

## The Modern Trend in Techniques for Reconciling Differing Natural-Gas Production and Distribution-System Load Characteristics

It is assumed that the peak load of the distribution system has been trimmed by the interruption of industrial supplies where this is economical, as dealt with in the preceding section. It is also assumed that the smoothing-out of gas-demand variations within the day will be the function of gas stored in holders and gas mains. In practice seasonal and peak load-shaving facilities may also make a small contribution to this.

The object, therefore, of the techniques detailed below is to relieve the natural-gas supply system, to the desired extent, of the seasonal variations in output remaining after planned load-shedding.

### 1 The Use of Seasonal Storage

As has already been stated the only economic form of seasonal gas-storage is that provided by natural underground structures as described in Chapter 18. To be effective such structures must be appropriately sited relative to the gas consumers. Commonly they are not available and the alternative techniques described below must be used.

### 2 The Use of Supplementary and Substitute Gases

As stated in Chapter 20 the predominant element in peak-gas cost is that of capital service. The capital involved in LPG and LPG/air installations is from a third to a half of that involved in a comparable natural-gas liquefaction, storage and vaporization system. Comparison of stored LPG or LNG installation costs with peak or seasonal shaving gas-making plant is complicated, and produces different results according to the period over which the gas load is spread. This arises from the fact that the capital cost of gas-manufacture plant

275

would be fixed, whether it was planned to operate for five days or one hundred days, whereas the cost of LPG storage, for example, would increase in proportion to the time of operation, *ie* the cumulative capacity required less the scale effect.

The choice of route can be further complicated if peak or seasonal gas-shaving equipment of any type is already available producing gas of acceptable quality and pressure, *ie* if a capital commitment has been made in advance. Process material and operating costs, which can be negligible for extreme peak-shaving operations, acquire significance in seasonal gas-shaving.

The most economical route or combination of routes can be determined only after taking account of all the characteristics, including the probabilities of the peak loads involved. A likely outcome is that LPG or LPG/air would prove the cheapest climatic peak and output fringe-shaving technique, within the limits imposed by its incompatibility or the dewpoint of the mixed gas. These limitations are likely to prevent LPG from assuming more than a fraction of the load. LNG facilities are likely to provide the cheapest gas source for the remainder (that is, the greater part) of the climatic and output fringe peak gas. A computer model designed to assist in the planning of the optimal sizing of LNG plants, when used for peak-shaving purposes in competition with alternatives such as LPG/air or underground storage, has been described (115).

A prolonged seasonal gap between natural-gas production rates and gas demand is likely to be met most economically by the manufacture from light distillate of a rich gas, for example by the UK Gas Council's Catalytic Rich-Gas Process. For small admixtures a supplementary gas differing slightly in quality could be made, and for proportionally higher admixtures this gas could be methanated and washed to produce a completely interchangeable gas.

In all cases peak and seasonal load-shaving gas should be considered for stand-by duty in case of temporary failure of supply. This consideration favours LNG and manufactured natural-gas substitutes for peak-shaving and seasonal-load gas production respectively since they can be distributed undiluted.


## The Use of Natural Gas in the Context of High-Flame-Speed Town-Gas Supplies

When adequate natural-gas supplies become available to a supply undertaking providing a service with manufactured high-flame-speed town gas, it is normal to convert the appliances to the use of the lower-flame-speed natural gas. Certainly this will be the economical solution when the natural-gas supply and tariffs are at such levels as to allow massive increases in consumption, owing to the increased capacity of mains when carrying natural gas instead of high-flame-speed gas of lower Wobbe number.

In the circumstances of a more limited but adequate supply at little cost advantage, a compromise that has been adopted is the distribution of methane/air at approximately the same Wobbe number as the high-flame-speed gas, thus minimizing the cost of appliance conversion.

On the fringes of natural-gas supply areas it may become available on a scale to supply a part of a gas-undertaking's demand. It can then be used either to supply the whole of the demand of part of the supply area, or it can be integrated into the manufactured gas. The latter is normally the more economical when, as is normal, the natural gas is cheaper than the current sources of enrichment available for the high-flame-speed gas. Furthermore, the substitution of methane, and methane plus ballast gas, for other forms of enrichment, results in substantial increases in gas output using given lean-gas sources.

## The Consequences of the Depletion of Natural-Gas Supplies

Natural-gas reserves, both proven and prospective, are substantially smaller than the earth's solid and liquid fossil-fuel resources. Methane to replace natural-gas supplies can readily be manufactured from either of these other fuels; see pages 43 to 50 and 132 to 134. In these circumstances it should be safe to leave the conservation of gas resources to the operation of market forces; the conservation argument, whatever its strength, should be directed to coal and oil.

The only restraint needed, therefore, on the production of gas at such a rate that it overflows from high-premium uses into bulk fuel uses, to be sold at even lower prices than alternative bulk fuels, is that provided by the balance of the current bulk-fuel gas price plus interest, against the future premium fuel price. This could be compounded partly from the price of indigenous natural gas and imported LNG and, increasingly as depletion approaches, the cost of manufactured methane.

The free operation of the market would result in a price increase back to the well, as resources fell in relation to demand, thus encouraging exploration resulting in the discovery of further resources, and discouraging the lower-priced bulk-fuel uses, thus conserving gas for premium uses. Where gas price levels are influenced or controlled by local, state or national authorities rather than free market forces, the controlled price should be manipulated to the same end.

# APPENDIX: UNITS, EQUIVALENTS AND CONVERSION FACTORS

## SI Units

All units in the International System (SI) are derived from seven basic units: metre, kilogramme, second, ampère, kelvin (temperature), candela (luminous intensity) and mole (quantity of a substance which has a weight in grammes numerically equal to its molecular weight). Decimal multiples and sub-multiples for these units are indicated by use of the following prefixes:

| Prefix | Symbol | Factor |
|--------|--------|--------|
| tera | T | $10^{12}$ |
| giga | G | $10^{9}$ |
| mega | M | $10^{6}$ |
| kilo | k | $10^{3}$ |
| hecto | h | $10^{2}$ |
| deca | da | $10^{1}$ |
| deci | d | $10^{-1}$ |
| centi | c | $10^{-2}$ |
| milli | m | $10^{-3}$ |
| micro | $\mu$ | $10^{-6}$ |
| nano | n | $10^{-9}$ |
| pico | p | $10^{-12}$ |
| femto | f | $10^{-15}$ |
| atto | a | $10^{-18}$ |

The following units and physical constants are of special interest to the gas industry:

| Unit | Symbol | Definition |
|------|--------|------------|
| newton (force) | N | $1 \text{ kg m/s}^2$ |
| pascal (stress or pressure) | Pa | $1 \text{ N/m}^2$ |
| joule (energy) | J | $1 \text{ N m}$ |
| watt (energy rate or power) | W | $1 \text{ J/s}$ |
| tonne | t | $1\,000 \text{ kg}$ |
| litre (1964 definition: $1 \text{ dm}^3$) | l | $0\cdot001 \text{ m}^3$ |

| Unit | Symbol | Definition |
|---|---|---|
| hectare | ha | $10\ 000\ m^2$ |
| bar | bar | $100\ 000\ N/m^2$ |
| millibar | mbar | $100\ N/m^2$ |
| centistokes (kinematic viscosity) | cSt | $1\ mm^2/s$ |
| centipoise (dynamic viscosity) | cP | $0 \cdot 001\ N\ s/m^2$ |
| International Table calorie | $cal_{IT}$ | $4 \cdot 186\ 8\ J$ |
| 15°C calorie | $cal_{15}$ | $4 \cdot 185\ 5\ J$ |
| thermochemical calorie | $cal_{TC}$ | $4 \cdot 184\ 0\ J$ |
| | (sometimes $cal_{th}$) | |
| International Table British thermal unit | $Btu_{IT}$ | $1\ 055 \cdot 06\ J$ |
| 15°C British thermal unit | $Btu_{15}$ | $1\ 054 \cdot 73\ J$ |
| thermochemical British thermal unit | $Btu_{TC}$ | $1\ 054 \cdot 35\ J$ |
| therm | | $100\ 000\ Btu_{15}$ |
| thermie | | $1\ 000\ kcal_{15}$ |

| Physical constant | Abbreviation or symbol | Definition |
|---|---|---|
| standard atmosphere | atm | $101\ 325\ N/m^2$ |
| technical atmosphere | at. | $98\ 066 \cdot 5\ N/m^2$ |
| standard gravity | $g_n$ | $9 \cdot 806\ m/s^2$ |
| ideal gas constant | R | $8 \cdot 314\ 34\ J/mol\ K$ |
| ideal gas volume, at 0°C and 1 atm, based on R | – | $22 \cdot 413\ 6\ dm^3/mol$ |
| ideal gas volume, at 15°C and 1 atm, based on R | – | $22 \cdot 644\ 5\ dm^3/mol$ |

## Definitions

The following definitions apply throughout the text, unless otherwise stated:

**Heat units**
The heat units most commonly employed by the European gas

industry to express calorific values are the 15°C kilocalories (kcal$_{15}$) and the 15°C British thermal unit (Btu$_{15}$), rather than the International Table units kcal$_{IT}$ and Btu$_{IT}$. The corresponding thermochemical units kcal$_{TC}$ and Btu$_{TC}$ are used mainly in the USA, the former in data compilations by the American Petroleum Institute.

1 Btu$_{15}$ = 0·252 kcal$_{15}$ = 1 054·73 J
1 kcal$_{15}$ = 3·968 Btu$_{15}$ = 4 185·5 J
1 Btu$_{IT}$ = 1 055·06 J
1 kcal$_{IT}$ = 4 186·6 J
1 Btu$_{TC}$ = 1 054·4 J
1 kcal$_{TC}$ = 4 184·0 J
1 therm = 100 000 Btu$_{15}$ = 105·473 MJ
1 thermie = 1 000 kcal$_{15}$ = 4·185 5 MJ

## Units and reference conditions for measuring gas volume

**UK gas industry:**
cubic feet, 60°F, either dry or saturated with water vapour, 1 013·74 mbar (the pressure exerted by 30 inches of mercury at 60°F under the gravity appropriate to the latitude 53°N).

**International Gas Union (IGU):**
cubic metres, 15°C, dry, 1 013·25 mbar.

**US gas industry:**
cubic feet, 60°F, either dry or saturated with water vapour, 1 015·92 mbar (the pressure exerted by 30 'conventional' inches of mercury– i.e. at the conventional density corresponding to 0°C and standard gravity). An alternative standard pressure is 1 013·25 mbar, as adopted by the IGU.

1 ft$^3$ = 0·028 32 m$^3$ (under the same conditions)
1 ft$^3$ (sat) UK gas industry standard = 0·027 78 m$^3$ (st) IGU standard
1 ft$^3$ (dry) UK gas industry standard = 0·028 28 m$^3$ (st) IGU standard
1 m$^3$ = 35·315 ft$^3$ (under the same conditions)
1 m$^3$ (st) IGU standard
= 35·99 ft$^3$ (sat) UK gas industry standard
= 35·37 ft$^3$ (dry) UK gas industry standard.

## Specific gravity

The specific gravity of a gas relative to air

$$= \frac{\text{density of gas at 1 013·74 mbar, 60°F, dry}}{\text{density of air at 1 013·74 mbar, 60°F, dry}}$$

Note: The practice of the UK gas industry is to base the specific gravity of saturated gas on the density of dry air:

$$\text{Sp gr} = \frac{\text{density of gas at 1 013·74 mbar, 60°F, sat}}{\text{density of air at 1 013·74 mbar, 60°F, dry}}$$

## Wobbe Number

UK standard: calorific value in $Btu/ft^3 \div \sqrt{\text{specific gravity}}$
IGU standard: calorific value in $MJ/m^3 \div \sqrt{\text{specific gravity}}$

## Efficiency of gas production

The method that comes nearer than any other to giving a comprehensive index of the overall thermal efficiency of a process is the efficiency of gas production, determined as follows.
A total is made up of the thermal equivalent of all the fuel and energy brought into a works for use directly and indirectly in the processes of gas manufacture and treatment, up to the point at which the purified gas enters the gas-holder. From this total the thermal value of the net output of products other than gas is deducted, leaving as the difference the thermal value of the gas made plus that of the fuel and energy used up or unaccounted for in the process of gas manufacture and treatment. The efficiency of gas production (EGP) is the thermal value of the net gas made, expressed as a percentage of that difference:

$$\text{EGP} = \frac{\text{Thermal value of gas made}}{\left(\begin{array}{c}\text{Total energy}\\\text{supplied}\end{array}\right) - \left(\begin{array}{c}\text{Thermal value of}\\\text{by-products}\end{array}\right)} \times 100$$

This equation expresses the efficiency of three processes:
a Manufacture of gas;
b Production of energy required for gas manufacture and treatment;
c Utilization of the energy in b.

# Equivalent gas volumes under various conditions of measurement

| UK Gas Industry standards | | Normal temperature and pressure* | IGU standard |
|---|---|---|---|
| 1 013·74 mbar 30 inHg (60°F, 53°N) 60°F, saturated stp (sat) | 1 013·74 mbar 30 inHg (60°F, 53°N) 60°F, dry stp (dry) | 1 013·25 mbar (760 mmHg) 0°C, dry ntp | 1 013·25 mbar (760 mmHg) 15°C, dry st |
| 1·000 | 0·983 | 0·930 | 0·981 |
| 1·018 | 1·000 | 0·947 | 0·999 |
| 1·075 | 1·056 | 1·000 | 1·055 |
| 1·019 | 1·001 | 0·948 | 1·000 |

# Equivalent calorific values and Wobbe numbers

| UK Gas Industry standards | | Normal temperature and pressure* | | IGU standard |
|---|---|---|---|---|
| Btu$_{15}$/ft$^3$ stp (sat) | Btu$_{15}$/ft$^3$ stp (dry) | kcal$_{IT}$/m$^3$ ntp | kcal$_{IT}$/m$^3$ st | MJ/m$^3$ st |
| 1·000 | 1·018 | 9·56 | 9·07 | 0·037 96 |
| 0·983 | 1·000 | 9·40 | 8·91 | 0·037 30 |
| 0·104 5 | 0·106 3 | 1·000 | 0·948 | 0·003 969 |
| 0·110 3 | 0·112 3 | 1·055 | 1·000 | 0·004 187 |
| 26·34 | 26·82 | 252·0 | 238·8 | 1·000 |

# Equivalent calorific values

| UK Gas Industry standards | | Normal temperature and pressure* | | IGU standard |
|---|---|---|---|---|
| Btu$_{15}$/ft$^3$ stp (sat) | Btu$_{15}$/ft$^3$ stp (dry) | kcal$_{IT}$/m$^3$ ntp | kcal$_{IT}$/m$^3$ st | MJ/m$^3$ st |
| 100 | 101·8 | 956 | 907 | 3·80 |
| 200 | 203·5 | 1 913 | 1 813 | 7·59 |
| 300 | 305·3 | 2 890 | 2 710 | 11·39 |
| 400 | 407·1 | 3 860 | 3 627 | 15·18 |
| 500 | 508·9 | 4 782 | 4 533 | 18·98 |
| 600 | 610·6 | 5 738 | 5 440 | 22·78 |
| 700 | 712·4 | 6 695 | 6 346 | 26·57 |
| 800 | 814·2 | 7 652 | 7 253 | 30·37 |
| 900 | 915·9 | 8 608 | 8 160 | 34·16 |
| 1 000 | 1 017·7 | 9 564 | 9 067 | 37·96 |

*These conditions are the 'standard temperature and pressure' (stp) of B.S. 350 :1963

283

# Conversion Factors

The factors shown in the table below apply to conversions between traditional units and those that may be used with the International System, as recommended by the Institute of Petroleum.

| To convert | into | multiply by | reciprocal |
|---|---|---|---|
| inches | mm | 25·400 0 | 0·039 370 1 |
| feet | m | 0·304 800 | 3·280 84 |
| yards | m | 0·914 400 | 1·093 61 |
| land miles | km | 1·609 34 | 0·621 371 |
| $in^2$ | $mm^2$ | 645·160 | 0·001 550 |
| $ft^2$ | $m^2$ | 0·092 903 | 10·763 9 |
| $yd^2$ | $m^2$ | 0·836 127 | 1·195 99 |
| acres | ha | 0·404 686 | 2·471 05 |
| $ft^3$ | $m^3$ | 0·028 316 8 | 35·314 7 |
| UKgal | litres | 4·546 09 | 0·219 969 |
| USgal | litres | 3·785 41 | 0·264 172 |
| barrels (bbl) | $m^3$ | 0·158 987 | 6·289 81 |
| | | | |
| lb | kg | 0·453 592 37 | 2·204 62 |
| ton | tonne | 1·016 05 | 0·984 207 |
| $lb/ft^3$ | $kg/m^3$ | 16·018 5 | 0·062 428 |
| mile/UKgal | km/litre | 0·354 005 | 2·824 81 |
| ft/min | m/s | 0·005 08 | 196·850 |
| lbf | N | 4·448 22 | 0·224 809 |
| kgf ($=$kp) | N | 9·806 65 | 0·101 972 |
| $lbf/in^2$ | bar | 0·068 947 6 | 14·503 8 |
| inHg | mbar | 33·863 9 | 0·029 530 |
| mmHg | mbar | 1·333 22 | 0·750 062 |
| $inH_2O$ | mbar | 2·490 89 | 0·401 463 |
| $mmH_2O$ | mbar | 0·098 066 5 | 10·197 2 |
| $tonf/in^2$ | $MN/m^2$ | 15·444 3 | 0·064 749 |
| $kgf/cm^2$ ($=$at.) | bar | 0·980 665 | 1·019 72 |
| | | | |
| Btu | MJ | 0·001 055 06 | 947·817 |
| Btu | kW h | 0·000 293 071 | 3 412·14 |
| kW h | MJ | 3·600 00 | 0·277 778 |
| hp h | MJ | 2·684 52 | 0·372 506 |
| Btu/lb | MJ/kg | 0·002 326 00 | 429·923 |
| Btu/lb | kW h/kg | 0·000 646 111 | 1 547·72 |

| To convert | into | multiply by | reciprocal |
|---|---|---|---|
| Btu/ft³ | MJ/m³ | 0·037 258 9 | 26·839 2 |
| Btu/ft³ | kW h/m³ | 0·010 349 7 | 96·621 1 |
| Btu/UKgal | MJ/litre | 0·000 232 080 | 4 308·86 |
| Btu/UKgal | kW h/litre | 0·000 064 466 | 15 511·9 |
| hp | kW | 0·745 700 | 1·341 02 |
| ch (=CV) | kW | 0·735 499 | 1·359 62 |
| Btu/h | kW | 0·000 293 071 | 3 412·14 |
| Btu/lb °F | kJ/kg °C | 4·186 8 | 0·238 846 |
| Btu/lb °F | kW h/kg °C | 0·001 163 | 859·845 |
| Btu/ft² h | kW/m² | 0·003 154 59 | 316·998 |
| Btu/ft³ h | kW/m³ | 0·010 349 7 | 96·621 1 |
| Btu/ft h °F | W/m °C | 1·730 73 | 0·577 789 |
| Btu/ft² h °F | W/m² °C | 5·678 26 | 0·176 110 |
| ft²/h | mm²/s (=cSt) | 25·806 4 | 0·038 750 1 |

The litre employed in the above table is the 1964 litre (dm³) and the Btu is the $Btu_{IT}$. However, the $BTU_{15}$ is used throughout this book to express the calorific values of gases.

Throughout this book, all calorific values are gross unless otherwise stated.

# BIBLIOGRAPHY

## PART 1

1 'Report of the Committee on Utilization of Gases,' Paper E-64, International Gas Union's 9th International Gas Conference, The Hague, 1964

2 VAN DER LINDEN, A, 'La Signification de la Qualité et de la Pression du Gaz pour les Techniques de Distribution et de Consommation', IGU's 8th International Gas Conference, Stockholm, 1961

3 DEWHURST, J R, and HOLBROOK, C G, 'A Test for the Sooting Propensity of Town Gas', *Journal of the Institution of Gas Engineers*, **6**, 1966 (IGE Communication 695)

4 WEAVER, E R, 'Formulae and Graphs for Representing the Interchangeability of Fuel Gases', *Journal of the National Bureau of Standards*, **46**, 1951

5 DELBOURG, P, 'The Control of the Quality and Interchangeability of Gases', Association Technical de l'Industrie du Gaz en France Congress, 1951

6 DELBOURG, P, and SCHRENCH, H, 'Interchangeability of Gases (Improvement of Methods)', Association Technical de l'Industrie du Gaz en France Congress, 1956

7 GILBERT, M G, and PRIGG, J A, 'The Prediction of the Combustion Characteristics of Town Gas', *Transactions of the Institution of Gas Engineers*, **106**, 1956-7 (Gas Council Research Communication GC35)

8 HARRIS, J A, and LOVELACE, D E, 'Combustion Characteristics of Natural Gas and Manufactured Substitutes', *JIGE*, **8**, 1968 (Research Communication GC142)

9 HENSHILWOOD, C P, 'The Modification of Domestic Appliances for Gases of High Calorific Value', *JIGE*, **6**, 1966 (Research Communication GC119)

10 *Erdöl und Kohle*, pp 364-7, May 1961 (German language)

11 'Process for Heating Coke Oven Batteries with Hydrocarbons, Particularly Petrol', *UK Patent Specification 879117*, Didier Werke AG, 1961

12 ELLIS, SIR CHARLES, 'Some Aspects of Coal Pyrolysis', *TransIGE*, **103**, 1953-4 (IGE Communication 436)

13 Abstracts, *British Chemical Engineering*, p 50, January 1962

14 *Coal and Coke Industry*, USSR, pp 31-2, No 12, 1961

15 OLIVER, G F, and OLDEN, M J F, 'The Development of Gas Production in the South West', *JIGE*, **4**, 1964 (IGE Communication 657)

16 STEENSTRUP, N V, 'The Use of Propane/Butane for Gas Making in Vertical Retorts', *TransIGE*, **108**, 1958-9 (IGE Communication 545)

17 DENT, F J, 'The Ninth Coal Lecture', *BCURA Quarterly Gazette*, October 1960

18 DAVIS, J E, 'Thermal Efficiency in Gas Production and Utilization', *TransIGE*, **102**, 1952-3 (Research Communication GC2)

19 MACCORMAC, M, and WROBEL, J, 'The Gasification of Coal in an Experimental Rummel Double-Shaft Slag-Bath Gasifier,' *JIGE*, **5**, 1965 (Research Communication GC113)

20 'Commercial Potential for the Kellogg Coal Gasification Process', report by M W Kellogg Co. for the US Office of Coal Research, Piscatawny, NJ, 1968

21 LINDEN, DR HENRY R, 'Sources of US Gas Supply — Now to the 21st Century', *American Gas Journal*, January 1969

22 TSAROS, C L, and JOYCE, T J, 'Comparative Economics of Pipeline Gas from Coal Processes', 1968 American Gas Association Synthetic Pipeline Gas Symposium, Office of Coal Research, Washington, DC, 1968

23 TSAROS, C L, KNABEL, S J, and SHERIDAN, L A, 'Process Design and Cost Estimate for Production of 266 Million SCF/Day of Pipeline Gas by the Hydrogasification of Bituminous Coal — Hydrogen by the Steam-Iron Process', Office of Coal Research, Washington, DC, 1967

24 TSAROS, C L, KNABEL, S J, and SHERIDAN, L A, 'Process Design and Cost Estimate for Production of 265 Million SCF/Day of Pipeline Gas by the Hydrogasification of Bituminous Coal', Office of Coal Research, Washington, DC, 1965

25 KNABEL, S J, and TSAROS, C L, 'Process Design and Cost Estimate for a 258 Billion Btu/Day Pipeline Gas Plant – Hydrogasification Using Synthesis Gas Generated by Electrothermal Gasification of Spent Char', Office of Coal Research, Washington, DC, 1968

26 TSAROS, C L, *et al*, 'Cost Estimate of 500 Billion Btu/Day Pipeline Gas Plant via Hydrogasification and Electrothermal Gasification of Lignite', *Research and Development Report No 22*, Office of Coal Research, Washington, DC, 1968

27 'Pipeline Gas from Lignite Gasification, a Feasibility Study' report by Consolidation Coal Co. for the Office of Coal Research, Library, Pennsylvania, 1965

28 INGRAM, L P, 'An Approach to the Use of Oil Gas in an Integrated System', *TransIGE*, **106**, 1956-7 (IGE Communication 506)

29 DENT, F J, 'Principles of New Gas-Making Processes', Gas Council Midlands Research Station, Solihull, 1965

30 SHPOLYANSKII, M A, and LEIBUSH, A G, *TransGIAP*, p 126, Issue 5 1956

31 ROZHDESTVENSKII, V P, and YEROFEYEVA, V I, *Neftekhimiya*, pp 204-10, No 2 1956 (Russian language)

32 ANDREW, S P S, 'Research Leading to the ICI Naphtha Reforming Process', *Proceedings of Eastbourne Conference*, Institute of Fuel, London, 1965

33 MASLYANSKII *et al*, *Neftekhimiya*, pp 328-34, No 3 1956 (Russian language)

34 WARD, E R, 'The Use of Light Petroleum Distillate for Gas Making', *TransIGE*, **107**, 1957-8 (IGE Communication 515)

35 DUNPHY, T E, 'Onia-Gegi Plant in Cork', *JIGE*, **2**, 1962 (IGE Communication 615)

36 NICKLIN, T, FARRINGTON, F, and WHITTAKER, R J, 'Further Developments in the Nickel/Urania/α-Alumina Catalyst System', *JIGE*, **10**, 1970 (IGE Communication 813)

37 MURTHY, P S, and EDGE, R F, 'The Hydrogenation of Oils to Gaseous Hydrocarbons', *JIGE*, **3**, 1963 (Research Communication GC88)

38 BROOKS, C T, 'Some Chemical Aspects of Processes Occurring in the Gas Recycle Hydrogenator', *JIGE*, **6**, 1966 (Research Communication GC123)

39 As 36, Discussion

40 COCKERHAM, R G, PERCIVAL, G, and YARWOOD, T A, 'The Catalytic Gasification of Petroleum Feedstocks', *JIGE*, **5**, 1965 (Research Communication GC106)

41 DAVIES, H S, *et al*, 'Applications and Development of the Catalytic Rich-Gas Process', *JIGE*, **7**, 1967 (IGE Communication 737)

42 WEBSTER, A G, *et al*, 'Operational Results with the New Gas-making Processes', *JIGE*, **9**, 1969

43 DAVIES, H S, LACEY, J A, and THOMPSON, B H, 'Processes for the Manufacture of Natural-Gas Substitutes', *JIGE*, **9**, 1969 (Research Communication GC155)

44 TEER HAAR, L W, and VOGEL, J E, 'The Shell Gasification Process', 6th World Petroleum Congress, Frankfurt, 1963

45 WITHEY, D S, 'Endothermic Gas Production from Commercial LPG', *Industrial Process Heating*, **7**, January 1967

46 BORGARS, D J and BRIDGER, G W, 'Catalysts Used in the Manufacture of Ammonia', *Chemistry & Industry*, 19 November 1960

47 RICKETTS, T S, 'The Operation of the Westfield-Lurgi Plant and the High-Pressure Grid System', *JIGE*, **3**, 1963 (IGE Communication 633)

48 HOPTON, G U, 'Research on New Methods of Gas Treatment', *JIGE*, **3**, 1963

PART 2

49 ERDMAN, J G, 'Geochemical Origins of the Low Molecular Weight Hydrocarbon Constituents of Petroleum and Natural Gases', 7th World Petroleum Congress, **2**, page 13

50 *Ibid*

51 KATZ, D L, *et al*, *Handbook of Natural Gas Engineering*, p 209, McGraw-Hill Book Co. Inc, NY, 1959

52 COPP, A D L, HILDREW, R G, and COOPER, L S, 'The Design, Commissioning and Operation of the United Kingdom Gas Industry's Methane Pipeline', *JIGE*, **6**, 1966 (IGE Communication 708)

53 SHERWOOD, T K, and PIGFORD, R L, *Adsorption and Extraction*, 2nd Edition, McGraw-Hill Book Co. Inc, NY, 1952

54 PERRY, J H, *et al*, *Chemical Engineer's Handbook*, 4th Edition, McGraw-Hill Book Co. Inc, NY, 1963

55 KOHL, A L, and RIESENFELD, F C, *Gas Purification*, McGraw-Hill Book Co. Inc, NY (out of print)

56 'Report of the Committee on Natural Gases and Mass Storage', 11th International Gas Conference, Moscow, 1970

57 MARKBOCITER, S J, and WEISS, I, 'Expander Cycles for LNG', *Cryogenic Engineering News*, March 1968

58 DENSHAM, A B, *et al*, 'The Odorisation of Natural Gas', 36th Autumn Research Meeting of the IGE, November 1970 (Research Communication GC178)

59 HUEBLER, J, *et al*, 'Physical Properties of Natural Gas at Cryogenic Conditions', Vol. 1, Second International Conference on LNG, Paris, 1970

60 ROWLINSON, J S, and WATSON, I D, 'The Prediction of Thermodynamic Properties of Fluids and Fluid Mixtures', *Chemical Engineering Science*, 24, 1969

61 CLAR, R, JONES, D M, and OWENS, P J, 'Meeting Peak and Seasonal Loads with LNG and Manufactured Natural-Gas Substitutes', *JIGE*, 7, 1967 (IGE Communication 743)

62 DARREDEAU, B, 'Dévelopement du Cycle à Cascade Incorporée pour la Liquifaction du Gaz Naturel', International Conference on LNG, London, 1969

63 LINNETT, D T, and SMITH, K C, 'The Process Design and Optimisation of a Mixed Refrigerant Cascade Plant', International Conference on LNG, London, 1969

64 SNYDER, J A, 'A Second-Generation LNG Peak Shaving Cycle', International Conference on LNG, London, 1969

65 WICKER, P, 'Reliquefaction of Boil-off Gas from LNG Storage Tanks', Vol. 1, Second International Conference on LNG, Paris, 1970

66 VOGELHUBER, W W, and PARISH, H C, 'Compact LNG System Using Large Stirling Cycle Cold Gas Refrigerator', 28, First International Conference on LNG, Chicago, 1968

67 IGU/A-70 Report of the Committee on Natural Gas and Mass Storage, Section 1.2, 11th International Gas Conference, Moscow, 1970

68 FÖRG, W, and WIRTZ, P, 'Helium and Nitrogen Removal from Natural Gas', *Linde Reports on Science and Technology*, 15, 1970

69 FÖRG, W, 'Some Considerations on Peak Shaving with Dutch Natural Gas', International Conference on LNG, London, 1969

70 RIGOLA, M, 'Recovery of Cold in a Heavy LNG', Vol. 2 Second International Conference on LNG, Paris, 1970

71 CHANSKY, S H, and HALLY, H E, 'How to Use the Cold in LNG', *American Gas Journal*, August 1968

72 KATAOKA, H, *et al*, 'Utilization of LNG Cold for Production of Liquid Oxygen and Liquid Nitrogen', Vol. 2, Second International Conference on LNG, Paris, 1970

73 FÖRG, W, 'Cryophores for the Short-Term Storage of LNG', Vol. 2, Second International Conference on LNG, Paris, 1970

74 GUTHRIE, J K, and GREGORY, E J, 'Design of Base-Load Evaporators for LNG', International Conference on LNG, London, 1969

75 WALDMANN, H, 'Development of a High-Performance Evaporator for Liquefied Gases', International Conference on LNG, London, 1969

76 COPP, D L, *Gas Transmission and Distribution*, Walter King Ltd, London

77 SHEBEKO, B C, *Polyflo Flow Computer*, Polyflo Incorporated, San Rafael, California, USA

78 EWING, G H, 'The Design Features of a Major Natural-Gas Transmission System', *JIGE*, 7, 1967 (IGE Communication 742)

79 'Recommendations Concerning the Installation of Steel Pipelines for High-Pressure Gas Transmission', *Publication 674*, IGE, London, 1967 (partially revised in 1970, as Communication 674A)

80 WALTERS, J R, 'Recommendations of a Joint Committee for the Co-ordination of the Cathodic Protection of Buried Structures', Section 7, GPO Engineering Dept, London

81 'Recommendations for Mainlaying', *Publication 734*, IGE, London, 1966

82 WHITCHURCH, D R, and COLLINS, H H, 'The Resistance of Ductile Iron to Corrosion by Soils', *JIGE*, 7, 1967 (IGE Communication 732)

83 BRAMWELL, D J, *et al*, 'Dry-Gas — Controlling Dust and Leakage in a Distribution System', *JIGE*, 9, 1969 (IGE Communication 783)

84 PICKERING, E W, *et al*, 'Leakage Control in the Natural Gas Era', *JIGE*, 11, 1971 (Research Communication GC 175)

85   CAIRNS, K F, and WHITE, J D, 'Mains Cleaning and Joint Sealing by the Fuelling Method', *JIGE*, **9**, 1969 (IGE Communication 798)

86   BRIGHTON, C A, and BENTON, J L, 'Modified PVC Pipes', *JIGE*, **8**, 1968 (IGE Communication 756)

87   WALKER, A, and CLEREHUGH, G, 'Modern Development of Plastics Systems for Gas Distribution', *JIGE*, **11**, 1971 (IGE Communication 835)

88   O'SHEA, J T, *et al*, 'The Effects on Plastics Pipes of Gas Conditioning Agents and Other Additives', *JIGE*, **11**, 1971 (Research Communication GC 173)

89   HANNAH, K W, *et al*, 'Transient Flow in Natural Gas Transmission Systems', American Gas Association Inc, January 1965

90   GOACHER, P S, 'Steady and Transient Analysis of Gas Flows in Networks', *JIGE*, **10**, 1970 (Research Communication GC157)

91   HEATH, M J, and BLUNT, J C, 'Dynamic Simulation Applied to the Design and Control of a Pipeline Network', *JIGE*, **9**, 1969 (Research Communication GC149)

92   LANGFORD, R G, and LUCAS, T A, 'The Design and Control of an Integrated High-Pressure Grid System', *JIGE*, **9**, 1969 (IGE Communication 782)

93   TROLLUX, J, 'Transporting Gas under Pressure and at Ambient Temperature', Paper 31, First International LNG Conference Chicago, 1968

94   IVANTZOV, O M, 'Problems of LNG Transmission Pipeline Construction', International Conference on LNG, London, 1969

95   IVANTZOV, O M, *et al*, 'Liquefied Natural Gas Mains', Vol. 1, Second International Conference on LNG, Paris, 1970

96   WALKER, G, *et al*, 'Liquefied Natural Gas Pipelines for Arctic Gas Recovery,' International Conference on LNG, London, 1969

97   McMULLEN, J J, 'A Systems Approach to the Marine Transportation of LNG', Paper 36, First International LNG Conference, Chicago, 1968

98   JACKSON, R G, and KOTCHARIAN, M, 'Testing and Technology of Modes of Integrated Tanks for LNG Carriers', Paper 35, First International LNG Conference, Chicago 1968

99 KVAMSDAL, R, *et al*, 'The Design of an 88 000 m³ LNG Carrier with Spherical Cargo Tanks and no Secondary Barrier', Vol. 1, Second International Conference on LNG, Paris, 1970

100 BROEKER, R J, 'A New Process for the Transportation of Natural Gas', Paper 30, First International LNG Conference, Chicago, 1968

101 FILSTEAD, C G, 'World LNG Trade in the Seventies', Vol. 1, Second International Conference on LNG, Paris, 1970

102 EIFEL, P J, 'Railroad and Highway Transportation of LNG', Paper 38, First International LNG Conference, Chicago, 1968

103 LATHAM, W N, 'The Design of Optimum LNG Highway Tankers', International Conference on LNG, London, 1969

104 JAMES, D P, 'Some Design Aspects of High-Pressure Pipelines and Storage Systems', *JIGE*, **10**, 1970 (Research Communication GC160)

105 BENTZ, K, 'Long-Distance Transmission and Underground Storage', *JIGE*, **2**, 1962 (IGE Communication 609)

106 WARDALE, J K S, 'Storage of LNG in Metallic Containers', International Conference on LNG, London, 1969

107 CLOSNER, J J, 'Very Large Prestressed Concrete Tanks for LNG Storage', Vol. 1, Second International Conference on LNG, Paris, 1970

108 GIBSON, G H, and WALTERS, W J, 'Some Aspects of LNG Storage', Vol. 1, Second International Conference on LNG, Paris, 1970

109 BERGE, H, 'Liquefied Natural Gas Storage Units in a Densely Populated Area', Vol. 2, Second International Conference on LNG, Paris, 1970

110 CLOSNER, J J, 'LNG Storage with Prestressed Concrete', Paper 32, First International LNG Conference, Chicago, 1968

111 SNELL, P A, and CRESSWELL, P J, 'Conversion of a Power Station Water-Tube Boiler to Natural Gas Firing', *JInstF*, XLIII, July 1970

112 CULSHAW, J W, and PRIGG, J A, 'Combustion Characteristics and Appliance Design', *JIGE*, **10**, 1970 (IGE Communication 809)

293

113 DESTY, D H, and WHITEHEAD, D M, 'In Search of a Burner', *BP Shield*, September 1969

114 HARRISON, W P, *et al*, 'The Design of Self-Recuperative Burners', *JIGE*, **10**, 1970 (Research Communication GC164)

PART 3

115 VAN DINTEREN, W J K, and ELLIS, D C, 'Planning of Optimal Sizing of LNG Plants for Peak-Shaving Purposes', Vol. 2, Second International Conference on LNG, Paris 1970

# INDEX

Acid gas, removal from natural gas **181-4**
  *statutory levels for* **181**
Active carbon, use in desulphurization **101**
Aerated burners **3, 259-61**
Air Liquide of France **191**
Air Products and Chemicals Incorporated **194**
Alkazid process **35**
American Gas Association **44**
American Office of Coal Research **44**
American Petroleum Institute, Standard 620 for design of storage tanks **240**
Amine **220** demulsifying agent **55, 85**
Ammonia, catalytic splitting of **124**
  *synthesis of* **8**
  *characteristics of gas for* **9**
Annular reactor tubes in continuous reformers **113, 120**
Anthracite, composition of **15**
Aquifer, cross-section through **239**
  *for high-pressure storage of natural gas* **238**
ARC (*see* Auto-refrigerated cycle)
Aromatic hydrocarbons **10, 79, 110**
Associated gas **171, 178**
Autocaloric process (*see* Autothermic processes)
Automatic control, of endothermic generators **149**
  *of gas transmission systems* **226-7**
Auto-refrigerated cycle **191, 193-4**
Autothermic processes **135-47, 148**
  *catalytic* **144-7, 148**
  *non-catalytic* **135-44**

Balsa wood, as insulation for LNG containers **229**
Base load, cost considerations of plant **139, 269**
  *in gas output* **268, 269**
BASF Lurgi process **126**
BASF Flesch-Demag process **36**
Benzole recovery in recycle hydrogenation **110**
Bituminous coating for steel pipes **214, 216**
Blue water-gas, characteristics of **26**
  *enrichment of* **52, 53, 55**

*manufacture of* **30**
  (*see also* Water gas)
Blue-water-gas process **28, 30**
  *capital costs of* **166**
  *gas-making costs of* **167**
BOC-Airco plant **194**
Boil off, economic optimum rate of **241**
  *for temperature control* **190**
  *in underground storage of LNG* **246**
Boil-off gas, from LNG cargo **229**
  *re-liquefaction of* **195-6, 241**
Boudouard reaction **75, 78, 112**
British Petroleum Company Matrix burner **262**
Brown coal, for manufacture of water gas **41** (*see also* Lignite)
Brown-coal tar, characteristics of **16**
Bubiag Didier process **32**
Burner design, for domestic appliances **259-62**
  *for large-scale appliances* **262-5**
Burners, aerated **3, 259-61**
  *Foster Wheeler system for continuous tubular reformers* **124, 126**
  *neat flame* **3, 13, 259-60, 263, 264**
  *SELAS system for continuous tubular reformers* **124-5**
  *self-aerated* **260-1**
  *self-recuperative* **258, 265**
  *SE-NEAT* **264**
Butane, catalytic reforming of **25**
  *characteristics of* **18**
By-products of liquefaction, separation of **196-8**

Calorific value, determination of **5**
Canvey Island, LNG evaporators on **199**
Carbonate processes for removal of acid gas **183**
Carbon-black production **65-7**
Carbon deposition, on catalysts **75, 149**
  *in catalytic steam reforming* **77**
  *in cyclic catalytic processes* **84, 85**
  *in fuel bed of carburetted-water-gas plant* **59**
  *in UK Gas Council fluidized-bed hydrogenator* **151**
Carbon dioxide removal **181-3**
Carbon dioxide acceptor process **50-1**

Carbon: hydrogen ratio, of coking coal 63
*of fuel gas* 259
*of various fuels* 63
Carbonization 19-25
*application of liquid hydrocarbons in 24-5*
*coal/oil mixtures for* 24
*catalytic reforming of butane in* 25
*in coke ovens* 21-3
*high-temperature* 20-3
*in horizontal retorts* 20, 24
*light-distillate reforming in* 24-5
*LPG reforming in* 25
*low-temperature* 23
*in vertical retorts* 20-1, 24-5
Carbon monoxide conversion 29, 35, 82, 94, 106, 110, 139, 144, 158-63
Carbon removal in partial-combustion processes 139, 144
Carbonizing processes 20-4
Carbonyl sulphide, conversion to hydrogen sulphide 139, 144
Carburetted water-gas, manufacture of 41
Carburetted-water-gas plant 52-62
*capital costs of* 166
*enriching feedstock for* 55
*fuel-bed reforming in* 55, 57-60
*gas-making costs in* 167
*hydrocarbon reforming in* 60-2
*operational data for* 56
*results of LDF reforming in* 58
*role of, in town-gas supply* 53
Cascade cycle 191-2
Cast-iron mains, dust removal from 218
*for gas distribution* 203
*leakage from* 218
*sealing shrunken joints in* 218
Cast-iron pipes 213, 216-19
*cost of* 224
*cost of laying* 221-2
*types of joint for* 217
Catacarb process 183
Catalysts, for ammonia splitting 124
*for carbon monoxide conversion* 106, 158-63
   *chromia-promoted iron oxide* 106
   *chromium-promoted iron oxide* 159-60, 162
   *cobalt-molybdenum* 35, 162, 163
   *Girdler G-66B* 160-2, 163
   *ICI brown oxide* 106
*for hydrodesulphurization, Nimox* 112
*for hydrogenation, cobalt/molybdenum Comox* 104
   *nickel/molybdenum* 127
*for methanol reforming, chromium-oxide/zinc-oxide* 124
*for organic sulphur removal* 163-4
*regeneration of* 115, 117, 150
*for steam reforming, alkalized-nickel* 73, 104
   *BASF* 113
   *lime* 81, 83, 87
   *nickel* 81, 82, 85, 87, 91
   *nickel-on-alumina* 101
   *nickel/urania* 113, 120, 121, 122
   *nickel/urania/α alumina* 102
   *nickel/uranium* 73, 82
   *Stickstoffwerke M1* 94
Catalytic reforming of butane 25
*of methanol* 124
Catalytic rich gas, methanation of 133-4
*production of, by BASF Lurgi process* 126
   *by Gas Council process (see* UK Gas Council)
   *by Japan Gasoline Osaka MRG process* 126
   *by Lurgi Gasynthan process* 126
Catalytic splitting of ammonia 124
Catalytic steam reforming 73-80, 103-6
*chemical and thermodynamic principles in* 73-9
*naphthenic and aromatic hydrocarbon behaviour in* 79
*scope and limitations of* 80
*(see also* Continuous catalytic steam reforming)
Cathodic protection of steel pipes 216
Centralized control of gas-transmission networks 226-7
$C_f$ factor, in gas-flow formulae 205, 208
*for paraffinic hydrocarbons* 205-6
$C_r$ factor, in gas-flow formulae 205, 208
*for paraffinic hydrocarbons* 205-6
Charcoal, composition of 15
Characteristics, of blue water-gas 26
*of brown coal tar* 16
*of butane* 18
*of coal gas* 7
*of the constituents of natural gas* 4, 188
*of crude oil* 16
*of fuel gases* 256-9
*of fuel oil* 16
*of gas from LDF* 130
   *from solid-fuel gasification* 26
*of gas oil* 16
*of hydrocarbon feedstocks* 16
*of light distillates* 16
*of LPG* 117
*of natural gas* 7, 172

296

of natural-gas test gases 13
of producer gas 26
of propane 18
of refinery gases 17, 18
of shale oil 16
of substitutes for natural gas 14
of test-limit gas 11
of town gas 7, 111
of total-gasification gas 26
Chequer-filled carburettor 53, 55
Chequerless carburettor 53, 55
Classification of gases 7
Claude cycle 189
Claus process 42, 184
Coal, methane manufacture from 277
   composition of 15
   for synthesis-gas manufacture 273
   for town-gas manufacture 273
Coal gas, characteristics of 7
   impurities in 19
Coal hydrogenation reaction 33
Coke, composition of 15
Coke ovens 21-3
   capital costs of 166
   gas-making costs in 167, 169
   light hydrocarbons for under-firing of 21
Coking coal, carbon: hydrogen ratio of 63
Cold, conservation of, in natural-gas liquefaction 188
   from evaporation of LNG, utilization of 198
Combustion prediction diagram, for natural gas 12
   for town gas 10
Complete gasification (see Total gasification)
Composition, of ammonia synthesis gas 9
   of blue water-gas 26
   of butane 18
   of coal gas 7
   of gas from endothermic generators 148
   of gas from Silamit P3 process 96
   of gases for synthesis and hydrogenation 9
   of liquefied petroleum gas 117, 121
   of methanol synthesis gas 9
   of natural gas 7, 172
   of natural-gas substitutes 14
   of producer gas 26
   of propane 18
   of refinery gases 18, 121
   of solid fuels 15
   of total-gasification gas 26
   of town gas 7, 111, 117, 130

Compressibility factor, chart for prediction of 207
   in gas-flow formulae 205, 208
   of liquefied natural gas 228
Compressors, gas 211-3
Computer model, for optimal sizing of LNG plants 276
Computer programmes, for simulation of pipeline networks 225
Conradson carbon content, of fuel oil 55, 68
   of hydrocarbon oils 151
Continuous catalytic steam reforming 99-134
   catalysts used for 101-2
   catalytic rich-gas processes for 100-3
   Didier continuous reformer for 119-21
   feedstocks for 100-3
   Haldor-Topsøe continuous tubular reformer for 112-13
   heating feedstock for 101
   for hydrogen manufacture 122, 124, 126
   ICI continuous reforming processes for 103-12
   Koppers Kontalyt continuous tubular reformer for 112-3
   Onia-GI continuous tubular reformer for 112-3
   Otto continuous tubular reformer for 116-9
   pretreatment of feedstock for 101
   process yields from 102
   product gas from 99-100
   for reducing-gas manufacture 122, 124
   for synthesis-gas manufacture 122-3
   utilities for 102-3
   Vickers-Zimmer continuous tubular reformer for 113-6
Continuous tubular reformers 81, 103-19
   annular reactor tubes in 113, 120
   capital costs of 166
   Foster Wheeler heating system for 124, 126
   gas-making costs in 167, 169
   SELAS burner system for 124, 125
Control, of pipeline networks 225-7
   information for gas transmission 203, 226-7
Conversion, of carbonyl sulphide to hydrogen sulphide 139, 144
   of domestic appliances for natural-gas burning 259-62
   of industrial appliances for natural-gas burning 262-5
Cost calculations, notional fuel prices for 165

297

Costs, of construction of LNG storage systems 240-1
*of detoxification in gas manufacture* 169
*of gas compression* 169, 211-2
*of gas manufacture* 165-9
*of gas transmission* 210, 220, 223
*of liquefaction* 228
*of organic-sulphur removal* 169
*of pipelaying* 221-2, 224
*of pipes for gas transmission* 220-2
*of transportation of LNG* 230-2
CRG (*see* Catalytic rich gas)
Crude oil, characteristics of 16
*as feedstock for town-gas manufacture* 65, 272
Cryogenics, in natural-gas liquefaction 187-95
Cryophores, for storage of cold 198
CWG (*see* Carburetted water gas)
Cyclic catalytic reforming 81-98
*CCR (UGI) process for* 62, 93-4
*feedstock specification for* 82, 93
*gas yields from* 83
*IBEG/CCR process for* 93-4
*MS process for* 91-3
*Onia-Gegi process for* 85, 87-9
*regenerative plant for* 81, 83-5
*Segas process for* 83-5, 86
*Silamit P3 process for* 94, 96
*SSC process for* 96
*'uniflow' plant for* 81, 87-98
*W-D/CCR process for* 93-4

Dayton oil-gas process 136-7
Demag coal-fed producer 30
Demulsifying agents 55, 85
Depletion of natural-gas reserves 274-5, 277-8
Design factor (f) for pipe-wall thickness 214, 215
Desulphurization, by absorption using zinc oxide 101, 103-4, 112, 120-1, 127
*by adsorption on active carbon* 101
*of feedstocks* 107, 120
(*see also* Hydrodesulphurization)
Detoxification, cost in gas manufacture 169
Didier continuous reformer 119-21
*capital costs of* 166
*annular reactor-tube of* 120
*feedstocks for* 121
*gas-making costs in* 167
Didier gasification process 138
Didier partial-oxidation process 147, 148
Diethanolamine (DEA) process, for acid-gas removal 182

Distribution of gas by pipes 203
Distrigaz autothermic catalytic process 144
*conversion of CWG plants to* 60
Dust removal, from cast-iron mains 218
Dynamic simulation of pipeline networks 225, 233

Economics, of gas manufacture and output 268-70
*of natural-gas production and supply* 274-8
*of pipeline routing* 276
*of station spacing on transmission lines* 209, 211
Electronic Associates Inc. 225
Electrothermal gasification 48
Emissivity, of fuel flames 258
Endothermic generators 147-50
*automatic control of* 149
Enrichment, of water gas 52-5
*in gas recycle hydrogenator* 108, 111
*of lean gas* 94, 132, 272
*with methane* 277
*with natural gas or LPG* 94, 107, 255
*with propane* 14, 154, 157
Epoxy-resin pipes 220
Equilibrium constant, for Boudouard reaction 78
*for carbon monoxide shift reaction* 74, 158
*for steam/methane reaction* 74
Equilibrium gas composition, catalytic shift of 148
*for steam reforming of light distillate* 75-6
ERS computer programme 225
Ethylene, manufacture of 198
*re-liquefaction of* 195-6
Evaporation in pipelines 228
Evaporators for LNG 198-202
*base-load* 198-9
*high-performance, for peak shaving* 200-2
*indirect* 199
*Marston Excelsior* 199-200
*open-surface* 198-9
*steam-heated* 201
Expansion-cycle process, for natural-gas liquefaction 188-90
*modification (Claude cycle)* 189

Fatchemko TEB demulsifying agent 55, 85
Feedstock enrichment in CWG plant 55
Field tubes, in Vickers-Zimmer continuous reformer 113

298

Flame speed **9-12, 256**
Flame-speed factor, Weaver **11**
Flame stabilization **262-5**
  *by flame impingement* **263-4**
  *of self-aerated burners* **260-1**
  *by self-recuperative burners* **265**
  *two-stage gas injector for* **264-5**
Flesch-Winkler process **36**
Fluidized-bed hydrogenator (*see* UK Gas Council)
Fluor Solvent process **183**
Formulae for gas-flow **204-5, 208-9**
Foster Wheeler burner system, for continuous tubular reformer **124, 126**
Friction in pipes **204-5, 211**
Friction factor in gas-flow **204-5**
Frost heave in frozen in-ground storage of LNG **246**
Fuel-bed reforming, in CWG plant **55, 57-60**
Fuel gases, carbon: hydrogen ratio of **259**
  *catalytic removal of sulphur from* **163-4**
  *characteristics of* **256-7**
  *industrial applications of* **248-56**
  *sooting propensity of* **10-11**
  *sulphur in* **164, 259**
Fuel oil, carbon: hydrogen ratio of **63**
  *characteristics of* **16**
  *for fuel-bed reforming* **55**
  *sulphur content of* **138**
  *thermal cracking of* **65**
  *vanadium and nickel in* **138**

Gas characteristics, from CWG plant **58-9**
  *from Gaz Integrale process* **26**
  *from Hall-type processes* **69**
  *from Howe-Baker Sun/Thermal process* **138**
  *from ICI continuous reformer* **106**
  *from IGT hydrogenation process* **46**
  *from Koppers-Totzek process* **39**
  *from Lurgi process* **27**
  *from Marischka producer* **26**
  *from MS process* **92**
  *from Onia-Gegi process* **89**
  *from Onia process* **146**
  *from Power Gas process* **26**
  *from Segas process* **86**
  *from Shell gasification process* **143**
  *for transmission* **213**
  *from tubular reformers* **111**
  *from UK Gas Council CRG process* **130**
  *from UK Gas Council fluidized-bed hydrogenator* **155**

  *from Vickers-Zimmer reformer* **117**
Gas compressors **211-3**
  *for large-scale high-pressure gas transmission* **211-2**
  *for reticulation and line packing* **212**
Gases, classification of **7**
  *interchangeability of* **8-13**
Gas-flow formulae **204-5, 208-9**
  *compressibility factor in* **204-5, 207, 208**
  *friction factor in* **204, 205**
Gas holders, for low-pressure storage **234-5, 236**
Gasification, electrothermal **48**
  *of lignite* **50**
  *of solid fuel* **26-62**
  *underground, of coal* **43**
Gas-making materials **16-8**
Gas modulus, calculation of **8**
  *of fuel gases* **256, 257**
Gas oil, characteristics of **16**
Gas output, economic and technical considerations of **268-70**
  *load elements in* **267-270**
  *variations in* **266-70**
Gas purification processes **35, 93**
Gas recycle hydrogenator (*see* UK Gas Council)
Gas storage (*see* Liquefied-natural-gas storage, Natural-gas storage)
Gas transmission (*see* Transmission)
Gaz de France **91, 94, 144, 198**
GEIM (Gegi) process **136**
General Electric Company **225**
Generators, endothermic **147-50**
GE Simulator computer programme **225**
Giammarco Vetrocoke process, for carbon-dioxide removal **183**
  *for removal of hydrogen sulphide* **35, 181**
Gilbert and Prigg, work on combustion prediction **11**
  *diagram for natural gas* **12**
  *for town gas* **10**
Groningen, characteristics of natural gas from **172**
  *liquefaction of natural gas from* **197**
  *origin of natural gas from* **171**

Harris and Lovelace combustion prediction diagram **11, 12**
Haldor-Topsøe continuous tubular reformer **112**
Hall process **57, 62, 72**
Hall-type processes **68-71**
Helium, in expander cycle LNG **195**
  *recovery from natural gas* **197**

High-flame-speed gas 6, 8
*manufacture in CRG process* 129-32
High-pressure gas storage 235-8
Homogeneous partial combustion 136
Howe-Baker process, for feedstock desulphurization 107
Howe-Baker Sun/Thermal process 137
*gas characteristics from* 138
*operational data for* 138
Humphreys & Glasgow CWG plant 53
Hydrate formation, in natural-gas transmission 175, 176, 177
Hydrocarbon dewpoint, adjustment for natural-gas transmission 174-7
Hydrocarbon feedstocks, characteristics of 16
*hydrodesulphurization of* 80
*thermal cracking of* 65
Hydrocarbons, aromatic 10, 79, 110
*catalytic steam reforming of* 73-80
*effect of, in catalytic carbon-monoxide conversion* 163
*separation of, in natural-gas liquefaction* 196-7
*sorption by plastic pipes* 219
*removal from natural gas* 176-81
Hydrodesulphurization 101, 103
*of hydrocarbon feedstock* 80
Hydrogasification, carbon-dioxide acceptor process for 50-1
*processes IGT (HYGAS)* 44
*of hydrocarbon oils* 151-7
*of solid fuels* 43-51
Hydrogen, manufacture of 8, 99
*in continuous catalytic reformer* 121-6
*in IGT hydrogasification process* 48
*from liquid hydrocarbons* 271
*load factor in* 270
*in partial-combustion processes* 135
Hydrogen sulphide, removal of 35, 181
Hydrogenation reaction of coal 33
HYGAS processes 44

IBEG/CCR process 93-4
ICI continuous reforming processes 103-12
*characteristics of gas from* 106
*feedstock quality for* 107
*flow diagram of* 105
*gas yield from* 107-8
*lean-gas process* 103-8
*Power Gas/ICI continuous reformer* 108-9
*lean-gas manufacture in* 272
*town-gas (ICI '500') process* 108, 272
IGT hydrogasification processes 44-50

Imperial Chemical Industries (ICI) 78, 101
Institute of Gas Technology 44, 221
Insulation of LNG containers 229, 231, 242
Intermediate gas types 6, 12-13

Japan Gasoline Osaka MRG process 126
Joints in pipes 217-9
Jones process 65, 72, 83, 87
*modified for carbon-black manufacture* 66-7
Joule-Thomson effect 178

Kellogg molten-salt process 41-42
Kerpely producer 37
Koppers Kontalyt process 112-3
Koppers recycling process 32
Koppers-Totzek process 37, 38-9
*capital costs of* 166
*characteristics of gas from* 39
*gas-making costs in* 167
*operational data for* 39
*for synthesis-gas manufacture* 273

LDF (*see* Light-distillate feedstocks)
Legal aspects of pipeline routing 224
Leman Bank, characteristics of gas from 172, 186
Lean-gas process 103-8
Leuna producer 37
Leuna BASF producer 37
Light distillates, characteristics of 16
Light distillate feedstocks, carbon: hydrogen ratio of 63
*reforming of* 24-5, 57-9, 113, 116, 117
*for synthesis gas and hydrogen manufacture* 271
*for town-gas manufacture* 272
Lignite, gasification of 48, 50
*hydrogasification of* 43-4
*properties of* 15
Line-storage or line-packing 212, 220, 233-4, 267
Liquefied natural gas, compressibility factor of 228
*computer model for optimum sizing of plants* 276
*evaporation of* 198-202
*insulation of containers for* 229, 231, 242
*re-liquefaction of* 195
*storage of* 240-7
*frozen in-ground* 244, 246, 247
*in above-ground metallic tanks* 241-2, 243

300

*in pre-stressed concrete tanks* **242, 244, 245**
*to relieve natural-gas supply* **275-6**
*transmission of* **227-32**
  *costs of* **230-2**
  *by pipeline* **277-8**
  *by road and rail* **231-2**
  *by sea* **229-30**
Liquefied petroleum gases, for
  carburetted-water-gas manufacture **62**
*characteristics of* **117**
*as chemical-synthesis feedstock* **255**
*as gas-making materials* **17**
*industrial applications of* **250-6**
*as natural-gas substitutes* **275-6**
*odorizing or stenching of* **184-6**
*reforming of* **25, 113, 116-9, 144**
*for synthesis-gas and hydrogen manufacture* **271**
*for town-gas manufacture* **255, 271-2**
*underground storage of* **240**
Liquid hydrocarbons, application in
  carbonization **24-5**
*for methane manufacture* **277**
*for synthesis-gas and hydrogen manufacture* **271**
*for town-gas manufacture* **271-3**
LNG (*see* Liquefied natural gas)
Load elements, in gas output **267-70**
*in town-gas manufacture* **272-3**
Load-factor, in natural-gas supply **274**
*in synthesis-gas and hydrogen manufacture* **270**
Low-flame-speed gases **6, 11**
Low-pressure storage, gas holders for **234-6, 267**
Low-temperature carbonization, formation of semi-coke in **23**
LPG (*see* Liquefied petroleum gases)
Lummus plant **194**
Lurgi process **29, 33-6**
*capital costs of* **166**
*characteristics of gas from* **27**
*estimated efficiency of* **36, 139**
*gasification rates in* **35**
*gas-making costs in* **167**
*purification of gas from* **35**
*for synthesis-gas manufacture* **273**
*upgrading of gas from* **36**
Lurgi Gasynthan process **126**
Luxmasse, as sulphur absorbent **127**

Magnetohydrodynamic (MHD) system, for gas production **48**
Marischka producer **31**
Marston Excelsior evaporator **199-200**

Matrix burner, of British Petroleum Company **262**
Mechanical refrigeration of natural gas **190-6**
*auto-refrigerated cycle for* **191, 193-4**
*cascade cycle for* **191, 192**
*cold-gas refrigeration systems for* **195**
*liquid-nitrogen refrigerant process for* **194**
*mixed-refrigerant cycle for* **191, 194**
Medium-condition liquefied-gas process **229**
Methanation, of raw CRG **133-4**
*of synthetic natural gas* **45-7**
Methane, manufacture from coal and oil **277**
*re-liquefaction in Stirling cycle* **195**
Methane: ethane ratio of natural gas **171**
Methanol, catalytic reforming of **124**
*injection for natural-gas transmission* **178**
*for Rectisol process* **183**
*synthesis of* **8**
*characteristics of gas for* **9**
Micro-Simplex process (*see* MS process)
Mined cavities for underground storage **238, 240**
Mineral wool, as insulation in LNG containers **242**
Mixed-refrigerant cycles **191, 194**
Molecular sieves, for hydrogen sulphide removal **181**
*for moisture reduction* **178**
Monoethanolamine (MEA) process, for acid-gas removal **182**
Montecatini gasification process **138**
MRC (*see* Mixed-refrigerant cycles)
MS process **91-3**
*feedstock specification for* **93**
*flow diagram of* **90**
*operational data for* **92**
*for town-gas manufacture* **271**
Multiple-refrigerant cycle (*see* Mixed-refrigerant cycle)

Naphthalene, deposition in water-gas plants **60, 65**
*sorption on plastic pipes* **219**
Natural gas, acid-gas removal from **181-4**
*as chemical-synthesis feedstock* **255**
*carbon: hydrogen ratio of* **63**
*characteristics of* **7, 172**
*combustion prediction diagram for* **12**
*conversion of domestic appliances for* **259-62**

conversion of industrial appliances for
262-5
decompression of 210
depletion of reserves of 274-5, 277-8
dust removal from 174
from Groningen 171-2
hydrocarbon content of 17
hydrocarbon removal from 174-5,
179-81
industrial applications of 248-56
liquefaction of 187-98
  conservation of cold in 188
  expansion-cycle processes for 188-90
  mechanical-refrigeration cycles for
  190-6
  separation of by-products from 196-8
  use of cryogenics in 197
  utilization of cold from 198
methane: ethane ratio of 171
from the North Sea 171-2
odorizing or stenching of 184-6
origins of 171
production and supply of 274-8
  economics of 274-8
  load factors in 274-6
  seasonal storage in 275
properties of constituents of 4, 188
storage of 233-47
  in gaseous phase 233-9
  in high-pressure systems 235, 237-8,
  267
  line-storage or line packing for 233-4,
  267
  low-pressure gas holders for 234-6, 267
  underground 238-9, 266-7
substitutes for 275-6
  characteristics of 14
sulphur removal from 174, 184
in town-gas manufacture 255
in town-gas supply 276-7
transmission of 203-32
  control of networks for 226-7
  costs of 210, 223
  flow formulae for 204-5, 208-9
  as gas 204-29
  gas compressors for 211-3
  hydrate formation in 176, 177
  hydrocarbon-dewpoint, adjustment
  for 174-6
  hydrocarbon removal for 176-81
  as liquid (see Liquefied natural gas,
  transmission of)
  notional cost of pipes and pipelines
  for 220-4
  in pressure vessels 227
  retrograde condensation during 175-6

  routing of pipelines for 224-5
  water-dewpoint adjustment for
  174-8, 184
Natural-gas fields, formation pressure
in 174
  temperatures in 174
Neat-flame burners 3, 13
  for burning natural gas 259-65
Nitrogen, as by-product of liquefaction
197
Non-aerated burners (see Neat-flame
burners)
North Sea, characteristics of natural gas
from 7, 172
  load factors in supply of gas from 274
  origin of natural gas from 171
  stratigraphic section through gas field
  in 173

Odorizing of gas 107, 184-6
Office of Coal Research 44
Onia autothermic catalytic process 144-6
Onia-Gegi process 85-9
  capital costs of 166
  gas-making costs in 167
  operational data for 89
  for town-gas manufacture 271, 272
  'uniflow' plant for 87-9
Onia-GI continuous tubular reformer 113
Organic sulphur, removal of 184
Osaka CRG plant 154
Otto continuous catalytic reformer 116-9
  for town-gas manufacture 271
Otto-Rummel generator 41

Pacific Coast oil-gas processes 65
Partial-combustion processes 135-50
  carbon removal in 139, 144
  Dayton oil-gas process 136-7
  Didier process 138, 147
  Distrigaz process 144
  GEIM (Gegi) process 136-7
  Howe-Baker Sun/Thermal process
  136-7
  manufacture of hydrogen in 135
  Montecatini process 138
  Onia autothermic process 144-6
  P2 (Gaz de France) process 94, 144
  Shell gasification process 138-44
  Texaco gasification process 138-44
  Topsøe-SBA process 147
Peak load, capital cost aspects of 269-70
  in gas output 267-70
  process costs for 269
Peak-load shaving, high-performance
evaporators for 200-2

302

*in large-scale manufacture* 273
*low-cost techniques* 270
*production of LNG for* 194
*seasonal contributions* 275
Peat, composition of 15
Perlite powder, as insulation for LNG containers 229, 231, 242
P2 (Gaz de France) process 94, 144
P3 (Silamit) process 94
'Pigs' for scavenging pipelines 228
Pinhole neat-flame burner 262
Pintsch Hillebrand process 32
Pipelines, control of 225-7
*for LNG transmission* 227-8
*network simulation* 225, 233
*progressive evaporation in* 228
*routing of* 224-5
  *economics of* 276
  *legal considerations in* 224
*scavenging of* 228
*two-phase flow in* 228
Pipes, cast iron 216-9
*expansion and contraction of* 215
*epoxy resin* 220
*factors affecting size of* 220-1
*friction in* 204-5, 211
*for gas distribution* 203
*for gas transmission and reticulation* 213-28
*grades of steel for* 215
*high-pressure steel* 213-6
*joints in* 217-9
*materials and specification for* 213-20
*plastic* 213, 219-20
*wall thickness of* 214, 215
*wrought iron* 203, 213
*yield strength of* 214
Pipetram computer programme 225
Plastic pipes 213, 219-20
*cost of* 224
Plastic tape, for cladding steel pipes 216
Polyflo calculator, for natural-gas flow data 204, 220
Polyurethane foam, as insulation for LNG containers 229
Power Gas Corporation CWG plant 53, 54
Power Gas/ICI continuous reformer 108-9
Power Gas process 30, 32
Pressure vessels, for natural-gas transmission 227
Prichard Rhodes plant 194
Producer gas, characteristics of 26
*manufacture of* 48
Producer-gas process 29-30, 37

*capital costs of* 166
*gas-making costs in* 167
Producer-gas reaction 27
Propane, characteristics of 18
*use in synthetic-natural-gas manufacture* 132-3
Purification processes 35-93
Purisol process 183
PVC foam, as insulation for LNG containers 229

Re-compression stations, on long-distance transmission lines 209
Rectisol process, for acid-gas removal 183
Recycle hydrogenation, benzole recovery in 110
Reducing-gas manufacture 122, 124
*in endothermic generators* 147
Refinery gases 17-8
*characteristics of* 18
Reforming of LDF 24-5, 57-60, 113, 116-9
Re-liquefaction, of boil-off gases 195-6, 241
*of ethylene in Stirling cycle* 195-6
*of LNG* 195
*refrigeration cycle for* 196
Reticulation of gas, by pipes 213-29
*pressures used in* 209-11, 233
Retorts 20-1, 24-5
*capital costs of* 166
*gas-making costs in* 167
Retrograde condensation 175-6
Rummel generator 40-1
*for natural-gas manufacture* 273

Sabatier reaction 33
Seasonal load in gas output 267, 268, 269
Segas process 83-5, 86
*capital costs of* 166
*gas-making costs in* 167
*for town-gas manufacture* 65, 272
SELAS burner system, for continuous tubular reformers 124, 125
Selexol process 183
Self-aerated burners 260-261
Self-recuperative burners 258, 264-5
*for flame stabilization* 265
Semet-Solvay process 69-71
Semi-coke, composition of 15
*formation in low-temperature carbonization* 23
SE-NEAT burner 264
Shale oil, characteristics of 16
Shell gasification process 138-44, 157

303

capital costs of 166
characteristics of gas from 143
design of combustor for 140
gas-making costs in 167
operational data for 143
for synthesis-gas manufacture 271
for town-gas manufacture 272
Shift conversion (see Carbon monoxide
conversion)
Silamit Indugas 94
Silamit P3 process 94, 96
Société Belge de l'Azote (SBA) 147
Solid fuels composition of 15
gasification of 26-51
for synthesis-gas manufacture 273
Sooting propensity of fuel gas 10-11
SSC process 96, 98
Steam reforming, equilibrium gas
composition for 75-6
Steel pipes, with bitumen or coal-tar
coatings 214, 216
corrosion protection for 216
cost of 224
high-pressure 213-6
with high tensile strength 209
for LNG transmission 227
with pitch coating 216
plastic-tape cladding for 216
for storage and reticulation 233
Stein & Roubaix 91
Stenching (see Odorizing)
Stirling-cycle refrigerator for re-
liquefaction 195
Storage, design of LNG tanks for 240-7
underground, mined cavities for
238, 240
Strache 'double gas' plant 32
'Styrpor' panels, to insulate LNG
storage tanks 242
Sulfinol process, for acid-gas removal
183
Sulphur, catalytic removal from fuel
gases 163-4
in fuel gases 164, 259
in fuel oil 138
in gaseous or liquid feedstocks 139
in light-distillate feedstock 104
removal from natural gas 174, 184
Sulzer re-liquefaction system 195-6
Synthesis gas, composition of 9
description of 8
manufacture of in ICI continuous
reformer 122, 123
in Kellogg molten-salt process 41-2
in Koppers-Totzek process 273
from liquid hydrocarbons 271

load-factor effect in 270
role of hydrocarbon oils in 72
from solid fuels 273
sulphur in feedstocks for 139
in Winkler-type processes 36
Synthetic natural gas as bulk fuel 230
manufacture of, by carbon-dioxide
acceptor process 50-1
from hydrocarbon oils 151
in IGT hydrogasification process 44-8
in UK Gas Council's CRG process
132-4, 197
in UK Gas Council's recycle
hydrogenator 154
purification and methanation of 45-7
Synthetic pipeline gas (see Synthetic
natural gas)

Tankers for LNG transportation by road
and rail 231
by sea 229
Test-limit gases 11-12
characteristics of 13
Texaco gasification process 42, 48,
138-44, 157
capital costs of 166
gas-making costs in 167
for synthesis-gas manufacture 271
for town-gas manufacture 272
Thermal-cracking processes 63-71
Hall-type processes 68-71
Jones process 65
Pacific Coast oil-gas process 65
reaction sequence in 64
Segas process 65
Thyssen Galoczy producer 37
Total gasification gas, composition of 26
Town gas, combustion prediction
diagram for 10
composition of 7, 111, 130
crude oil as feedstock for manufacture
of 65, 272
high-flame-speed 6
low-flame-speed 6
manufacture, by continuous tubular
reformer 271
from coal 273
from liquid hydrocarbons 271-3
output in systems 266-70
Transmission, automatic control of
226-7
control information for 203, 226
of gas by pipes 213-28
of LNG 227-32
re-compression stations on long-
distance lines 209

Transportation of LNG, by road and rail **231**
*by sea* **229**
Tubular reformers, continuous **103-20**

UK Gas Council
*Catalytic Rich-Gas Process* **69, 78-9, 126-34, 154, 197**
*capital costs of* **166**
*catalyst-bed temperature profile of* **78-9**
*characteristics of gas from* **130**
*feedstock quality for* **127**
*flow-diagram for* **128**
*gas-making costs in* **167**
*lean-gas enrichment by* **132**
*LPG reforming by* **133**
*methods of applying* **129-31**
*movement of reaction zone in* **129**
*natural-gas substitutes from* **276**
*supplementary-gas manufacture by* **132-4**
*synthetic natural-gas manufacture by* **132-4, 197**
*town-gas manufacture by* **129-32, 272**
*fluidized-bed hydrogenator of* **151-5**
*characteristics of gas from* **155**
*hydrogenation of crude oil in* **155, 272**
*operational data for* **155**
*town-gas manufacture by* **272**
*gas-recycle hydrogenator of* **108-10, 154, 156-7**
*heat balances in* **157**
*light-distillate cracking reactions in* **154**
*methane: ethane ratio of gas from* **154**
*preheat/reheat process of* **132**
*recommendations for high-pressure steel pipelines of* **213-16**
*research station of* **78, 163, 225, 230**
Underground gasification of coal **43**
Underground storage, in mined cavities **240**
*of natural gas* **238-9, 266-7**

'Uniflow' cyclic processes **81, 87-9**
*capital costs of* **166**
*gas-making costs in* **167**
Uniplane neat-flame burner for natural gas **262**
United Engineers & Constructors **93**
United Gas Improvement Company of America **93**

Vetrocoke process (*see* Giammarco Vetrocoke process)
Viag synthesis-gas process **32**
Vickers-Zimmer continuous tubular reformer **113-6**
*design and arrangement of reactor tubes in* **113**
*feedstock quality for* **115**
*general layout of* **114**
*operational data for* **117**
*for town-gas manufacture* **271**

Wall thickness of pipes **214-5**
Water dewpoint adjustment, for natural-gas transmission **174-5, 184**
Water-gas, carburetted (*see* Carburetted water-gas)
Water-gas plant, fuel-bed reforming of **55-60**
Water-gas reaction **28**
Weaver flame-speed factor **11**
Winkler process **36, 273**
Winkler-type processes **36**
Wood, composition of **15**
Wobbe Number **6, 8-12, 260**
*definition of* **8**
Woodhall Duckham W-D/MS plant **90**
*W-D/CCR plant* **93, 95**
Wrought-iron pipes **213**
*for gas transmission,* **203**

Yield strength of pipes **214**

Zinc oxide, use in desulphurization **101, 103-4, 112, 120-1, 127**